Political Ideologies in Contemporary France

Two week loan

Please return on or before the last
date stamped below
Charges are

Edit
Ch   r Flood and Laurence Bell

PINTER

London and Washington

Pinter
A Cassell Imprint
Wellington House, 125 Strand, London WC2R 0BB, England
PO Box 605, Herndon, VA 20172

First published in 1997
© Christopher Flood, Laurence Bell and the contributors 1997

British Library Cataloging in Publication Data
A catalogue record for this book is available from the British Library.

ISBN 1 85567 237 5 (Hardback)
     1 85567 238 3 (Paperback)

Library of Congress Cataloging-in-Publication Data
Political ideologies in contemporary France/edited by Christopher Flood and Laurence Bell.
    p. cm.
  Includes bibliographical references and index.
  ISBN 1-85567-237-5 (hc).   ISBN 1-85567-238-3 (pbk)
  1. Political science–France. 2. Ideology–France. I. Flood, Christopher. II. Bell, Laurence, 1952– .
  JA84.F8P65   1997
  320.5'0944'09045—dc21   96-47167
                                                                         CIP

Typeset by York House Typographic Ltd, London
Printed and bound in Great Britain by Biddles Limited, Guildford and King's Lynn

Contents

List of Contributors

Laurence Bell is Lecturer in French Studies at the University of Surrey. He is the author of chapters in books and articles on subjects such as higher education in France, the political thought of Pierre Mendes's France, and French socialism and May '68.

Máire Cross is Senior Lecturer in French Studies at the University of Sheffield. She is co-author of *The Feminism of Flora Tristan* (Berg, 1992) and of *Early French Feminisms 1830–1940* (Elgar, 1996), editor of *La Société Française* (Newcastle Polytechnic, 1991) and co-editor of *Voices of France: Social, Political and Cultural Identity* (Pinter, 1997) and *Population and Social Policy in France* (Pinter, 1997).

Christopher Flood is Senior Lecturer and Head of European Studies at the University of Surrey. He is author of *Pensée politique et imagination historique dans l'oeuvre de Paul Claudel* (1991), *Political Myth: A Theoretical Introduction* (1996), and numerous articles or chapters on aspects of French politics and culture. He co-edited a collection of essays on French intellectual responses to the Occupation (1993) and is currently co-editing a collection dealing with French debates over decolonization, immigration and postcolonialism.

Peter Fysh is Senior Lecturer in French at Nottingham Trent University. He has published articles in journals such as *Parliamentary Affairs, Modern and Contemporary France* and the *International Journal of Public Opinion Research*. His most recent work is a chapter on the candidates and parties of the right in R. Elgie (ed.) *Electing the French President: The 1995 Presidential Election* (1996). He is currently co-writing a book on racism and anti-racism in contemporary France, to be published by Macmillan in 1998.

Alec Hargreaves is Professor of French and Francophone Studies at Loughborough University. His recent publications include *Voices from the North African Immigrant Community in France* (second edn 1997), *Immigration, 'Race' and Ethnicity in Contemporary France* (1995) and, co-edited with Jeremy Leaman, *Racism, Ethnicity and Politics in Contemporary Europe* (1995).

Jeremy Jennings is Reader in Political Theory at the University of Birmingham. He is author of *Georges Sorel* (Macmillan, 1985) and of *Syndicalism in France* (Macmillan, 1990) and editor of *Intellectuals in Twentieth-century France* (Macmillan, 1992). He has also published extensively in journals.

Brendan Prendiville is Lecturer in British Area Studies at the University of Poitiers. He is author of *Environmental Politics in France* (1994), articles on the French Green movement in *Modern and Contemporary France* and *Environmental Politics*, and contributions to collections published in Britain and France.

Acknowledgements

We wish to thank the contributors to the collection for responding so generously to our invitation to participate in the project. We are also very grateful to Nicola Viinikka, now at Manchester University Press, and to Petra Recter and Helena Power at Cassell for their helpfulness and patience.

Introduction

CHRISTOPHER FLOOD

When approaching the study of any set of political ideologies, it is useful to give some thought to the concept of ideology itself, since it has been the subject of considerable dispute. Rather than embark here on a lengthy review of the history of the concept and of its many permutations, suffice it to say that the present work is based on a neutral, inclusive notion of ideology. Political ideologies are taken, as in Martin Seliger's widely quoted definition, to be 'sets of ideas by which men [and women] posit, explain and justify ends and means of organized social action, and specifically political action, irrespective of whether such action aims to preserve, amend, uproot or rebuild a given social order' (1976, p. 14). This type of definition offers a particularly useful perspective for focusing on ideological production by political elites who offer leadership to mass publics. Political theorists, publicists, politicians and other proselytizers – sometimes termed ideological carriers – are obliged to systematize and to offer more or less rational justification of their ideas for purposes of coherent communication to audiences.

Following Elinor Scarbrough (1984), ideologies can be said to comprise core beliefs, including fundamental assumptions (about the nature of human beings and of society), values (such as liberty, equality and justice) and ultimate goals (such as the establishment of a democratic socialist society embodying values of liberty, equality and justice). They also incorporate principles of action, relating to classes of action which are deemed acceptable and appropriate in the light of core beliefs, on the one hand, and of the context of action, on the other. However, as Michael Freeden (1994) observes, individual ideologies do not have exclusive ownership of particular values and principles.

Attachment to the principles of liberty and equality, for example, may be shared by more than one ideology; but their meaning and significance for any particular ideology are determined by their relationship with other elements in a specific combination, which involves a hierarchy of components such that some have precedence over others. Given that each particular combination may vary in its composition and/or in the hierarchical ranking of its components in response to changing circumstances over the course of time, it is important to avoid the temptation of viewing ideologies as if they were solid, immutable blocks.

For analytical purposes, the definition is neutral and inclusive in the sense that it takes all such sets of ideas to be ideologies, regardless of the particular beliefs which any set contains. Whereas Marxists have excluded Marxism itself from the category of ideology or have at least given it a privileged epistemological status among ideologies, the neutral conception considers all ideologies to be of the same order. Similarly, it stands apart from those non-Marxist conceptions which have restricted the designation of ideology to sets of ideas which they consider extremist and totalitarian, in contrast to other types of political doctrine that they take to be fundamentally different from, and superior to, ideologies.

Depending on the context of action, an ideology may legitimate the established political and social order. It may thereby seek to promote acceptance of present authority, because people will not have to be coerced if they feel a sense of political obligation. Conversely, ideology is also a weapon of contestation and opposition, since conflicts occur both horizontally and vertically within societies of all sizes. Ideologies furnish explanations and justifications for political or even military confrontations. They are oriented towards practical action in the sense that they involve models of how society ought to be. The conception of what ought to be the case colours the perceptions and evaluations of social reality which shape descriptions and arguments in political discourse. They also generate myths, which may be defined minimally as ideologically marked narratives which purport to give true accounts of past, present or predicted events – not merely the grand narratives contained in histories, biographies or sweeping prophecies, but those in everyday journalism, interviews and speeches, for example (Flood, 1996). The desire to produce change or continuity from a present state of affairs to a desired future state – subject to the possibilities available in the historical/political context – informs collective action, which is normally channelled through political parties or pressure groups, assuming that legal and other conditions make that a possibility.

Clearly, political parties are constrained by contingent factors relating to their internal structures, practices and traditions as well as to the external distribution of power and support within a given political system at a particular period. Core beliefs interact with calculations of strategy, and strategy interacts with questions of tactics. Policy programmes represent a trade-off between the ideal and what is believed to be sellable. It is useful to recognize the distinction between what Seliger (1976) calls fundamental ideology, which is distilled from theoretical writings, and operative ideology, which corresponds to arguments supporting the adoption of policies by a party or other organized group. Seliger's bifurcation appears too sharp, given the infinite variability of movement between general principles, ideologically coloured analyses of situations, longer- or shorter-term strategies and so on, through to the formation of policies. Nevertheless, it is useful to note the increasing degree of flexibility at the operative end of the scale as compared with the fundamental end. Because operative ideology functions under the constraints of immediate social contexts, there is often deviation from the principles of fundamental ideology. At any time there may be a more or less close correspondence between a political group's fundamental ideology and its operative ideology on a range of principles, but a greater or lesser divergence on others. A party holding power may also find that practice highlights underlying contradictions within its fundamental ideology as well as between the fundamental and the operative. The temptation is to ignore or dissimulate such contradictions for as long as possible. Under the best of circumstances there are likely to be conflicts of interpretation and emphasis between different sections of any party or other group, but explicit revision of core beliefs is particularly divisive.

Ideological change also raises wider problems relating to the identity of ideologies. On the one hand, to win support and to maintain the loyalty of its activists, a political party or other group must maintain its ideological distinctiveness. Its core beliefs must appear sacrosanct. Its policies must be presented not only as consistent with its core beliefs, but also as significantly different from and better than those of other parties representing other ideologies. However, the climate of public opinion may favour a more consensual posture, involving dilution of ideological principles on the operative level and eventually, by implication, on the fundamental level. This kind of dilemma can lead to discursive contortions and to various forms of doublespeak, especially for groups on the extreme left or right when they attempt to broaden their electoral appeal.

The development of communications in the modern period has meant that ideological currents are not restricted by national borders. Some ideologies claim to be based on principles and values which are valid for humankind as a whole. Others may claim only to articulate the nature and the needs of a particular society or of a specific group within that society, but the observer may view them as variant expressions of a generic ideology common to several societies, as in the case of some types of nationalism. Conversely, every society gives its own colouring to the ideologies which are shared by its members, regardless of whether the claims made in the name of those ideologies are universalistic or not. That is why it is meaningful to analyse a range of ideologies as they present themselves in a particular society – in the present case, France.

French society has an important place in the history of ideology. The concept of ideology was invented in France during the period of the French Revolution by the philosopher Destutt de Tracy. He and his circle used the term *idéologie* as the name for a new field of knowledge deriving from the scientific study of how ideas are formed and combined together in the human mind (Head, 1985). Over the two centuries since it was first coined, the term has passed into worldwide use with a range of different meanings, though none of them correspond closely to the original intention of de Tracy and his fellow *idéologues*.

The French Revolution also played a vital role in the emergence of most of the main ideological currents of the modern period, including various versions of what we would now call liberalism, conservatism and socialism, although they were not called ideologies at the time. Since then, France has developed a rich ideological heritage. It has produced major theoretical contributors to all of the main Western currents of political thought. It has developed a strong tradition of political commitment by intellectuals, whose role in French society is accorded considerable prestige. Their influence may have been less significant than they themselves have often assumed, but their activity has been a fertile source of ideological communication in books, periodicals, the press and broadcast media. As befits the country which also gave rise to the convention of categorizing ideologies and political parties in terms of the topographical metaphor of left–centre–right, France has developed a multi-party system which accommodates a broad range of ideological currents. Outside the party system, furthermore, other ideologies have been sustained by adherents in the absence of significant institutional expression.

Our approach to the subject of this book is somewhat different from the perspective adopted in many surveys of political ideologies. We do not offer a systematic study of great thinkers who are deemed to have made seminal contributions to the ideological currents in question. We have not, in general, aimed to offer a history of political ideas which would trace the development of the different ideologies since the Revolution, or from some other historical juncture which can be taken as a point of origin. In works of those types the contemporary – however it is defined – usually receives rather limited treatment, even in studies which present their subject on the basis of themes rather than chronological development. The emphasis is usually on the ways in which the main lines of the ideology formed in the more distant past, so the contemporary figures are treated as an extension or variant of earlier beliefs. There is often an implicit assumption that recent developments cannot be viewed with sufficient critical distance to distinguish the essential from the ephemeral. By the same token, the history-of-ideas approach leads to a concentration on core beliefs at the expense of the operative end of ideology, where it informs the policies and strategic objectives of organizations engaged directly in the political arena.

There is nothing wrong with the traditional approach. Nevertheless, it can be interesting to look at the subject from the opposite angle by placing the contemporary phenomenon at the centre of attention, seeking to explain what it is and how its components fit together. Of course, this does not imply a purely synchronic approach. It does not exclude attention to historical antecedents. But the emphasis is different, and the treatment of those antecedents is in terms of the explanation of the present. While there is always the risk of dwelling excessively on features which will prove to have been transitory or trivial in the longer term, there is the opportunity to convey something of the colour of the ideology in relation to a particular context – the issues that its adherents face, the priority which is given to particular concerns, and the affective dimension, without which it could not exist as a mobilizing ideology. If it is assumed that ideologies are action-oriented, there are good reasons for taking account of the operative end of ideologies, without, however, focusing too exclusively on policy programmes at the expense of core elements, as studies of political parties often do. Ideally, a balance can be struck between treatment of the fundamental and the operative ends of the range so that attention can be paid to the relationship between them.

That is the aim of the present book. Contributors have framed their topics in whatever way they considered most appropriate to make the recent development of the ideologies intelligible. The history of any particular ideology has been included to the extent that the author of the chapter concerned thought it appropriate for the purposes of explanation. The objective has been to produce a book which is up to date without merely being topical at the time of writing but stale by the time it reaches the reader. For reasons of coherence and concentration of focus, where it was possible to single out a particular political party as the primary – though not necessarily the exclusive – conduit of a major ideological current in France, chapters have been centred on those parties. Thus, democratic socialism is discussed particularly in relation to the Parti Socialiste (PS), communism (Marxism-Leninism) in relation to the Parti Communiste Français (PCF), Gaullism and liberalism in relation to the Rassemblement pour la République (RPR) and the Union pour la Démocratie Française (UDF) respectively, national populism in relation to the Front National (FN) and ecologism in connection with Les Verts. The treatment of feminism and multi-culturalism is different. They have been taken up piecemeal by one or more parties at different times, and they have inspired pressure groups, but in both cases their core assumptions, values and goals have not given rise to a particular party or mass movement. Part of the analysis of these two ideologies is devoted to the question of why this has been the case.

From what has been said so far it will be evident that we have not set out to cover the full range of ideologies extant in France today. The scope was necessarily limited in order to give reasonably detailed attention to those selected for inclusion. On the one hand, we have excluded republicanism and its antithesis, monarchism. Republicanism can certainly be treated as a distinct ideology (Hazareesingh, 1994), but in the context of modern France there are good reasons for consider-ing it rather as a dominant paradigm which defines the framework within which a number of ideologies operate. In other words, it is a superordinate category in so far as many political ideologies in France are variant forms of republicanism. Conversely, monarchism can be considered as the paradigm for authoritarian ideologies since the time of the Revolution, even though very few people nowadays are seriously committed to a restoration of the monarchy. We have preferred to treat ideologies at the next level down, each in its own right, rather than reduce them to common denominators.

On the other hand, we have not included a number of ideologies which no longer have a significant influence on the political/ideological fields, if they ever did so. For example, we have excluded anarchism and Trotskyism on the left, Christian democracy and radicalism in the centre, and neo-Nazism on the extreme right. In some cases they have always been minority tastes. In others they once had a distinctiveness which has largely dissolved. Radicalism and Christian democracy are cases in point. Both exerted a powerful influence in French political life at one time. In the later nineteenth century radicalism meant something distinctive as a form of republicanism, but the periods of the Parti Radical et Radical-Socialiste in power from the 1900s to the fall of the Third Republic in 1940 eroded its ideological force. Although it did not entirely disappear thereafter, and although two small parties still exist in its lineage, radicalism can no longer be counted a significant ideology. Similarly, Christian democracy, which became a potent political force in the immediate post-war years through the medium of the now-defunct Mouvement Républicain Populaire, has increasingly lost its distinctiveness of ideological expression, even though it is still represented among the federation of parties within the UDF by the Force Démocrate.

Some of the ideologies selected for inclusion can be placed along the conventional left–right axis of classification, moving across from communism to democratic socialism, liberalism and Gaullism to national populism. These could be considered as older ideologies in comparison with the newer ones of ecologism, feminism and multiculturalism. The distinction can be made on the grounds that the older ones have been identified as ideologies and propagated by political parties or organized mass movements throughout all or most of the post-war period, at least. The newer ones crystallized as identifiable ideological currents in the late 1960s and 1970s out of the developing interest in grass-roots issues of civil society, quality of life, self-determination and minority rights – although the label of multiculturalism has seldom been used. Of course, the older ideologies are also the contemporary variants of broad ideological currents and cross-currents which can be traced back much earlier in France's history, with the Revolution usually serving conveniently as a symbolic point of emergence. But French feminists can cite pioneering figures from the period of the Revolution and the early nineteenth century. Ecologists can cite Rousseau and the romantics. Only multiculturalism appears to lack historical purchase.

The newer ideologies do not fit the left–right spectrum in a straightforward way. As ideologies they start from a preoccupation with a particular wrong committed by, or within, society – maltreatment of the natural environment, the dominance of men over women, intolerance of the native cultures of ethnic minorities – and prescribe principles and methods for righting that wrong in the light of particular values. The problem and its solutions do not exist in isolation from other features of society. On the contrary, they invite being viewed as symptomatic of wider, underlying characteristics, so ecologism, feminism and multiculturalism are not so much single-issue ideologies as partial ideologies which can agglomerate into larger sets of ideas. They may be incorporated as components of ideologies which offer more comprehensive worldviews. Political parties committed to those comprehensive ideologies will often adopt elements of a newer ideology in more or less diluted form, as the PS did, for example, with all of the three considered here during the late 1970s and the early 1980s. Alternatively, they may remain at the core of new syntheses, as both ecologism and feminism have done by drawing on and rethinking ideas associated with older currents, such as anarchism or socialism, or even fusing with each other, as in the case of what is sometimes called eco-feminism. New syntheses can also be enriched by adopting and adapting insights based on theoretical developments in scientific or other fields (Boudon, 1989), as when ecologism appeals to systems theory or feminism draws on psychoanalytic theory.

Ideologies enjoy varying fortunes over the course of time. They emerge, they become widely established or they remain marginal, they may achieve dominance, they may decline and become merely residual, they may re-emerge later. If measured by their expression in the discourse of political parties, the newer ideologies – ecologism, feminism and multiculturalism – have achieved varying but limited success so far. Of the three, multiculturalism has shown very slight appeal within French political circles. In Chapter 7 Alec Hargreaves explains how the permissiveness of multiculturalism clashes with a range of values and cultural assumptions which underpin the particular conception of nationhood associated with the French republican tradition. In policy terms multiculturalism was also ill served when measures were introduced in the name of cultural diversity under Giscard d'Estaing's presidency in the late 1970s, but were, in reality, part of a strategy to facilitate mass repatriation of immigrants. Equally, although the PS came to power in 1981 with a commitment to multiculturalism (under another name) as a positive, long-term goal for a multi-ethnic French society, this was a fairly peripheral element of the party's ideology. From the mid-1980s onwards, faced with electoral and opinion-poll evidence of increasing public sympathy for the anti-immigrant stance of the FN, the PS largely retreated from support for a multiculturalist agenda.

Feminism has made larger advances than multiculturalism in some respects, although it has not been translated into an organized mass movement, let alone a political party committed to a project of reform in the light of feminist principles. In fact, its political profile has faded since the heyday of the Mouvement de Libération des Femmes in the 1970s. The PS's creation of a new ministerial post for women's rights under Mitterrand's first presidency did not pave the way for a major increase of female representation in public life. Indeed, if participation in public life is taken as an indicator, the picture is not encouraging. At the time of writing, the increasing number of female MEPs (29 per cent) is counterbalanced by the generally low levels in other areas – for example, among members of the Assemblée Nationale (5.5 per cent – 32 members out of 577), of the Sénat (5.9 per cent – 18 members out of 303), among mayors (8.3 per cent – 2,824 out of 33,948), among regional councillors (12 per cent), among prefects (less than 3 per cent), among ambassadors (2 per cent) or among top civil servants in the ministries (5.5 per cent). In the economic sphere, to name another area, the presence of increasing numbers of women in the workplace must be set against the persistence of gender-related differences of job security, and access to senior positions, for example. Nevertheless, as Máire Cross points out in Chapter 6, the feminist movement in France can boast an impressive theoretical output. Feminist scholars have also worked to constitute a growing body of gender historiography. And with regard to formal politics, the demand for rectification of the gender imbalance in representation remains on the agenda. It was illustrated, for instance, in the summer of 1996 with the launching of a manifesto by ten leading female politicians from different political parties to demand a range of measures such as parity in governmental and senior civil service appointments, the use of quotas by parties in elections until at least one third of the seats in all assemblies are held by women, differential financing of political parties in the light of their respect for the principle of parity, and legislation against sexism comparable to existing laws against racism (Barzach *et al.*, 1996).

Of the newer ideologies discussed in this book, only ecologism has inspired the creation of a political party whose policies are centred on concerns relating to that particular ideology. However, its popular appeal, as measured by electoral performance, has been inconsistent. The emergence of the ecologist movement from the 1960s onwards coincided with the wider international development of environmental awareness. Among the signs of the times, the first UN Conference on the Environment was held in 1972 and the first of the EC's Environmental Action Programmes was launched in 1973. During the 1970s established organizations such as the World Wildlife Fund were joined by new pressure groups, including Friends of the Earth and Greenpeace. France's first anti-pollution laws date from the 1960s and further legislation was to follow. A junior ministerial post for the environment was created in 1971. Although the funding levels have inevitably remained far lower than campaigners believe necessary, the state has created a range of agencies and promoted numerous initiatives for environmental protection and enhancement since that time.

To that extent, political ecologism derived benefit from an increasingly favourable climate. But this did not guarantee overwhelming support for ecologism as a political ideology. Political ecologism was a diverse phenomenon, both ideologically and organizationally, and it has remained so. The strand examined by Brendan Prendiville in Chapter 5 represents the more radical end of the range. The ideology of Les Verts, a party founded in 1984, has been anti-statist, anti-productivist, anti-materialist, communitarian, attracted to small-scale organization and inspired by a holistic conception of the natural world. The early steps taken by ecologist groups into electoral politics during the 1970s had been intended more to gain publicity than to participate in a political system to which many of them were hostile (Journès, 1982). Nevertheless, they were sufficiently successful by the late 1970s – for example, scoring an average of 4.5 per cent in constituencies where they put up candidates in the 1978 parliamentary elections, and 4.39 per cent in the 1979 European election – to encourage the PS to court the ecologist vote (Sainteny, 1994). The pattern of fragmented participation by different ecologist groups in national and local elections continued throughout the 1980s, with variable success until the apparent breakthrough in the European elections of 1989, when a joint ecologist list gained 10.6 per cent of the vote, which brought nine MEPs. The municipal elections of that year yielded nearly 1,400 councillors, and the momentum continued until the regional elections of 1992 produced a combined total of 14.7 per cent for the various ecologist electoral lists, giving them more than 200 councillors. Yet the disappointing green vote in the parliamentary elections of 1993 (7.8 per cent), the European elections of 1994 (4.9 per cent) and the presidential election of 1995 (3.3 per cent) showed that widespread public concern over environmental issues had not translated into solid support for the variegated ecologist movement as a whole, let alone for Les Verts in particular. Whatever other reasons can be adduced to explain the failure to break through in national elections since the early 1990s, it also suggests that the political ideology of ecologism has not yet established a genuine mass following committed to the fundamental changes of social, economic and political organization which practical implementation would entail.

At the time of writing, communism could be considered a residual ideology in France, as in most other Western countries where it was once an established oppositional current. For a range of reasons the appeal of Marxism-Leninism has dwindled from its high point during the two decades following the Liberation. The PCF was extremely late to de-Stalinize its internal practices, in so far as it has yet done so. As Jeremy Jennings shows in Chapter 2, it identified itself too closely for too long with the USSR. Its parallel identification of itself as the patriotic bearer of all that was best in France's own revolutionary tradition brought diminishing returns. By the later 1960s it had lost much of the support which it had previously attracted from intellectuals, and it had failed to appeal to the younger generation, as was evident in the students' movement of May 1968. It was outmanoeuvred by the PS in the 1970s and 1980s in competition for votes from the dwindling industrial working class and from the new middle-class strata (Ross, 1987). It was taken hostage by the PS in government from 1981 to 1984. The party which had scored over 26 per cent at its post-war peak saw its electoral support fall to a low of 6.8 per cent in the 1988 presidential election, so that its score of 8.6 per cent in the first round of the 1995 presidential election could be claimed by the leadership as a sign of revival.

Nevertheless, it does not have to be assumed that communism is doomed to fade away definitively. Attempts have already been made to reconceptualize, or at least to repackage, the ideology, even if room for manoeuvre is limited by unwillingness to sacrifice core beliefs, or to risk losing distinctiveness in relation to the PS, by espousing what the PCF regards as social democracy. There is always the possibility of renewal, given the right combination of personalities, organization and political environment. That much is evident from what has occurred at the other end of the political spectrum. National populism could be described as a resurgent ideology. It offers a modernized synthesis of ideas largely deriving from earlier currents of the radical right, combined with some borrowings from other areas of the ideological spectrum. Paradoxically, it too owes something to the climate of ideological ferment and the launching of new projects in the wake of the massive, quasi-revolutionary protests by students and workers in May 1968. Throughout the post-war period until that time the authoritarian extreme right had lacked ideological and organizational direction. Apart from short-lived flurries of serious agitation during the later 1950s and early 1960s, its political impact was marginal. However, the desire to respond to the rise of the new left-wing counter-culture symbolized by the events of May 1968 provoked a desire among activists on the extreme right to find new ways to respond to the situation.

The main impetus towards ideological renewal from the end of the 1960s onwards originated with the intellectuals associated with the Groupement de Recherche et d'Etudes pour la Civilisation Européenne (GRECE) and with the Club de l'Horloge, formed by breakaway members of GRECE in 1974. The conscious aim of these groups was to create a new right-wing culture (Duranton-Crabol, 1988; Taguieff, 1994). While GRECE remained aloof from direct reflection on politics, the Club de l'Horloge concerned itself with exerting influence on the political parties of the mainstream right. Some of its members became active in the Gaullist party, the UDF or the ultra-conservative Centre National des Indépendants et Paysans (CNIP).

During the same period the organizational impetus towards political renewal came from the Front National, which had been formed in 1972 from a number of neo-fascist and ultra-nationalist groups in an attempt to unify the extreme right and present a more acceptable face to the electorate. Throughout its first ten years of existence the party followed the sterile tradition of the post-war extreme right by spending much of its time on internal divisions, personal animosities, expulsions, rivalry with breakaway groups, and occasional self-inflicted violence: it made no significant electoral impact, never receiving even 1 per cent of the national vote. The 1981 presidential election was particularly humiliating for its leader, Jean-Marie Le Pen. Having scored a mere 0.74 per cent in the 1974 election, he failed even to gain the necessary 500 signatures of public office holders to qualify as a candidate in 1981. Yet, within three years of that disaster, the FN had started to make its breakthrough into the national arena, where it achieved national scores ranging from just under 10 per cent to 15 per cent from 1984 to the mid-1990s.

What makes the FN particularly interesting in the present context is the fact that its early successes, and the hope of better things to come, allowed it to attract an increasing number of leading lights of the Club de l'Horloge, including some of those who had previously established themselves as rising stars within the RPR, the UDF or the CNIP. Several intellectuals from GRECE had also moved into the FN by the end of the 1980s. Although the New Right did not establish a monopoly of ideological discourse within the FN, its incorporation into this highly activist party has produced a potent combination in which ideological production has spurred, and been spurred by, the struggle to capture an increasing share of the electorate. My discussion of national populism in Chapter 4 gives some indication of the substantial range of theoretical argument which lies behind the FN's policy positions.

What of the other ideologies – democratic socialism, liberalism and Gaullism? Although they come from different directions, it might appear that they have reached a considerable degree of convergence. In bringing together elements of the previously fragmented non-communist left in 1969 and absorbing others in the following years, the formation of the PS offered the possibility of ideological renewal through cross-fertilization between diverse subcurrents. In the course of the 1970s the PS did, in fact, assimilate a number of themes associated with the New Left into its programmes. However, with the exception of administrative decentralization, and to a lesser extent worker self-management (*autogestion*), these themes did not have a central place. In the interests of cooperation/competition with the PCF, the strategic decision was taken to centre the party's official line on a traditional Marxist analysis of capitalism, coupled with a statist model of development towards socialism through economic planning, massive extension of public ownership, tight regulation of the private sector, redistributive taxation, increased negotiating power for employees, reductions in working hours and a wide range of other economic, social or cultural reforms, to be financed by Keynesian methods of deficit spending and demand management.

After the great hopes when the PS took power in 1981, and the initial wave of sweeping reforms, the ensuing economic and financial crisis, the gradual retreat from unfulfilled objectives, and the reversal of some of the earlier reforms all paved the way for the evolution of policy towards a broadly social democratic combination of technocratic economic management and increasing acceptance of free-market practices. The silence of the left-wing intelligentsia during this period has been the subject of much comment by political analysts. Following its two years out of power after the 1986 election, the return of the PS to government from 1988 to 1993 on a weaker electoral mandate reinforced the retreat from traditional socialist objectives, to the accompaniment of inconclusive soul searching and factional in-fighting on the issue of ideological self-definition – a process which was exacerbated by the electoral disaster of 1993 and which has continued since that time. The complex trajectory of democratic socialism is analysed by Laurence Bell in Chapter 1.

It might therefore seem that the real ideological winners of the 1980s and 1990s will have been the parties of the mainstream centre-right, notwithstanding endless personal rivalries and internal competition for ascendancy. The constitutional programme of post-war Gaullism – itself a synthesis of republican and neo-Bonapartist elements – was achieved by the establishment of the Fifth Republic, subject to some later modifications. By the late 1970s and early 1980s, the highly inter-ventionist attitude to the economy and the rather vague notions of industrial relations reform had given way to enthusiasm for neo-liberal ideas and the objective of developing a French counterpart of the Reaganite and Thatcherite models. Neo-liberalism also found fertile ground in the UDF, in which the version of liberalism with a social conscience propagated by Giscard d'Estaing had already been a domi-nant ideological force in the 1970s. In Chapter 3 Peter Fysh examines the development of Gaullism, Giscardian liberalism and the meeting between them.

The opportunity to enact a radical programme substantially shaped by neo-liberal economic principles in combination with a conservative social agenda came in 1986, with the election of an RPR/UDF parlia-mentary majority; but the failure to achieve re-election in 1988 showed, among other things, that public enthusiasm for privatizations, dereg-ulation, and other neo-liberal policies had diminished in the aftermath of the stock market crash in October 1987. Though more cautious in its electoral programmes during the 1990s, the RPR/UDF block remained largely wedded in theory, though not always in practice, to a liberal worldview (Godin, 1996). But it was a more pragmatic, chastened liberalism which had to face public resentment of persistently high unemployment, unpopular decisions concerning the finances of the welfare state, resistance of employees to rationalization or privatization of public services, and constraints on monetary policy in the light of convergence criteria for future participation in the European Monetary Union (EMU) – not to mention the whole gamut of economic pres-sures affecting Western economies under the impact of globalization.

During the 1995 presidential election campaign, Jacques Chirac accused his fellow-Gaullist rival, Edouard Balladur, of slavishly follow-ing the liberal approach, regardless of its damage to the fabric of French society (Windebank, 1996, p. 346). Regardless of the incon-sistencies of Chirac's own position, his criticism of Balladur echoed the increasingly widespread charge that liberalism was tending to become a stifling orthodoxy, whether it was espoused with enthusiasm or with resignation. The maverick anti-establishment journalist and essayist,

Jean-François Kahn (1995), captured this tendency under the label of *la pensée unique*, which subsequently passed into wide circulation in political and media circles. Although his diatribes on the subject were given to polemical overstatement, Kahn's argument was persuasive when he asserted that large sections of French society were being reduced to a state of desperation – and attraction in increasing numbers to the FN's national populist appeal – by the repeated, deterministic message from the formerly socialist (now social liberal) left as well as the centre-right to the effect that, beyond limited measures around the edges, there was no real alternative at national or international level to the remorseless logic of liberal capitalism. The communicators of every ideology invariably claim that the beliefs in question are natural, normal and ultimately beneficial to all sections of society because they are inescapably valid and true (Thompson, 1994). It is difficult at present to imagine that liberalism – with either a conservative liberal or a social liberal slant – could be challenged seriously in France in the short to medium term, except perhaps from the radical right. But that assumption may itself be an ideologically induced distortion of thought.

References

Barzach, M. *et al.* (1996) 'Le Manifeste des dix pour la parité'. *L'Express*, 6 June, pp. 32–3.

Boudon, R. (1989) *The Analysis of Ideology* (trans. M. Slater). Cambridge: Polity Press.

Duranton-Crabol, A.-M. (1988) *Visages de la Nouvelle Droite: le GRECE et son histoire*. Paris: Presses de la Fondation Nationale des Sciences Politiques.

Flood, C. (1996) *Political Myth: A Theoretical Introduction*. New York: Garland.

Freeden, M. (1994) 'Political Concepts and Ideological Morphology'. *Journal of Political Philosophy* **2** (2), 140–64.

Godin, E. (1996) 'Le Néo-libéralisme à la française: une exception?'. *Modern and Contemporary France* NS4 (1), 61–70.

Hazareesingh, S. (1994) *Political Traditions in Modern France*. Oxford: Oxford University Press.

Head, B. (1985) *Ideology and Social Science: Destutt de Tracy and French Liberalism*. Dordrecht: Martinus Nijhoff.

Journès, C. (1982) 'Les Ecologistes, l'Etat et les partis', in P. Bacot and C. Journès (eds) *Les Nouvelles Idéologies*. Lyon: Presses Universitaires de Lyon.

Kahn, J.-F. (1995) *La Pensée unique*. Paris: Fayard.

Ross, G. (1987) 'Destroyed by the Dialectic: Politics, the Decline of Marxism, and the New Middle Strata in France'. *Theory and Society* **16**, 7–38.

Sainteny, G. (1994) 'Le Parti socialiste face à l'écologisme'. *Revue française de science politique* **44** (3), 424–61.

Scarbrough, E. (1984) *Political Ideology and Voting: An Exploratory Study*. Oxford: Oxford University Press.

Seliger, M. (1976) *Ideology and Politics*. London: Allen and Unwin.

Taguieff, P.-A. (1994) *Sur la Nouvelle Droite: jalons d'une analyse critique*. Paris: Descartes.

Thompson, J.B. (1994) *Ideology and Modern Culture*. Cambridge: Polity Press.

Windebank, J. (1996) 'Economic Review of the Year 1995'. *Modern and Contemporary France* NS4 (3), 345–8.

1

Democratic Socialism

LAURENCE BELL

Introduction

Democratic socialism in France is represented in the party political system by the Parti Socialiste (PS), the heir of the Section Française de l'Internationale Ouvrière (SFIO), founded in 1905 following the unification of a variety of different, pre-existing socialist movements. Throughout its existence its real nature and aims have often been in dispute, both within the party and among outside observers. The origins and evolution of democratic socialism in France have made this question particularly problematic. In addition, the ideological changes which French socialism has undergone in recent years, largely (although not entirely) as a result of its experience in power in the period from 1981 to 1993, have not really clarified the question. If the 'normalization' of French socialism since 1983 poses the question, 'What is socialism now and what can it be in the future?', it still places a question mark over what it *really* was in the past, prior to these changes.

For many political scientists French socialism seems most readily identifiable with the European social democratic tradition. However, French socialists themselves – until the changes of the 1980s at any rate – generally refused such an identification and claimed that their own project represented a 'third way', distinct from both Soviet-style communism and reformist social democracy. Seasoned observers of European social democracy have rejected this claim as being based on little more than radical rhetoric, bearing little relation to the 'true' nature of French socialism (Padgett and Paterson, 1991, pp. 20, 32). Others, in line with this, have argued that the deliberate move of the PS in the mid-1980s to rally to the banner of social democracy was merely a somewhat disingenuous acknowledgement of an already existing state of affairs (Bell and Criddle, 1988, pp. 250–1). Proponents of the social democratic nature of the Socialist Party tend to base their argument on analysis of policy objectives and the means proposed for achieving them.

French observers are usually uncomfortable with the assimilation of French socialism to a 'foreign' tradition and tend to define changes in the identity of the PS in more specifically French terms. Thus Duverger (1955, pp. 19–24) argued that the SFIO had by the middle of the twentieth century stepped into the shoes of the declining Parti Radical (a middle-class, small-town provincial, republican-liberal party founded in 1901), albeit without revising its doctrine accordingly. Portelli (1980, pp. 89–105) later took up the same theme, applying it to the renovated PS of the 1970s. Proponents of the 'neo-radicalization' argument deny that the PS is or can be social democratic, on the grounds that it has always lacked social democratic structures (a mass membership bound together in a 'solidarity community', close organizational ties with the trade union and cooperative movement, etc.). They base their argument on other structural factors, such as electoral geography and the social composition of the PS electorate. The PS, they claim, is like the Parti Radical of the Third Republic: it is the defender of the interests of the professional (and largely provincial) middle classes, particularly teachers; it is inextricably tied to a republican vision of democracy, whose defence has been, at certain periods in its existence, virtually its *raison d'être*; it is happy to manage the system rather than transform it; and it clings to a rather hollow notion of *laïcité* (secularism in public affairs). This explanation, while enlightening in many respects, has the disadvantage of dismissing decades of socialist discourse on radical social change as nothing more than symbolic gesturing in bad faith. One also has to question whether the term *radicalisation* (in the French sense of becoming like the Parti Radical) can really explain very much in the second half of the twentieth century and, particularly, under the regime of the Fifth Republic.

Other authors acknowledge some of the evidence supporting the neo-radicalism argument, but reject it as inadequate to explain the nature of the PS and its evolution (Bergounioux and Grunberg, 1992, pp. 183, 477–85). However, while not unsympathetic to social democracy, they do not interpret that evolution in terms of a process of 'social democratization' either. Rather the identity of the PS, both before and after the ideological sea change of the mid-1980s, should be understood in terms of a '*dégradation*' (a gradual weakening) of the original socialist model, which marked the SFIO from its creation in 1905 and which has not been replaced by a coherent, alternative model.

An approach in terms of the way in which a collective identity was structured and has since been stripped away is an appropriate one for the present examination of socialism as an ideology or ideological discourse. It lends itself to the idea of discursive constraint, that is (in this context), the factors which have constrained the discourse that structured the identity of socialism in France and forced it in a particular direction or prevented it from evolving. Ideology is, after all, one of the factors which determine what is and what is not sayable at a given moment in history.

The main themes which will be examined in this retrospective view are: the tension between the republican and socialist poles of PS identity; a comparison between French socialism and the social democratic model, and some indications of why the latter was not possible in France; the bases on which the PS was relaunched in the 1970s, and the role ideology played in positioning the party and in internal rivalries; the ideological 'baggage' with which the PS came to power in the 1980s; and how the experience of government affected its discourse.

A Dual Republican and Socialist Identity

The ideological complexion of the early SFIO was profoundly affected by the two major figures who presided over its foundation, Jules Guesde and Jean Jaurès. The followers of Guesde were influenced by the thought of Karl Marx, but while they accepted his revolutionary conclusions, they did not adopt his method in order to analyse contemporary society, but instead tended to reduce his materialism to a series of dogmatic affirmations (Willard, 1967, pp. 51–4). One of these was that the political rights of the parliamentary Republic were illusory and that fighting for them diverted socialists from their real goal – a social revolution which would overthrow the bourgeois order in all its forms. However, as socialism had developed in an organized political form in the late nineteenth century, it had inexorably been drawn towards electoralism and the reformism that this implied.

On the other hand, the socialism of Jaurès, who had begun his political life as a radical republican, was strongly coloured by the idea of the potential of the Republic for realizing not only political rights, but also social and economic rights, and therefore reforms which would lead to the achievement of socialism. The Republic thus had to be defended and developed (Willard, 1967, pp. 75–6). It has often been thought that the dilemma of French socialism (and many of its difficulties of self-definition in the twentieth century) lay in the contradiction between these two positions. However, with hindsight, we can say that there was an equally important cleavage *within* Jaurès's thought and the tradition he bequeathed to his party.

Jaurès was profoundly attached to democracy and saw socialism as the fulfilment, in concrete, socioeconomic terms, of its humanist message. Socialism was to be achieved by 'calm deliberation and the legal will of the majority of the nation' (cited in Lévy, 1947, p. 143). In this respect he was in tune with the re-evaluation of liberalism going on within German social democracy and associated with Eduard Bernstein (Wright, 1993, pp. 83–5). However, he also adhered to Marx's theory of value, to the absolute distinction between the bourgeoisie and the proletariat (in which property ownership was the main criterion), and to the centrality of class struggle to historical development. He attempted to reconcile this materialism with his own moral idealism in what he called 'revolutionary evolution' (Lévy, 1947, pp. xiv, 120). While Jaurès believed in the value of reform, he derived his model of change from the French Revolution and viewed socialism as a break to be achieved in the possibly distant future. Thus, despite his attachment to the Republic (with its ideal of a unified citizenry) and acceptance of electoral means, Jaurès repudiated Bernstein's revisionist view that socialism was a process, not a final goal. French socialism accordingly adopted a distinction between short-term reform programmes and long-term revolutionary aims.

Owing to Guesdist influence the SFIO declared itself, at its foundation in 1905, to be not a party of reform but a revolutionary, workers' party. However, within a matter of years Jaurès's preponderant influence led the party to support such reform demands as workers' pension schemes and the nationalization of the railways. On the other hand, despite its growing number of parliamentary seats, the party held to its stance of not participating in 'bourgeois' governments (Bergounioux and Grunberg, 1992, pp. 73–4). In addition to this tension between the poles of reform and revolution, a number of other factors structured the identity of French socialism in the early decades of the twentieth century.

The first of these was the absence of strong links with the trade union movement. This weakened the supposed working-class nature of the SFIO and forced it to look elsewhere for support. The increasingly prominent role of teachers, in particular, reinforced the identification of the party with *laïcité*. Second, the SFIO abandoned its pacifism and belief in international working-class solidarity when it opted to join in a bourgeois-led government to support France's war effort in World War I. It thus put the nation before class. Finally, following disagreement in the SFIO in 1920 over whether the party should join the new Soviet-dominated Communist International or not, those who opted for membership split from the SFIO to form the Parti Communiste Français (PCF). The SFIO, now led by Léon Blum, henceforth had a rival on its left, and one whose revolutionary profile would challenge its identity and make any adjustment of it difficult.

All of the above factors had a mutually contradictory effect, in that they both reinforced the identification of French socialism with the Republic and led it to reject revisionism and cling to the doctrine of its founding period. In common with the PCF, the SFIO continued to adhere to a revolutionary critique of capitalism derived from Marx. Likewise, even socialists such as Blum held that the transition from capitalism to socialism would not be a gradual and seamless one, but would involve a revolutionary break and might require a temporary 'dictatorship of the proletariat' (Lacouture, 1977, p. 160).

On the other hand, the SFIO held that these aims should, if possible, be achieved without violence, and emphasized the importance of reforms in the business of preparing the working class to assume its historical role. However, by the 1920s the SFIO had become an important parliamentary party, and this placed it in a dilemma: on the one hand electoral success was pushing it towards the mainstream of republican politics and the achievement of reforms, which it might try to negotiate with the Parti Radical; on the other hand its doctrine – with its long-term aims – made collaboration within the existing system with a 'class enemy' problematic. Léon Blum, who in the inter-war years led the majority centre tendency of the party, sought to provide a way out of this ideological discomfiture with his famous distinction between the 'exercise' and the 'conquest' of power (Lacouture, 1977, pp. 197–9; Portelli, 1980, p. 53). The 'exercise' of power involved taking part in coalition governments in order to defend democracy and achieve piecemeal reforms. It implied legal action within the system with no pretence of transforming it in the direction of socialism. The (revolutionary) 'conquest' of power was placed in a more distant future. Thus, despite growing support in the SFIO for reformism, the distinction between a maximal programme and a minimal one was maintained and, in the 1930s, the SFIO rejected the new idea of socialist planning of the (existing) economy (Lacouture, 1977, p. 388; Willard, 1967, pp. 114–15).

In certain other European countries socialism or social democracy had by this time moved, more decisively than in France, towards a thorough-going socialist reformism. Within the British Labour Party, for example, the work of the Fabian Society, the Webbs and R.H. Tawney had led to a dual critique of capitalism, in terms of both economic efficiency and moral values (Wright, 1993, p. 86). These people were confident that history was on their side and that democratic politics could – through economic planning, socialization, welfare and redistribution – use the state to reform capitalism into socialism. This breed of reformism, which had no Marxist past to come to terms with and which had not been founded on the rock of anti-clericalism, was quite happy to ground itself in Christian ethical values. French socialism, with its republican, anti-clerical background, could not articulate its project in such terms. In addition, the SFIO was unwilling to acknowledge the irreversibility of the 1920 schism, which had given birth to its rival on the left, by undertaking a thorough revision of its doctrine. Social reform within capitalism was a good thing, but it was not socialism, which was something qualitatively quite different.

French socialists were comforted in this view by the fact that reformist confidence was dented by the crisis years of the 1930s: far from being able to convert a robust capitalism – ready to give way to its fundamentally socialized nature – into socialism, socialists (in those countries where they were associated with government) appeared to be propping up an ailing capitalism. The recession of the 1930s gave the Marxist idea of the crisis of capitalism renewed credibility. For the left of the SFIO the final crisis of capitalism was at hand, and even Blum viewed the causes of the recession as specific to capitalism and quite inconceivable in socialism (Bergounioux and Grunberg, 1992, p. 121).

The SFIO's first experience of power was in the 1936 Front Populaire government led by Léon Blum. This relatively short-lived socialist-led coalition of the left, brought to power by opposition to the rising tide of fascism, is usually remembered for its significant social reforms and its disastrous economic policy. Faced with difficulties which its doctrine did not equip it to deal with, the SFIO was driven to practise a conservative economic policy, which its left wing repudiated as a betrayal of socialism (Guérin, 1970, p. 201). This notion of a betrayal of principles, along with electoral evidence, has been used to support the argument that the 'radicalisation' of the socialist party was already under way in 1936 (Portelli, 1980, pp. 54–5). However, it is possible to view the lessons learnt from the Front Populaire in a different light.

Reflecting on the difficulties and opposition which even a minimal programme had encountered, Blum concluded that the problem had been, in large part, that a minimal programme without an extensive plan of structural reforms had lacked the coherence of an overall strategy which could attract enough broad-based support to overcome political obstacles. This implied an end to the distinction between the minimal and the maximal programme, and suggested that acting within the existing political framework with a reinforced armoury of means offered better prospects. This pointed in the direction of a reinforced social state acting within a mixed economy (Bergounioux and Grunberg, 1992, pp. 155–6) and was in step with the thinking in certain European social democratic parties, which had begun to find a solution to the dilemma in which the 1930s slump had placed them in Keynesian economics (Wright, 1993, pp. 88–9). However, the impact of Keynes's ideas on both socialist and social democratic movements was not really felt until after World War II, and even then French socialists were reluctant to integrate the perspective opened by their application into their political outlook.

Compromise and Retrenchment

In the immediate post-war period the need for state intervention to bring about national reconstruction was unquestioned in France. Structural reforms and rebuilding the country were the order of the day, and economic planning, nationalization and welfare provision were the central plank of the reform programme advocated by the National Resistance Council and supported by the socialists. The generation of socialists who had cut their political teeth in the clandestine action of wartime resistance was more pragmatic than doctrinaire, and the old argument over participating in government or not now seemed obsolete (Quilliot, 1972, p. 21). However, the precise significance to be attached to nationalization was not clear. Did it imply state control of important sectors of the economy, simply with a view to rationalizing them to facilitate reconstruction, or did it imply socialization? Was a partly socialized economy – in an intermediate position between liberal capitalism and socialism – a culminating point or merely a staging post on the road to socialism, which would, at some indefinite time in the future, involve a qualitative transformation achieved by the accumulation of reforms? Providing clear answers to these questions, which had important implications for both socialist doctrine and strategy, proved difficult in the circumstances in which the post-war SFIO found itself.

In the generally reformist climate of the Liberation the SFIO had an opportunity to relaunch itself on a new footing, with a new following drawn from the Resistance. This, however, would have required it to abandon its traditional anti-clericalism and revise or abandon its Marxist doctrine. Blum, who in wartime captivity had formulated a revised 'humanist' socialism, according to which revolution would essentially be a moral transformation, favoured such a change. His vision, in which 'class struggle' was replaced by 'class action', emphasized the primacy of democratic liberties and the development of the individual in harmony with society (Lacouture, 1977, pp. 518–19).

However, an opposing tendency, soon to be identified with the neo-Guesdist Guy Mollet, held that the way forward for the party lay in a return to its revolutionary Marxist doctrine and viewed reforms as just one aspect of 'socialist preparation' (for revolutionary change, that is), not as socialism in themselves (on these ideas, see the party text reproduced in Quilliot, 1972, pp. 785–803). That Mollet's tendency gained the upper hand within the SFIO was largely due to the political context of the time. The post-war SFIO found itself in a governing coalition, uncomfortably wedged between two larger parties: to its left the PCF, to which it did not want to abandon the monopoly of revolutionary aims, and to its right the newly created and apparently reformist Christian democratic Mouvement Républicain Populaire (MRP), from which it had to distinguish itself clearly. It was also obliged to play a conciliatory hinge role in this coalition. The concessions socialist ministers had to make antagonized the party rank and file, who felt that the dilution of the party line was the main cause of the SFIO's increasingly poor election results.

Appreciations of the real doctrinal differences between the two camps and of whether Mollet's ideological position was held in good faith vary (Portelli, 1980, pp. 70–3; Quilliot, 1972, pp. 175–82). Perhaps the most important aspect of Mollet's charge that the party's difficulties stemmed from a dilution of its doctrine was its appeal to the party 'patriotism' of the rank and file, an attitude which exacerbated its attitude of retrenchment and inability to confront post-war political realities, notably the new dominance of the PCF.

Thus while the experience of the Resistance had converted the SFIO to the mixed economy, to structural reforms and to a necessarily reformist practice, its response to the post-war political landscape was to reaffirm its pre-war revolutionary doctrine. This contradiction between its principles and practice was to be exacerbated by the complicated circumstances of the Fourth Republic. With the onset of the Cold War and the dismissal of the communist ministers from the government in May 1947, the PCF went into a long period of isolation, from which it attacked not merely particular policies but the foundations of the political system itself. The new republic also had to withstand the onslaughts of the Gaullists, who were determined to replace it with a different set of institutional arrangements. The SFIO was therefore drawn into joining in 'Third Force' coalitions in which the political centre of gravity shifted increasingly to the centre right. It found itself acting as an alibi for policies it did not agree with in order to defend the Republic, a strategy which was presented as the defence of democracy and to which other considerations were subordinated.

Despite the fact that in the period 1946–58 the SFIO supported more governments than it squarely opposed, its electoral decline and the resurgence of the right meant that its reforming efforts were limited to relatively minor social questions (Bergounioux and Grunberg, 1992, pp. 203–4). However, rather than scaling down its doctrinal pretensions, the SFIO stiffened its doctrinal position in an attempt to preserve its threatened identity. The 'immobilism' of the regime and its involvement in ill-fated colonial wars also reduced the party's capacity to promote reforms. The doctrine of the SFIO therefore had little bearing on its political practice.

So while the German Social Democrats (SPD) were moving towards a sweeping revision of their doctrine and while the British Labour Party was engaged in a fundamental debate, their French counterparts were absorbed in colonial and regime conflicts and paid little attention to what was happening in northern European sister parties (Padgett and Paterson, 1991, pp. 28–32). At its Bad Godesberg Congress in 1959 the SPD, with an eye on the vote of the new middle classes, affirmed that it was a 'people's' party, rather than a workers' party, and abandoned its former class-based critique of capitalism for an eclectic humanist ethos, whose major principles were freedom, justice and solidarity. This signalled an acceptance of the liberal pluralist political model and of the market economy (and hence of the private ownership of the means of production), which were to be reconciled with democratic principles. The formulation 'as much competition as possible, as much planning as necessary' summed up this new stance (Wright, 1993, p. 90). The basic assumption of the revisionism of the northern European parties (although it was not universally shared) was that reformed and regulated capitalism was not merely the path to socialism but was already socialism in action. This was the 'social democratic compromise'.

Such revisionism found only faint echoes in the SFIO. While there were individuals who sought to narrow the gap between the party's doctrine and its practice (Quilliot, 1972, p. 755), they did not form an organized tendency and their proposals were marginalized by the leadership. The Fundamental Programme of 1962 acknowledged that there had been changes in the nature of capitalism, but did not view a reformed capitalism, based on a mixed economy, as the destination of socialism. Public ownership thus remained central to the doctrine of the SFIO. However, it was acknowledged that the appropriation of surplus value was not inherently bad, but bad because its rate and use were not democratically determined. This failing was to be corrected by democratic planning. Nevertheless, for this to be possible, private property deemed to be exploitative of labour had to be collectivized, although non-exploitative activities (essentially agriculture and small-scale production) could stay in private hands. The party was again declared to be a party of revolutionary reform (Codding and Safran, 1979, pp. 43–7).

Thus, there was little change in the SFIO's doctrine in relation to its 1945 definition, and little that reflected the significant changes taking place in French society as a result of rapid economic growth. Without a clear idea of how to respond to the new phenomenon of Gaullism, unable or unwilling to draw on a credible centre alliance and dwarfed on the left by the PCF, the SFIO clung blindly to its original identity and, in the early years of the Fifth Republic, seemed destined for terminal decline.

In order to understand how French socialism was resurrected and was again able to present itself as the future, some consideration of the political landscape of the 1960s is necessary here. In this period there were three different bids to revive the non-communist left, in order to confront the obstacle to change which the PCF constituted and to respond to the challenge of Gaullist dominance. The first of these attempted to rally the parties of the non-communist left, the Christian democratic centre and other organizations, such as trade unions and a variety of political clubs, around the reform programme of a presidential candidate, Gaston Defferre. This strategy, modelled more or less on the style of an American Democrat campaign, failed essentially because it ignored party sensibilities, lacked a realistic solution for dealing with the PCF and did not correspond to the new bipolar logic of the Fifth Republic (Chapsal, 1972, pp. 557–8; Suffert, 1966, pp. 106–10).

The second strategy was also based on a presidential candidacy, that of François Mitterrand, but took account of bipolarization. Mitterrand's aim was to unite the non-communist Left, that is the SFIO, the Radical Party and the nebula of 'republican' clubs he had brought together in the Convention des Institutions Républicaines (CIR), and take it into a tactical alliance with the PCF. This was a partisan strategy which excluded the Christian democratic centre and did not count simply on the rallying power of new ideas and proposals. Mitterrand considered ideological questions to be secondary and announced that he was prepared to accept that socialism was what the SFIO said it was at its party congresses, that is, the socialization of the means of production (La Pensée Socialiste Contemporaine, 1965, pp. 24–5). His calculated gamble was that a 'union of the left' strategy would eventually advantage the more moderate partner in such an alliance and erode the communist vote. It was therefore futile to begin by trying to arrive at an agreement on ideological grounds. What gave this strategy credibility was its electoral effectiveness: Mitterrand's relatively narrow defeat in the 1965 election suggested that this was the way ahead (Dreyfus, 1975, pp. 277–84).

The third strategy, associated principally with the 'modernist' branch of the small but intellectually influential Parti Socialiste Unifié (PSU), led from 1967 by Michel Rocard, had much more ideological aims (Poperen, 1972, pp. 27–31, 74–6, 362–5; Martinet, 1986, pp. 128–52). For them the SFIO was obsolete, but the PCF's ideological stranglehold on the left was an obstacle to renewal. The way ahead therefore lay in the definition of a doctrine which, thanks to the appeal of its modernity, could break the hegemony of communist doctrine.

The 'modernists' held that industrial societies, in both the East and the West, were converging towards technocratic forms of organization in which power lay less with those who owned the means of production than with those who controlled decision making. The 'modernists' therefore advocated an efficient managerial socialism, whose technocratic tendencies would be counterbalanced by the democratization of decision making, by means of democratic planning and employee participation in the workplace (Mallet, 1963, pp. 60–73, 174–5). Socialism would therefore not be a final result, achieved after the defeat and expropriation of an exploitative capitalist class, but rather an ongoing process in which the balance of social and economic power would be regulated by contractual relationships. This bears some relation to the compromise of social democracy, in that it could accommodate itself to a (regulated) market economy. However, it looked to a 'post-Fordist' economy, conferred little value on the traditional type of political party, and championed a form of decentralizing anti-statism which owed more to Tocqueville than to Marx (Servet, 1966).

Whatever their differences, the perspectives outlined above presented socialism as being above all about how to organize the relationships of production, and considered social actors first and foremost from the point of view of their role as producers. They were all blown off course by the events of May 1968 with their incongruous but explosive mixture of anarchic libertarianism and Marxist-inspired revolutionism (for an explanation of this incongruity see Hamon, 1989, pp. 10–22). May '68 saw the emergence of anti-productivist and anti-authoritarian themes and the politicization of identity and 'lifestyle' issues – such as feminism, sexual orientation, regionalism and ecologism – which were not directly connected to the question of socioeconomic class. It also affected the general political climate in France for several years in a number of ways. First, it legitimized an anti-bureaucratic and anti-authoritarian left-wing critique of the PCF, which signalled the beginning of the end of the PCF's ideological dominance. Second (despite the apparent paradox), it 're-ideologized' the climate on the left and gave Marxist phraseology a new lease of life.

The Refounding of French Socialism

The immediate political consequences of May '68 were disastrous for the parties of the left: their conflicting responses to the events exposed their lack of unity, and it was not until after a centrist strategy for the SFIO had again demonstrated its lack of promise (Defferre's humiliating defeat in the 1969 presidential election) that the union of the left was back on the agenda (Bell, 1989, pp. 82–99). But first the SFIO needed to be reinvigorated. This was done in two stages: first, in 1969, Mollet was replaced as leader by Alain Savary and the party was renamed the Nouveau Parti Socialiste; second, at the 1971 Epinay Congress, Mitterrand's CIR and a number of political clubs merged with the party to form the PS. Mitterrand, who claimed that his conversion to socialism came about in the wake of May '68 (Mitterrand, 1969, pp. 152, 163–84), simultaneously became a member and the leader of an enlarged party whose rejuvenation was predicated on a commitment to a union of the left strategy. In the light of subsequent and sustained electoral recovery, the 'Epinay line' was to assume mythical proportions as a (re-)founding moment and prove very difficult to deviate from. Mitterrand owed his party leadership victory to support from an incongruous alliance comprising both the right and the extreme-left tendencies within the party. His reliance on the support of the extreme-left group, the Centre d'Etudes, de Recherches et d'Education Socialistes (CERES), ensured that the PS would be firmly committed to the union of the left and that the PS's programme would be markedly left-wing in character.

Despite concessions to the post-'68 climate, the 1972 programme (significantly entitled *Changer la vie*), in whose drafting the CERES leader, Jean-Pierre Chevènement, played an important role, was more a reaffirmation of than a break with French socialist tradition. If progress had turned against humankind, it stated, it was because of the dictatorship of profit, which was the root cause of exploitation, social injustice, environmental degradation and the stress of modern urban life (Parti Socialiste, 1972, pp. 7–18). The liberation of humankind could only come from a break with the logic of capitalism, and central to this was public ownership of the means of production. The 'modernists' ' idea that it was possible to distinguish between the decision-making power of managers and power deriving from ownership, and that the democratization of the former was a sufficient condition of socialism, was explicitly rejected (Parti Socialiste, 1972, p. 62). However, it was principally banking, large monopolistic firms, multinationals and firms dependent on public procurement which were targeted for nationalization, and the future socialist economy was to be a mixed one. Furthermore, to achieve economic democracy, structures enabling workers' control (now referred to as *autogestion*) would be put in place. *Autogestion* was seen as a form of economic management which would take many years to establish, and which would be the result of a combination of legal norms established by the state and of the efforts of workers themselves to assume their responsibilities and overcome resistance. The period of transition inaugurated by an electoral victory of the left would thus not abolish class antagonism but, rather, make its significance for workers explicit (Parti Socialiste, 1972, p. 64). The PS thus presented its project as something more than a reform programme to be implemented by purely parliamentary means, and restated the idea of socialism as a future destination to be reached following a conflictual transitional phase which would bring about irreversible changes.

This was obviously an attenuated version of class struggle, even if the programme preferred the term 'workers' struggle'. But how could a 'catch-all' party, whose leadership structures were dominated by middle-class professionals, credibly put forward a strategy for change predicated on some sort of class struggle, however vaguely defined?

Here an idea borrowed from the PSU came to the rescue. This was the 'class front' (*front de classe*), according to which workers, peasants, technicians, engineers, almost the entire tertiary sector and even managers (*cadres*), were similarly oppressed by capitalism and therefore had converging interests. Only exploiters, profiteers and privileged groups would be excluded from this front. There was a Janus aspect to this discourse, since it was intended to have broad appeal without abandoning the terrain of revolution to the PCF in the run-up to the signing of the PS–PCF Common Programme of 1972.

The bulk of the PS's programme, however, was devoted not to doctrinal discussion but to the concrete changes the PS, once in government, would bring about in all areas of political, economic, social and cultural life within a five-year period. In keeping with the post-'68 climate, emphasis was placed on humanizing industrial-urban society, on decentralization, on the democratic management of many institutions, on educational equality and on women's rights. In the field of political institutions, the programme stated that the role of Parliament would be strengthened and the term of office of the president reduced from seven to five years. Apart from this, only relatively minor changes to the Constitution were envisaged. This indicated that the PS had come to accept the Fifth Republic, with its presidential logic. In Mitterrand it now had a credible presidential candidate, and under his influence in the 1970s the party became increasingly 'presidentialized', that is, it became an instrument whose primary purpose was to ensure Mitterrand's electoral victory. This effectively introduced a break with the past, in that the instrumentalization of the party meant that it was no longer simply an end in itself, there to bear witness to the personal commitment of its members and able to put the purity of its doctrine before the responsibilities of government. Likewise, tying the party to a comprehensive package of concrete measures to be achieved within the life of a Parliament, as the result of an historic alliance with a good chance of achieving a parliamentary majority, effectively put an end to the distinction between a maximal and a minimal programme.

Overall, this programme, which set the tone for the next decade, combined a doctrinal certainty (the break with capitalism was the key to all of France's problems) with a radiant and generous view of the future (citizens would be actively involved in all sorts of collective endeavours in a convivial society) and a catalogue of promises regarding improvements in living standards and the quality of life. While it promised not merely to democratize capitalism, as social democrats did, but to break with it, the definition it gave of capitalism was, in a sense, restrictive, since it was identified above all with big monopolies and in particular with *American* multinationals. This flattered a certain Jacobin national-ist sentiment particularly prevalent in the CERES.

Despite the inherent pragmatism of Mitterrand's strategy, the 1970s marked the high point of ideological debate within the PS. Ideological discourse played an important role in re-establishing the left-wing credentials of the party, enabling it to hold its own against its ally-cum-rival, the PCF. It was, for example, able to use the idea of *autogestion* (which increasingly became a catch-phrase suggesting not only work-ers' rights but, more generally, citizen empowerment in a partici-pationist democracy) to define an identity which was distinct both from 'reformist' social democracy, with its culturally unacceptable image of compromise, and Soviet-style communism, with its threat of totalitari-anism. That the term *autogestion* lent itself to a variety of interpretations and was rarely defined in a precise way mattered little. Second, ideology was the terrain on which internal leadership struggles were conducted. The PS was effectively a juxtaposition of different tendencies, which, with their own networks and press, operated like parties within the party, identifying with a leader in a somewhat clan-like manner. This was particularly the case after Michel Rocard (who with other PSU members rallied to the PS in 1974/5) formed his own tendency between 1977 and 1979 in order to oppose the other major tendencies – the Mitterrandist majority and the CERES. Although it often took the form of ideological skirmishes between the Rocardians and the CERES, the main focus of internal party competition between 1977 and 1981 was the rivalry between Mitterrand and Rocard, both over the definition of the party line and for nomination as the party's candidate for the 1981 presidential election (Hamon and Rotman, 1980, pp. 259–85; Schneider, 1987, pp. 247–58).

During this period the union of the left did in fact work to the electoral advantage of the PS rather than to that of the PCF – and indeed sometimes at the latter's expense. This led to a deterioration of relations between the two parties and to the virtual collapse of their alliance in 1977, which prevented the left from winning the 1978 elections as had been predicted. Mitterrand, however, continued to cling to the now rather hollow idea of the union of the left and to the priorities it had more or less imposed on the PS. His own legitimacy as leader was closely linked to it, and to abandon it would have been to admit defeat and open the way to his rival. Rocard, on the other hand, saw these setbacks as a confirmation of his criticism of the alliance strategy and its implications for the PS's policy commitments, and, with a battery of intellectuals largely marginal to the PS (for example, Pierre Rosanvallon, Jacques Julliard and Alain Touraine), pushed for a re-definition of the party's project.

The ploy of the Rocardian camp was to distinguish between two political 'cultures' on the French left and assign negative value to that of their adversaries, whose culture was 'Jacobin, centralizing, statist, na-tionalist and protectionist' (Rocard, 1979, p. 79). The logic of this culture had encouraged the working class to make demands without being prepared to accept a share in responsibilities, and had led it to look to the central state for solutions. Its dogmatic insistence on nationalization would engender bureaucratic statism, which would be neither economically efficient nor democratic. Against this, the need for the democratic control of production rather than public ownership was restated. However, while planning ought to provide the framework for economic activity and regulation, it was up to the market to anticipate the needs of consumers. The state ought not to be involved in production but, rather, ought to enable firms to create the wealth to pay for public services.

The other culture (that of the 'second left') was decentralizing, regionalist and against the domination of both bosses and the state. It was suspicious of administrative rule making, to which it preferred the autonomy of grass-roots communities and social experimentation. It placed *autogestion* at the centre of its project. However, *autogestion*, which had originally been a doctrine advocating workers' participation, was now the affirmation less of a 'natural' community of producers than of a political collectivity recognizing the autonomy of the individual, and regulated by contractual relations rather than by the state (Rosanvallon, 1976, pp. 14–16, 83–100). The autonomy of civil society from the state had to be ensured without this permitting the economic domination of one class, as traditional liberalism effectively did. This was to be done by developing a politicized but decentralized sphere between civil society and the state, a sphere which would develop new political rights and which Rosanvallon and Viveret (1977, pp. 129–39) called 'political society'. The constituent elements of this 'political society' were to be social movements, associations, trade unions and political parties. How-ever, the great obstacle to both the ideological and strategic success of the Rocardian vision remained the 'vertical' nature of the traditional parties of the left, with their imperative of the conquest of state power. This critical attitude towards parties also reflected Rocard's marginal and minority position in the PS, and was most vehemently expressed in Julliard's polemical attack on the 'professionals of politics' and Marxist intellectuals, who aspired to become a bureaucratic ruling class (Julliard, 1977, p. 52). This, he argued, was why they saw nationalization as the cornerstone of socialism.

Rocardism was thus clearly revisionist in relation to orthodox French socialist doctrine. Among other points it accepted the market not merely begrudgingly, but as a principle of good economics. However, while Rocard acknowledged the material achievements of social democracy and was not hostile to its sense of compromise, he was critical of its statist conception of social change, its conception of the party, its excessive faith in the automatically progressive nature of the development of productive forces, and the reliance of its key success, the welfare state, on capitalist expansion (Rocard *et al.*, 1979, pp. 11–25).

Mitterrand's response to Rocard's challenge was to allow him to accentuate his criticism of the Epinay line and thus further marginalize himself. However, in order to bolster his leadership position, Mitterrand had again to turn to the CERES for support, and this was to give Chevènement an important role in the drafting of the 1980 PS programme (Bauchard, 1986, p. 13). Although Mitterrand enjoyed considerable room for manoeuvre, this programme necessarily influenced the platform on which he stood – and on which he was elected – in the 1981 presidential election.

Preparing for Power

The 1980 *Projet socialiste* was essentially a restatement of the 1972 programme, although a new element was the emphasis it placed on responding to the recession, which was presented principally as the consequence of a capitalist strategy to overcome a tendential drop in the rate of profit (Parti Socialiste, 1981, pp. 35–42). In its bid to re-establish high rates of profit, capitalism was closing down a certain amount of productive capacity to keep prices high, and using unemployment to drive wages down. The deployment of new technologies, the conquest of new regions of the world and the commodification of social relations (for example, in the fields of health, education and culture) were also part of this strategy. The restructuring of the world economy was being brought about by multinationals, which moved production out of Europe to countries with cheap labour and low taxation. Multinationals were the beneficiaries of the crisis and were mostly American. This new international division of labour was reinforcing the hegemony of the USA over the rest of the industrialized world (1981, pp. 41–2). While the French economy was a victim of this system, the French right, with its liberal, integrationist policy, merely served the interests of the multinationals (1981, p. 18). In the light of all this, we can now see that the 'break with capitalism' was above all a bid to reassert French economic independence, and that PS strategy was going to be heavily dependent on the interventionist capacity of the nation state in a globalized economy. Indeed this was to be the Achilles' heel of socialist government policy in the 1980s.

How then was this 'break with capitalism' to be achieved? The PS proposed a new type of economic growth, which was to be motivated by social usefulness and not profit and was significantly called 'social growth'. Egalitarian reforms and improvements in working conditions would mobilize the effort of the people, needless waste would be avoided, production and consumption would be adjusted to match real needs, and unused productive capacity would be developed (1981, pp. 172–81). Full employment was the priority of priorities, and to achieve it a high rate of growth was necessary. The market would continue to play a role in the short-term adjustment of supply and demand, but planning would lay down the model of development and be the overall regulator. But how was this regulated growth to be achieved in an economy increasingly open to foreign competition and the vagaries of world markets? The key element here was a reduction of the share of foreign trade in France's gross national product: French firms would expand their share of the domestic market, and this would reduce the demand for imported goods and make a socialist government less dependent on external pressures. Keynesian demand management could then produce a consumption-led period of high growth. The socialists were aware (prophetically as it turned out) that the failure of this protectionist strategy, heroically named the 'reconquest of the domestic market', would either challenge the viability of their entire project or lead to a depreciation of the franc and a national debt crisis, or both (1981, pp. 222–3).

With its emphasis on nationalization, state regulation of the economy, the reduction of social inequalities, and industrial democracy, the PS programme was consonant with the post-war social democratic programme. However, what in particular made it appear radical was its refusal to downgrade expectations as social democrats had done in other countries, largely in response to the decreasing effectiveness of national instruments of economic regulation. What then made French socialists think that they could succeed where others had not?

The simple answer to this is that the PS's programme had never before had to face the test of being applied: it would have to be shown not to work before it could be modified or abandoned. In addition, there was the conviction that political will based on coherent ideas and vested in a strong state was a sufficient condition of success. Finally there was the idea that France, in order to remain France, had no choice but to follow an independent path: in all the great moments of history France had been inspired by a universal mission. If it ceased to identify with a universal mission and did not have a collective ambition, France would cease to exist (1981, p. 163). This clearly harks back to the mythology of the French Revolution, except that now France's mission was to be the political motor of a workers' Europe, allied to third world countries, in order to put an end to power-bloc domination and institute a new international economic order.

The government of the left did indeed, broadly speaking, attempt to apply the PS's programme. The presence of four communist ministers in the Mauroy government (1981–4), despite the fact that the PS by itself had an absolute majority of seats in the National Assembly, symbolized President Mitterrand's intention to remain faithful to the idea of the union of the left and carry out the programme outlined in his election campaign, as well as being a way of muting possible communist criticism. The policies of the first socialist government, led by Pierre Mauroy, can be characterized in a number of different ways. Some were liberal in nature (the abolition of the death penalty, the attempt to make television broadcasting more independent from state control, the authorization of independent radio stations, less heavy-handed policing methods). The Auroux labour laws aimed not to impose workers' control but to enhance employee protection and rights, and to institutionalize the practice (uncommon in France until then) of negotiating pay and conditions at company level. This was essentially an attempt to modernize industrial relations and make them less confrontational. It was also intended to bring about, by legislative means, the kinds of relations of compromise which had developed in a more organic fashion in northern European countries (Groux, 1986).

The major decentralization reforms aimed not only to enhance citizen participation in local affairs and make local and regional government more democratically accountable, but also to decongest an administrative system in which centralized bureaucracy had become increasingly bogged down in the detailed management of purely local affairs. In addition, decentralization was to encourage local economic development based on small and medium-sized firms, which, in the socialist scheme of things, were not tainted by identification with monopoly capitalism (Keating and Hainsworth, 1986, p. 115). Even taken together, however, the Auroux laws and decentralization hardly added up to the promised *autogestion*.

While an array of policies aimed to fulfil the promise of improvements in the quality of life (an additional week of paid holiday and the reduction of the retirement age for men to 60, for example), public sector job creation, substantial increases in a variety of social benefits, and an increase in the minimum wage were also part of the reflationary policy designed to boost demand in the economy. Likewise the nationalization programme, while ideologically motivated, was seen as instrumental in the growth strategy. Following years of low levels of investment, private enterprise had shown itself to be incapable of promoting dynamic growth. The state therefore had to take over to facilitate a rational investment plan. However, socialist policy foundered in two of the areas most closely linked to PS identity, namely the voluntarist 'break with capitalism' and the republican principle of *laïcité* in education. We shall look at these in turn.

The social character of the reflationary dash for growth, which was supposed to establish a new economic logic, was threatened by France's dependence on the international economic environment. As France reflated, other Western economies stuck to competitive deflationary policies. The upturn in the international economy, which had been forecast by socialist economists and which was to allow a reflated French economy to enjoy an export boom, did not come about. In addition, French productive capacity was much weaker than the socialists had expected and was unable to meet the increased level of demand they had created. Instead this demand sucked in imported goods, causing a balance of payments crisis and threatening the franc, while increased public spending without sufficient wealth creation led to a budget deficit and fuelled inflation. There was also speculation on the franc and a massive flight of capital abroad. In addition, the rise in unemployment had not been halted.

All of this suggested that France could not buck international trends and go it alone. The government responded to this situation by a move away from its growth strategy, punctuated by successive devaluations of the franc. A first package of austerity measures (including a wage and price freeze and public spending cuts) was adopted in June 1982, but was not yet clearly perceived as the beginning of the end of the experiment in 'social growth' (Bauchard, 1986, pp. 110–11). However, by the spring of 1983 the worsening crisis of the franc presented Mitterrand with a stark choice: France had to withdraw from the

European Monetary System (EMS), operate a massive competitive devaluation of the franc to reduce imports, and adopt protective measures to get the economy back on its feet for a resumption of the 1981 policy, or negotiate a more modest realignment of the franc and the mark within the EMS and accept the monetary rigours European partners (notably Germany) would demand in return for their support for the franc. The first option was advocated by Chevènement and Pierre Bérégovoy, the second by Mauroy, Jacques Delors and, eventually, Laurent Fabius. After considerable hesitation Mitterrand chose the second and, as Serge Bernstein (1996, p. 9) has put it, opted for Europe in preference to the socialist project. This choice implicitly meant an acceptance of market forces and an acknowledgement of the limits of state intervention.

This U-turn was not easily digested by the PS at large, and the party did not respond with a coherent overview regarding what direction it should now take. Its 1983 Congress put forward a number of unlinked imperatives: a determination to stay in power, acceptance of austerity, but also a restatement of fidelity to the original project (Bergounioux and Grunberg, 1992, pp. 441–2). A further débâcle in 1984 was to precipitate a redefinition of French socialism.

In its 1972 and 1980 programmes the PS, faithful to the principle of *laïcité*, had committed itself to the creation of a unified national education service, which supposed the integration of (predominantly Catholic) private schools into the state sector. While the government envisaged a relatively flexible arrangement, a large proportion of the public viewed its proposals as a straightforward nationalization of private schools. This sparked off a wave of mass protest in defence not so much of religious education as of educational pluralism. The right was able to accuse the left of threatening a major liberty (Bauchard, 1986, p. 251). The left, accustomed to viewing the defence of liberty as one its own prerogatives, was entirely wrong-footed. This showed that *laïcité* was no longer a value in which the socialists could successfully root their identity, and that this kind of republicanism could not provide an ideological fallback position after the ebbing of the tide of anti-capitalism. A beleaguered Mitterrand was obliged to withdraw the proposals and shortly afterwards announced a change of government.

Varieties of Revision

The appointment of a new prime minister provided Mitterrand with the opportunity to translate the change in logic implied by his choice of

Europe and austerity into a visible political form. With the appointment of Laurent Fabius (then only 38), the watchwords of the government changed. Gone were the 'break with capitalism', the logic of social growth and the primacy of social justice. The new priorities were 'modernization' and *'rassemblement'* (the rallying of broad support). 'Modernization' implied restructuring and rationalizing industrial structures to achieve greater competitiveness, at the cost of massive layoffs in unprofitable firms. Nationalized firms had to become profit makers, entrepreneurial initiative became a positive cultural value, and the market-oriented firm was seen as a key actor in creating the future. Competitiveness also meant giving priority to the reduction of inflation and wage restraint. Social redistribution was no longer the mainspring of policy. However, something missed by many observers viewing this in retrospect was the technocratic and administrative aspect of this approach to coming to terms with market imperatives: managerialism might be the new culture, but it was still an administrative managerialism, in a regime in which a frown of disapproval from the President of the Republic could lead to the dismissal of a senior executive of even a private firm remotely connected with the state.

'*Rassemblement*', a term borrowed from Gaullism, implied the abandonment of any reference to class in future socialist strategy. This reflected the final breakup of the union of the left, following the refusal of the PCF to remain in a government prepared, in the pursuit of other goals, to let unemployment rise (Bauchard, 1986, pp. 270–2). It implied that the PS would aim after the 1986 elections to constitute a parliamentary majority itself with any non-socialists who would agree to support its policies. In fact, the PS was unable to define an alternative alliance strategy to the union of the left and had to fall back on the notion of the 'presidential majority'. This reliance on a president who was becoming increasingly distant from his own party contributed to the weakening of the now uncertain identity of the PS.

The first major opportunity for the PS to respond collectively to the government policy U-turn and rethink its own orientation was provided by its 1985 Congress. The issue was clouded, however, by questions of rivalry. Rocard believed that the abandonment of the 'Epinay line' legitimized his own version of economic 'realism' and 'social compromise' (Rocard, 1986, pp. 37–62). The leadership should, therefore, now fall to him (Duverger, 1985, p. 7). However, Fabius also had leadership ambitions, while Lionel Jospin, as party leader, sought to preserve the left-wing character of the PS in any process of revision (Lhomeau, 1985, p. 7; Jospin, 1985, p. 7).

The final 'synthesis' motion of the 1985 Congress concluded that the experience of power had shown that, in an open and democratic society, there were constraints from which no government could escape. Society had become more complex and this affected the nature of political debate. This implicitly acknowledged that PS discourse had been too schematic and therefore unrealistic. However, certain values (now a key word) remained fundamental to the party's project: solidarity and social justice; faith in the value of reason and of work; democracy and a sense of responsibility; fidelity to a collective vision of France. In addition, while the socialists had come to accept the reality of market constraints and the need for firms to be profitable, they did not take on board the idea that market forces were the ultimate and legitimate decider, and reaffirmed that planning should determine the major economic priorities. Regulation should set out how these priorities should be achieved in order to prevent the market from being an instrument of oppression. Likewise, while the firm was a valuable unit of production, it was also the terrain on which different social forces confronted each other. In short, there remained a degree of ambiguity and reluctance to abandon the 1981 project in this revision of doctrine. Overall, the changes which the PS acknowledged in its outlook were characterized as a transformation from a culture of opposition to one which accepted the responsibilities of government (*Le Monde*, 15 October 1985). But was all of this enough to forge a new identity?

Certain observers proclaimed that the PS had at last become a social democratic party or had revealed its true social democratic nature (for example, Colombani, 1985, p. 7; Duverger, 1985, p. 1) and Jacques Delors spoke of 'a little Bad Godesberg' (*Le Monde*, 15 October 1985). However, this is to identify social democracy negatively, merely as the abandonment of anti-capitalism and as the repositioning of the PS as a party of the workforce in general. As Bergounioux and Manin (1989, pp. 183–9) argue, the originality of social democracy is not only to have introduced Keynesian economics, the welfare state and the redistribution of income, but to have substituted these for the collective appropriation of the means of production. The specificity of social democracy was this *quid pro quo*, not a particular economic policy. In the post-war period in Sweden, Germany and Austria (and to a lesser extent in Britain) close party–trade union links had facilitated the substitution of modest objectives for the project of a radical economic transformation. A political culture of moderation and a belief that a political force should acknowledge the interests of its adversaries had brought about an acceptance of both private property and market regulation. The recession of the 1970s had shown that another *quid pro quo* was possible: the protection of jobs in exchange for wage restraint, thanks to the integration of a strong and centralized trade union movement in decision making and a political culture based on solidarity and moderation.

French socialism, on the other hand, did not have close links with a unified and centralized trade union movement and did not accept the principle of 'frontal compromise' and voluntary moderation (Bergounioux and Manin, 1989, p. 187). This meant that the means of achieving a distribution of surplus value in favour of profit, after the 1983 U-turn, were different from those employed in social democratic regimes. French socialism did not offer a *quid pro quo* to unions, which were weak and divided and would not have accepted it in any case. Rather the government used a public opinion strategy in a series of improvisations carried out under the pressure of events. The 'republican monarchy' aspect of the regime and the greater dependence of the government on the president than on the party contributed to this phenomenon. In effect, in the absence of a culture in which an advantage is exchanged for a concession, French socialism had to invoke general principles and moral imperatives, such as the rehabilitation of profit owing to the external constraints of world markets, and the new value attached to entrepreneurship as a cultural model. This indeed may go some way to explaining why the U-turn in French socialist economic policy brought about such a traumatic sea change in French culture in general.

In addition to these arguments against the 'social democratization' of the PS, there is the fact that if the PS wanted to adopt the social democratic model, it had simply missed the boat: the social democratic model had by the 1980s lost much of its solidity and thus much of its specificity (Padgett and Paterson, 1991, pp. 257–63; Wright, 1993, pp. 93–4). Inflationary pressures made Keynesian demand management inoperable, unemployment and demographic pressures (among other factors) began to question the future of the welfare state, and new patterns of employment (added to unemployment) led to the breakup of the old model of the solidarity community. In addition, the idea of social transformation was now increasingly associated with 'green' and 'alternative' issues, which the social democratic model, with its trade unionist clientele and productivist outlook, could not easily address.

However, while on the one hand the decline of the PCF in the 1980s gave the undisputed leadership of the left to the PS and freed it from any remaining complex in relation to communism, and, on the other, the weakening of the social democratic model eased whatever historic sense of inferiority the PS had had in regard to it in the past, these phenomena were part of a more general collapse of the culture of the left which did not spare even its 'modernist' branch (Julliard, 1985, pp. 179–201; Rosanvallon, 1988, pp. 136–56). The main problem was of course how to respond to the new economic liberalism, which had undermined the age-old certainties of socialism. This was particularly difficult for the PS in that the government it was supporting was pursuing market-oriented policies, while the theme of economic liberalism was perceived by rank-and-file socialists as that of their adversaries on the right.

In the event, the French right was unable to imitate the example of Thatcherism and Reaganism and articulate a convincing political discourse to legitimize radical neo-liberalism, and certain aspects of French culture were more resistant to the neo-liberal ideology than was the case, for example, in Britain (Godin, 1996, pp. 61–9). Following his re-election to the presidency in 1988, Mitterrand could therefore plausibly stick to a '*ni–ni*' policy (neither privatization nor further nationalization). However, he was re-elected not because of a resurgence of the 1981 climate, but because of public doubts concerning the apparent volatility of his main opponent, Jacques Chirac. Indeed Mitterrand's 1988 campaign was extremely bland: it projected the image of a unifying grandfather of the nation. His main campaign ploy was a 'Lettre à tous les Français' (a message not to any one section of French society, but to the French people as a whole). The two priorities of his next term of office were to be 'Europe' and the reduction of social inequalities. Indeed 'Europe' came to replace 'socialism' as a provider of a sense of purpose in the Mitterrandist scheme of things. This foregrounding of European integration, accompanied by a vaguely defined intention to reduce inequalities, corresponded to the need to woo centrist voters, and foreshadowed the appointment of Rocard as prime minister in an attempt to gain the support of centrist members of Parliament for the forthcoming minority socialist government, which could not revive an alliance with the PCF.

The Rocard government (1988–91) was really the first unashamedly reformist French socialist government, and tried to make a positive virtue of the idea of compromise. For Rocard the recent experience of French socialism had shown that the state could not be the exclusive instrument of social transformation. However, he argued, social democracy was also in crisis owing to the difficulties of the welfare state. The alternative was therefore the 'method of social democracy working for the values of socialism' (Rocard, 1987, pp. 315–16). This was characterized by the negotiation of compromise, which would bring about convergence between opposing forces without denying their differences. However, what 'social compromise' meant in this context was that solutions to problems and proposed changes were only likely to be successful and durable if they could gain broad acceptance from the outset and go with the flow of society. This supposed an organic view of society regulating itself in an evolutionary fashion, and a kind of consensualism which was foreign to French socialist experience.

Rocard now defined the values of socialism in general terms: liberty (although this included the freedom of the consumer and acceptance of the market), democracy (although this extended to the economic field and was to be applied to power in the workplace and achieved by negotiation), solidarity (the refusal of an individualistic perspective), autonomy (which replaced *autogestion* and meant an ethic of personal responsibility, although this supposed that individuals would be free enough to be responsible), the primacy of the law (which in fact meant affirming the idea of rights and regulation in the face of market anarchy), protection from unacceptable technologies (which included the protection of the environment and was now the main business of planning), and the quest for world peace (Rocard, 1987, p. 316).

The main principles of Rocardism in government were thus a regulatory – but not *dirigiste* – state, organizing the rules of the game but leaving room for civil society (including the market) to conduct its own affairs by dint of negotiated contractual relations (Bréhier, 1989a, p. 9). The state ought also to be in permanent dialogue with civil society, and Rocard identified the re-establishment of social cohesion as a priority (Colombani and Lhomeau, 1988, pp. 1, 7). In practice this latter aim presupposed tackling unemployment and easing wage restraint, but the profitability of firms was seen as a condition of this and was dependent on international confidence, which in turn required wage restraint and the reduction of inflation to remain the priority. The government was thus caught between two logics (Andréani, 1988, p. 8) and, despite its easing of public sector wage restraint, was criticized within the PS for its 'social deficit' and inaction (Andréani, 1990, pp. 1, 10; Pierre-Brossolette, 1989, p. 16).

To counter criticisms that the socialists in government had presided over an increase in economic inequality, Rocard insisted that redistributive mechanisms and social benefits had in the preceding twenty years lost their effectiveness, and could only act on the margins of this situation (Bréhier, 1989b, p. 11). The real source of the problem was the primary distribution of incomes; that is, it was situated in the productive enterprise. The state could not resolve this alone: it was up to the 'social partners' to achieve progress through contractual relations, while the state would reform the taxation of property. Of those who were excluded from the workforce, young people trying to get started in life were the most preoccupying problem, and the solution to their predicament lay in the 'redistribution of knowledge', that is, in education and training (Rocard, 1989, p. 11).

There was, then, an attempt to shift the argument away from the traditional social democratic solution of complicated social engineering by means of redistributive state intervention. In response to claims that he was a neo-liberal, Rocard repeated that, like Keynes, he placed the real economy (production) above purely financial concerns and criteria and rejected the principles of monetarism (Andréani, 1989, pp. 1, 10). Monetarism reduced economics to the study of the circulation of money and ignored the role of public spending and human factors, notably unemployment. The dominance of monetarist policies was producing dysfunctional societies and there were many areas, such as public services, the protection of the environment and the distribution of knowledge, where the market could not be effective. However, Rocard had to admit his dilemma: that in the West he could see no coherent body of philosophy or values able to replace 'regulation by money' with anything else which could gain sufficient acceptance (Andréani *et al.*, 1991, pp. 1, 10). Rocardian socialism was therefore essentially a morality – an attempt to convert society to a process of self-regulation based on an ethic of responsibility, solidarity, dialogue and negotiation – and this process was basically seen as an end in itself.

In practice, the compromises of the minority Rocard government relied more frequently in parliament on the top-up support of the centre and moderate right than on that of the PCF (Andréani, 1991, p. 11). For many in the PS this cast doubts on this version of revisionism, which, with its blurring of the distinction between left and right, seemed to be throwing the baby out with the bathwater, and demobilized activists.

The PS's revision was thus undertaken in retreat, while many of its major personalities were still in government, and was therefore neither complete nor entirely coherent. Many of the party's rank and file were uncomfortable with the direction Mitterrand had obliged the party to take after 1983 and remained attached to the idea of the union of the left. This was visible in the election of Mauroy (a symbol of the old PS identity) as party leader in 1988, in preference to Fabius, Mitterrand's preferred candidate and, since 1984, a symbol of 'modernization'. In addition there was not one revisionism within the party, but several, and no single one could gain general acceptance. This was particularly so because the late 1980s saw the beginnings of a new struggle for control of the party (and therefore of the process of nominating its future presidential candidate) in anticipation of the post-Mitterrand era.

Throughout most of the 1980s the main dividing line in the PS had run between the Rocardians and the Mitterrandist majority. However, by 1990 the latter had split into two rival tendencies, led respectively by Laurent Fabius and Lionel Jospin (Philippe and Hubscher, 1991, pp. 109–11). In addition there were the smaller tendencies grouped around Jean-Pierre Chevènement, Jean Poperen and, later, the Gauche Socialiste. All the major tendencies acknowledged, in varying degrees, the mistakes of the 1981–2 period, the unavoidable constraints of an open-market economy, and the fact that a 'break with capitalism' was no longer on the agenda. Differences between the leaders of the three main party tendencies (Fabius, Rocard and Jospin) now centred much more on the nature of political contest and on the identity and role of the party. These questions may seem purely strategic ones, but in so far as they impinged on the very nature of the French socialist project, they had an ideological dimension.

For Fabius the PS had accomplished an '*aggiornamento*', which, although it involved a break first with its messianic attitude of the 1970s and second with its former radical anti-capitalism, was not a conversion to liberal ideology. Regarding the first of these 'breaks' Fabius argued that, while traditional socialism had been inspired by the utopia of a perfect society, the guiding principle of the 'modern left' was a 'democratic utopia', whose aim was the 'progressive extension of the rights and liberties of individuals, as citizens and producers' (Fabius, 1990, pp. 183–4). The error of nineteenth-century revolutionary socialists had been their excess of democratic zeal: they had demanded absolute equality for all, not only in terms of rights, but also in terms of real wealth, power and prestige. This had been mistaken, because the real role of political ideals was to challenge and alter the established order by bringing pressure to bear on power relationships and encouraging reform. While ideals were absolute by nature, their realization required the 'complexity of things' to be taken into account. Democracy was not, therefore, a future state of affairs to be achieved once and for all, but an historical process. The aim of the left was to achieve not 'perfect democracy' but the 'maximum amount of democracy compatible with the stage of development of society and the international context' (1990, p. 191). Thus, while democracy was a good thing, there could be grounds for limiting it.

Of the above we can also observe, first, that the idea that the socialist project was a process rather than a final victory to be won was now common to all the major PS tendencies. Rocard had always thought in such terms, and Jospin too now referred to the socialist movement as a movement *towards* socialism, whose task was to 'give birth progressively to new balances of power in a composite society' (quoted in Bergounioux and Grunberg, 1992, p. 452). Second, while Fabius sought to appropriate Jaurès's idea of the 'social Republic', equality of rights and of opportunity had now replaced effective equality of socioeconomic outcomes. Rocard likewise now preferred the term 'equity' to 'equality' and argued that certain inequalities could be justified when they produced a positive outcome for the collectivity (Rocard, 1993, p. 12).

How then was the second 'break' (that with radical anti-capitalism) accomplished without giving way to liberal market ideology? Fabius argued that a distinction could be made between capitalism and the market (1990, pp. 194–5). The assumption here seems to be that national economies are markets and may be subjected to the state regulation which all PS tendencies advocated, whereas the international economy, where big corporations fight each other for power and dominance, is real capitalism. Strangely, we seem here to be back in the realm of the PS's 1980 programme. However, added to this was the idea that, because the market is a means of exchange and therefore not inherently bad, there are 'good', socially useful capitalists (the captains of industry), who engage in market competition which is beneficial for the economy, and, on the other hand, 'bad' ones, who are speculators, 'archaic' and parasitical. Socialism wanted therefore not to abolish the distinction between bosses and employees but to encourage initiative and innovation (Fabius, 1990, p. 197). This is reminiscent of the discourse of the 'modernists' of the 1960s, except that now ('democratization' within the firm notwithstanding) the major partner of enterprise was to be the state. Fabius spoke in admiration of such an arrangement in the Japanese system and advocated a 'developmental' state which would provide backup for large firms, in order to encourage the emergence of 'national champions' in key sectors, and promote the even development of smaller firms and the regions (1990, pp. 55–6). His version of the 'mixed economy' was therefore not simply a resigned acceptance of the peaceful coexistence of a public sector and a private sector but a sort of dynamic partnership. At the same time, the scope of the market was to be limited so that it would not impose its logic on all areas of life, in particular, on the primary functions of the state and on 'areas where national cohesion requires a minimum [*sic*] of equality between citizens (education, health, culture and communications)' (1990, p. 196). This was, as he acknowledged himself, a journey from Marx to Saint-Simon and Schumpeter.

Fabius argued that it was possible to form a '*rassemblement*' of the left on the basis of these ideas because they were a synthesis of two traditions: the 'liberal-libertarian' tradition and the 'rationalist and Marxist' tradition. This meant that the PS ought not to form an alliance with the centre parties, but constitute the dominant pole on the left. Fabius, however, envisaged not an alliance with any other party but, rather, the rallying of their disillusioned troops, notably ex-communists. This suggestion of a synthesis of different traditions was clearly an attempt to follow Mitterrand's example and create a broad political force to support a presidential candidacy – his own, whenever that should be possible.

By contrast, as we have seen above, the party did not figure much in Rocard's conception of socialism or social transformation. His own presidential strategy was based much more on appeal to public opinion – especially to the 'central group' in the working population – and it did not exclude centrist alliances. The PS did not have to be conquered, simply neutralized. However, following the PS's poor electoral perform-ance in 1992 and crushing defeat in the 1993 parliamentary elections, Rocard had to put his shoulder to the party wheel, since its decline was threatening his intended 1995 presidential candidacy. Having taken over the leadership in 1993, he attempted to 'refound' the party by inviting ecologists, centrists, undogmatic communists and human rights activists to merge with it in a 'vast and open modern movement' (Jarreau, 1993a, p. 1; 1993b, pp. 7–8). However, these potential part-ners were not convinced that they would not simply be absorbed into an untransformed PS. The PS's disastrous score in the 1994 European elections under Rocard's leadership both postponed such a prospect and put an end to his presidential hopes. Having for so long expressed such critical views on the nature of traditional parties, he could not easily assume the mantle of a party leader.

Jospin, on the other hand, had a more traditional approach to the PS. He accused Fabius of seeking to turn it into a presidential 'party of supporters' rather than strengthening it as a party of activists. The role of the PS, he argued, should be kept separate from any presidentialist strategy, and the party should not turn its back on the future possibility of an agreement with the leadership of a renovated PCF. He wished to modernize the PS without entirely abandoning its past and what he viewed as its achievements (Philippe and Hubscher, 1991, pp. 114–16, 121–5).

While Jospin took issue with Fabius's intended 'presidentialization' of the PS, he was also critical of the kind of consensus politics which appeared to be an integral part of Rocard's largely extra-partisan presidential strategy. If consensus were based on assumptions which simply accepted an existing state of affairs, he argued, it could be used to justify immobilism and the avoidance of problems (Jospin, 1991, pp. 301–7). In a society in which contradictions and conflict necessarily existed and in which real choices were necessary, consensus should only apply *a posteriori*, that is, after there had been a confrontation between opposing positions and after a resolution had been arrived at. Political compromise based on the lowest common denominator did not modify initial positions and simply led to stagnation, whereas a real confrontation of positions shed light on the real issues at stake and could lead to convincing solutions able to rally the support of the majority. Jospin therefore rejected what he saw as the ideology of compromise in favour of what we may call a dialectical view of the process of political change, which justified a more left/right partisan approach.

This, of course, supposed that the distinction between the left and the right was still a valid one, whereas opinion polls showed that for a majority of French people it was now blurred. Jospin suggested that this was in large part due to the fact (just as in the economy, where supply often created its own demand) that 'political supply' was shaping public consciousness (1991, p. 307). The problem with this was that a political system which denied the possibility of alternatives produced apathy and led a large proportion of the population to turn its back on the democratic process. The weakening of the left/right distinction in favour of a supposedly more 'rational' approach merely produced irrationality and violence on the margins of this superficial consensus, and created a space for the Front National. The PS therefore had to reaffirm its own values.

This begged the question of what these values now were. What, for example, could be salvaged from the socialist tradition, given the magnitude of the ideological changes of the 1980s? In response to this question Jospin made a distinction between action and words. The language of the PS prior to the 1983 U-turn had been excessive, in particular because it did not correspond to what the party had actually done in power, even in the 1981–2 period. After all, the Auroux laws, while positive, were not supposed to be *autogestion*, and nobody really took the 1981 nationalizations to be the beginnings of a 'break with capitalism'. However, he added, PS discourse in this period had simply reflected a broader cultural phenomenon in post-'68 France, a certain *air du temps,* for which the PS could not bear sole responsibility (1991, p. 308). This suggests that while the party's pre-1983 language could now be seen to have been defective and that its abandonment was therefore justified, the same did not apply in a wholesale fashion to its basic values or to its policy objectives, although the latter needed to be adjusted to take account of a new context. In fact, Jospin held that the real mistake of the left in the early 1980s had been its attempt to do too much too quickly, rather than adopting a more gradual approach. The 'break with capitalism' had therefore, in large part, been a translation of the idea (left in the collective memory by the experience of the Front Populaire) that the left might only have a short period in power in which to achieve its objectives, or that its reform programme might become bogged down owing to resistance (as in 1936) if it were not conducted with the energy and speed of a revolution. Thanks to their long experience in power, socialists had learnt the virtues of a more gradual and evenly paced approach. This, however, did not mean that they had abandoned their values or that these were not still very different from those of the right.

For Jospin the main difference between the right and the left was that the right's discourse defended the established order, whereas the left, even when it was in government, could not confine itself to a manage-rialist – or even reformist – discourse: it had to maintain a critical discourse on society. The right, for example, believed in a natural order which had to be preserved and in a rigid notion of authority. It held to the importance of tradition, hierarchy and often religion, whereas the left believed in progress towards social harmony, which was to be achieved by a process of social and individual transformation in which authority was based on consent. So far this is a fairly traditional contrast between a conservative (not to say reactionary) right and a republican, humanist left. However, moving on to a different terrain, Jospin empha-sized that the right believed that the economy was best left to market forces and was often mistrustful of trade unions, whereas the left believed that the economy should be organized according to agreed objectives (which supposed state intervention), sought partnership with trade unions, and wanted to extend democracy beyond the polit-ical field to the economic one. Nevertheless, we are presented here not with two distinct entities (capitalism and socialism) but with two differ-ent approaches to the same entity (capitalism). This, of course, was the source of the socialists' uneasiness concerning their revision, and Jospin's 'critical discourse on society' was much the same as the 1991 PS programme's conclusion that socialists should maintain a 'critical relationship with capitalism' (Parti Socialiste, 1992). In other words, even if the prospect of replacing capitalism with something else now seemed remote, capitalism was not to be embraced wholeheartedly.

The same uneasiness can be seen on the question of class, for while Jospin sought to distinguish between the left and the right by saying that the latter denied the existence of class struggle, it is clear that this struggle was no longer central to the left's view of contemporary society either, and was replaced by the idea of 'the interplay of organized groups' (Jospin, 1991, p. 311). What, then, of the working class, formerly at the centre of the socialists' 'class front'? For Jospin, the disadvantaged situation of the working class, its aspirations for change and its continued, if attenuated, class consciousness could not be denied. However, the working class was now proportionally less numerous and had been enveloped by a larger, much less homogeneous group. It could therefore no longer play the historical role assigned to it by Marxists: that of emancipating workers and forging a new society. On the other hand, the electoral weight of the working class, its organizational capacity and presence in social movements, meant that socialist parties could not ignore it and view society as an undifferentiated whole.

Jospin thus sought to steer a course between tradition and renewal. His revision was characterized not by the construction of a new grand design for the future, but by an attempt to interpret the recent past in order to have a base from which to face an uncertain future. With some lucidity he acknowledged that the past (electoral) success of the PS had not been due to 'sociological' factors, as had been the case of certain social democratic parties, whose strength lay in their links with a solidarity community. This acknowledged that the PS was not social democratic, but also broke with the Mitterrandist myth that electoral victory in 1981 had resulted from a sociological majority finally being translated into a political one. Success had not been achieved thanks to 'historical' reasons either, as had been the case with the Spanish socialists, who had embodied the great democratic and modernizing changes in the post-Franco era. The success of the PS had been due to specifically political factors, one of which was its personalities (most obviously Mitterrand). We can extrapolate from this that the message to the PS was that it had no automatic right of occupancy of government, based on some law of history which gave it a natural legitimacy in the eyes of the electorate: it had to (re-)earn its place in the sun by reasserting a more ethical approach to political life (especially after the financial scandals implicating a number of socialists in power), highlight its differences with the right by giving them a concrete content, and make its priorities and choices clear to the public (1991, p. 316).

This elucidates the emphasis, outlined above, on values: socialism was now a moral choice for individuals, not a sociohistorical given. Nevertheless it involved a choice between fairly polarized values, and Jospin saw the party as the repository of such values and the means of amplifying them.

Conclusion

From its foundation until World War II, the French Socialist Party lived uneasily with the contradiction between the two major constituent elements of its original identity: republicanism and a commitment to a revolutionary perspective. The former tended to integrate the party within the established political and social system, whereas the latter preached the transcending of that system. In the post-war period the SFIO was not able to integrate the lessons of Keynesianism into its doctrine as northern European social democratic parties did, largely because of the defensive position it had to adopt in relation to a dominant communist party, because of its weak links with the organized labour movement, and because of the unattractiveness of the idea of compromise and moderation in a country accustomed to abrupt rather than gradual change.

The stripping away of the revolutionary identity of French socialism in the post-war period was halted in the 1970s by the ideological polarization which characterized the post-'68 years. The PS of the 1970s was able to instrumentalize a discourse of radical change, which a long period of opposition to a conservative regime helped to make credible. While the party's discourse was radical, its recipes for change were not markedly different from those of post-war social democracy. However, the PS attempted to apply these in a new context which made their achievement impossible. The abandonment of the discourse of radical transformation was made all the more difficult to come to terms with by the fact that social democracy, itself now in crisis, could no longer offer a comfortable fallback position.

This stripping away of socialist identity has therefore led the PS to rely on a republican identity centred on moral values, which tend to be formulated in imprecise terms. However, republicanism today is ideologically threadbare and cannot have the sense of future it had in the late nineteenth century. None of the major parties now contests the Republic, and *laïcité* is on the defensive and can easily be construed as veiled racism in contemporary multicultural France. The PS's present position may therefore be characterized as a sort of social liberalism operating in the context of a mixed economy and a welfare state. The PS has been through the mill of electoral defeat in recent years. This has undoubtedly been the result of a long period in power, but has also been linked to its inability to put forward a credible idea of change for the future. Nevertheless, Lionel Jospin's honourable defeat as the 'citizen candidate' in the 1995 presidential election may well have laid the ground for a more constructive, if more modest, post-Mitterrandist left, and has shown that in the bipolar logic of the Fifth Republic the Parti Socialiste occupies a space which – for the meantime – no other party can fill.

References

Andréani, J.-L. (1988) 'Gouverner autrement'. *Le Monde*, 27 May.

Andréani, J.-L. (1989) 'Les Deux Rocard'. *Le Monde*, 8 November.

Andréani, J.-L. (1990) 'Le Classicisme et la réforme'. *Le Monde*, 11 May.

Andréani, J.-L. (1991) 'M. Rocard a gouverné trois fois plus avec le centre et la droite qu'avec le PC'. *Le Monde*, 9 June.

Andréani, J.-L., Noblecourt, M. and Vernholes, A. (1991) 'Un entretien avec Michel Rocard'. *Le Monde*, 7 March.

Bauchard, P. (1986) *La Guerre des deux roses*. Paris: Grasset.

Bell, D.S. and Criddle, B. (1988) *The French Socialist Party*. Oxford: Clarendon Press.

Bell, L. (1989) 'May '68: Parenthesis or Staging-Post in the Development of the Socialist Left?', in D. Hanley and A.P. Kerr (eds) *May '68 Coming of Age*. Basingstoke: Macmillan, pp. 82–99.

Bergounioux, A. and Manin, B. (1989) *Le Régime social-démocrate*. Paris: Presses Universitaires de France.

Bergounioux, A. and Grunberg, G. (1992) *Le Long Remords du pouvoir*. Paris: Fayard.

Bernstein, S. (1996) 'Les Deux Septennats de François Mitterrand: esquisse d'un bilan'. *Modern and Contemporary France* NS4 (1), 3–14.

Bréhier, T. (1989a) 'Onze Travaux d'Hercule de M. Rocard'. *Le Monde*, 31 August.

Bréhier, T. (1989b) 'Le Projet social est de retour'. *Le Monde*, 21 December.

Chapsal, J. (1972) *La Vie politique en France depuis 1940*. Paris: Presses Universitaires de France.

Codding, G. and Safran, W. (1979) *Ideology and Politics: The French Socialist Party*. Boulder, CO: Westview Press.

Colombani, J.-M. (1985) 'Le Tournant de la social–démocratie'. *Le Monde*, 13/14 October.

Colombani, J.-M. and Lhomeau, J.-Y. (1988) 'Le Gouvernement se propose de rétablir la cohésion sociale'. *Le Monde*, 12 May.

Dreyfus, F.G. (1975) *Histoire des gauches en France*. Paris: Grasset.

Duverger, M. (1955) 'SFIO: mort ou transfiguration?'. *Les Temps modernes*, June, pp. 19–24.

Duverger, M. (1985) 'L'Heure de Bad Godesberg'. *Le Monde*, 8 October.

Fabius, L. (1990) *C'est en allant à la mer*. Paris: Seuil.

Godin, E. (1996) 'Le Néo-liberalisme à la française'. *Modern and Contemporary France* NS4 (3), 61–70.

Groux, G. (1986) 'La Modernisation des rapports sociaux en France: les logiques en présence'. *Problèmes économiques*, 10 September, pp. 12–15.

Guérin, D. (1970) *Front Populaire révolution manquée*. Paris: Maspéro.

Hamon, H. (1989) '68: The Rise and Fall of a Generation', in D. Hanley and A.P. Kerr (eds) *May '68 Coming of Age*. Basingstoke: Macmillan, pp. 10–22.

Hamon, H. and Rotman, P. (1980) *L'Effet Rocard*. Paris: Stock.

Jarreau, P. (1993a) 'M. Michel Rocard appelle à la naissance d'un "vaste mouvement ouvert et moderne" '. *Le Monde*, 19 February.

Jarreau, P. (1993b) 'Comment Laurent Fabius a perdu la direction du Parti Socialiste'. *Le Monde*, 6 April.

Jospin, L. (1985) 'Constituer une majorité de gauche'. *Le Monde*, 13/14 October.

Jospin, L. (1991) *L'Invention du possible*. Paris: Flammarion.

Julliard, J. (1977) *Contre la politique professionnelle*. Paris: Seuil.

Julliard, J. (1985) *La Faute à Rousseau*. Paris: Seuil.

Keating, M. and Hainsworth, P. (1986) *Decentralization and Change in Contemporary France*. Aldershot: Avebury.

Lacouture, J. (1977) *Léon Blum*. Paris: Seuil.

Lévy, L. (1947) *Anthologie de Jean Jaurès*. London: Penguin.

Lhomeau, J.-Y. (1985) 'A rénovateur rénovateur et demi'. *Le Monde*, 13/14 October.

Mallet, S. (1963) *La Nouvelle Classe ouvrière*. Paris: Seuil.

Martinet, G. (1986) *Cassandre et les tueurs*. Paris: Grasset.

Mitterrand, F. (1969) *Ma Part de vérité*. Paris: Fayard.

Padgett, S. and Paterson, W. (1991) *A History of Social Democracy in Postwar Europe*. Harlow: Longman.

Parti Socialiste (1972) *Changer la vie: Programme de gouvernement du Parti Socialiste*. Paris: Flammarion.

Parti Socialiste (1981) *Projet socialiste pour la France des années 1980*. Paris: Club Socialiste du Livre.

Parti Socialiste (1992) *Un nouvel horizon pour la France: Projet socialiste pour la France*. Paris: Gallimard.

La Pensée Socialiste Contemporaine (1965) *Actes des Colloques Socialistes de 1964*. Paris: Presses Universitaires de France.

Philippe, A. and Hubscher, D. (1991) *Enquête à l'intérieur du Parti Socialiste*. Paris: Albin Michel.

Pierre-Brossolette, S. (1989) 'La Chasse au Rocard'. *L'Express*, 14 September.

Poperen, J. (1972) *La Gauche française: le nouvel âge 1958–1965*. Paris: Fayard.

Portelli, H. (1980) *Le Socialisme français tel qu'il est*. Paris: Presses Universitaires de France.

Quilliot, R. (1972) *La SFIO et l'exercice du pouvoir*. Paris: Fayard.

Rocard, M. (1979) *Parler vrai*. Paris: Seuil.

Rocard, M. (1986) *A l'épreuve des faits*. Paris: Seuil.

Rocard, M. (1987) *Le Coeur à l'ouvrage*. Paris: Odile Jacob.

Rocard, M. (1989) 'Déclaration de M. Rocard'. *Le Monde*, 21 December.

Rocard, M. (1993) 'Perspectives pour la social-démocratie'. *Vendredi* 2, 10–14.

Rocard, M., d'Almeida, P., Martin, J.-P., Martinet, G. and Sandoz, G. (1979) *Qu'est-ce que la social-démocratie?* Paris: Seuil.

Rosanvallon, P. (1976) *L'Age de l'autogestion*. Paris: Seuil.

Rosanvallon, P. and Viveret, P. (1977) *Pour une nouvelle culture politique*. Paris: Seuil.

Rosanvallon, P. (1988) 'Malaise dans la représentation', in F. Furet, J. Julliard and P. Rosanvallon *La République du centre*. Paris: Calmann Levy.

Schneider, R. (1987) *Michel Rocard*. Paris: Stock.

Servet, G. (alias M. Rocard) (1966) *Décoloniser la province*. Paris: Bibliothèque de la Fondation Nationale des Sciences Politiques.

Suffert, G. (1966) *De Defferre à Mitterrand: la campagne électorale*. Paris: Seuil.

Willard, C. (1967) *Socialisme et communisme français*. Paris: Armand Colin.

Wright, A. (1993) 'Social Democracy and Democratic Socialism', in R. Eatwell and A. Wright (eds) *Contemporary Political Ideologies*. London: Pinter, pp. 78–99.

2

Communism

JEREMY JENNINGS

Introduction

In the opening pages of his biography of France's foremost post-war Marxist philosopher, Yann Moulier Boutang recounts that on his last visit to Louis Althusser in hospital the main question preoccupying the latter was 'What are they saying about Gorbachev in Paris?' (Boutang, 1992, p. 33) This small incident alone is sufficient to indicate the centrality of the Soviet Union to the thought patterns of the French (Marxist) left until well into the 1980s. However, this very subjective appreciation of what has undoubtedly been one of the constants of French politics since 1917 can be backed up by more detailed and extensive evidence. Shortly before the leadership of the French Communist Party (PCF) greeted the August 1991 coup by Moscow's 'hard-liners' with ill-disguised satisfaction,[1] an opinion poll amongst delegates at the PCF's 27th Party Congress in December 1990 revealed that no less than 57 per cent were prepared to identify the Soviet Union with socialism whilst 81 per cent had a 'very positive' assessment of the actions of Lenin. Only 29 per cent believed that the changes taking place in the Soviet bloc countries could be described as a good thing (SOFRES, 1990).[2] In short, the 'Soviet myth' lasted as long as the Soviet Union itself.

The methods of inculcation of this myth and the psychological needs that it met were various and say much about the human need for the certainty of ultimate victory. Fresh from the horrors of World War I, a rapidly 'bolshevized' communist party had little difficulty convincing its adherents that the USSR was the home of socialism, that Moscow (in the words of the PCF's general secretary, Louis-Oscar Frossard) was a 'holy city', and that a terrestrial Eden and 'superior civilization' were in the process of creation, which one day would bring forth the liberation of the working class everywhere (quoted in Desanti, 1975, p. 34).

Moreover, there appeared to be much evidence to support these claims. Between 1917 and World War II, no fewer than 125 (for the most part uncritical) accounts of visits to the Soviet Union were published in France alone. The list is even longer if the numerous novels inspired by the Soviet experience are included. Unfortunately there is little indication that many of these visitors left Moscow (or in some cases, the Kremlin or the Hotel Lux!), or that they spoke Russian and hence were able to free themselves from the influence of the Bolshevik propaganda machine (Kupferman, 1979). Nothing was left to chance by the Soviet authorities. Laid on for novelist André Gide, for example, was a swimming pool full of handsome young men from the Red Army, and even homosexual encounters were prearranged so that Gide could be blackmailed later if necessary. In addition, a whole series of front organizations (most notably Les Amis de l'URSS), designed to enhance the image of the Soviet Union as the land of peace and progress, complemented the PCF in its self-appointed role as the sole authoritative source of information on the subject. Thus, after the achievements of the Red Army at Stalingrad were translated within France into ideological ascendency in such diverse fields as art, literature and even science, there seemed little that could shake the faith in the Soviet Union. As Robert Desjardins (1988, p. 13) makes plain: 'Any person daring to level criticism against the Soviet Union was automatically accused of playing into the hands of the class enemy and labelled as a member of the imperialist and fascist camp.' Within this context even the existence of the gulag could be denied with apparent complete sincerity (and by such eminent figures as Jean-Paul Sartre as well as the PCF itself). And so, for example, Jeannine Verdès-Leroux (1983, p. 14) begins her magisterial account of the affiliation of French intellectuals to the PCF by commenting that she had been 'troubled by the obstinacy displayed by these intellectuals in denying or distorting the *long since well-established* reality of the USSR'.

Yet the USSR was not without its critics in France and the reality of the regime was not too hard to discover. In 1935, for example, former communist Boris Souvarine published his monumental denunciation of Stalin – arguably one of the most important books of the twentieth century – and after this there was no shortage of material denouncing the regime as a self-perpetuating military dictatorship, a form of 'total bureaucratic capitalism' or, later, a totalitarian system. Yet until well into the 1970s amongst large sections of opinion in France the revolution in Russia enjoyed respect and adulation, whilst the Soviet regime, despite its repressive nature and actions, continued to receive praise and to be viewed as a model for the future.

Among those institutions that best exemplified this devotion to the Soviet system was undoubtedly the PCF. And yet it also has seen itself as a party with deep roots in the cultural and political traditions of France, and since its 22nd Congress in 1976 it has proudly proclaimed its aim as finding 'a French way towards socialism and a French style of socialism' (Marchais, 1976, p. 62). Thus, Georges Marchais, general-secretary of the party, could announce at the beginning of his book *Démocratie*, published in 1990, that 'one of the greatest historical strengths of the Communist Party ... has been to reconcile the tricolour flag of the homeland with the red flag of socialism, the *Marseillaise* and the *Internationale*' (Marchais, 1990a, p. 19). The party, it is affirmed, is not something grafted upon the French body politic from the outside, and it is this in part which explains the decision to retain the title of *communist* party when its sister parties throughout Europe and else-where chose to abandon the name with unseemly haste. Communism comes not only from Russia, it is proclaimed, but from the glorious revolutionary tradition of France itself, a tradition made manifest in such events as the Revolution of 1789, the Paris Commune of 1871, the Popular Front of the 1930s and, in the case of the PCF, participation in the Resistance during World War II. It is then the twin symbols of the tricolour and the red flag that take us to the heart of communist ideology in contemporary France.

The Red Flag

When the party was created in 1920, initial adherence to the PCF was heavily influenced by the immense suffering associated with World War I and by the failure of the socialist-dominated labour movement to provide even the semblance of effective opposition to mass slaughter.[3] To this was added the unchallenged prestige of the October Revolution and the personal reputation of Lenin, even if adherents knew little of the ideas of the Bolsheviks or of their actions. Quickly Lenin's Third International began the process of turning the French party (indeed, all other communist parties) into a replica of its Soviet counterpart, a transformation that led not only to expulsions amongst its members but to acceptance of the famous 21 conditions covering not just party organization but doctrine and strategy. Defining itself as *the* party of the French working class, the PCF was henceforth to exist as the French section of the international communist movement, closely controlled by Moscow, committed to a rigid conception of Marxism-Leninism (most notably, the notion of the dictatorship of the proletariat), and run on democratic-centralist lines throughout what came to be a vast panoply of factory cells, trade unions, newspapers, clubs and associations. Frequently seen as a counter-church or as a society within a society, the PCF rapidly established a style, a language (the famous *langue de bois*), a culture and an identity all of its own (Lavau, 1981). Moreover, it was into this specific worldview that the party activist would be drawn, accepting its rules, its discipline, its cults and its objects of veneration; and so much so that no life seemed possible outside its confines (Thomas, 1995).

To what extent this ideological and organizational framework led inevitably to a willing embrace of the dictates of Stalinism is open to discussion (and touches upon questions that relate to the entire history of Marxism in the twentieth century), but there can be no doubt that the PCF fell victim to the personality cult: Stalin was at once father figure, spiritual leader, sage and undisputed expert in all fields of knowledge, the very exemplar of all that was finest in communist man. 'Comrade Stalin', Jacques Duclos told his national conference in a speech of profound emotion mourning their terrible loss in Stalin's death, was 'the greatest man of his age', the defender of peace who had devoted his entire life to the cause of proletarian revolution and the construction of socialism (Legendre, 1980, pp. 66–8). If the party's own leader, Maurice Thorez, received similar adulation, behind the reverence for Stalin lay a continued worship of the Soviet Union as the home of socialism. Surrounded by its enemies (and hence meriting unqualified loyalty), it held out the prospect of a new world of prosperity and emancipation, a civilization that was superior in every respect to that of capitalism, be it in the fields of art, literature, health care, housing or science. No praise seemed too excessive for its heroic leaders and people. And thus, in line with Soviet policy, French communism threw its weight behind the emerging 'popular democracies' of Eastern Europe, condemned the 'renegade' Tito in Yugoslavia, supported the invasion of Hungary in 1956, and celebrated the launch of the first Sputnik into outer space.

The 'awakening of the sleepwalkers' (title of Verdès-Leroux, 1987) began from the mid-1950s onwards, with the 1968 invasion of Czechoslovakia and the crushing of 'socialism with a human face' by Soviet troops doing irreparable damage to the image of the USSR. Yet still the vision of a promethean Russia lingered on in French communism. The best example is undoubtedly Georges Marchais's assessment of the 'achievements' of the Soviet Union as being 'generally positive' at the PCF's 23rd National Congress in 1979, but other examples are easily found. Typical of the style and mode of argument is the manner in which the party's principal newspaper, *L'Humanité*, covered Marchais's statement (made in Moscow) of his approval of the Soviet invasion of Afghanistan. Having drawn a distinction between the invasions of Czechoslovakia (which received the PCF's disapproval) and that of Afghanistan, Marchais characterized the latter as an impoverished, underdeveloped country in the grip of feudalism, with a largely illiterate population incapable of defeating imperialism on its own. To emphasize the point *L'Humanité* (1980) duly carried a eulogy of the four Soviet central Asian republics, concluding that 'Tadjikistan and the other Muslim republics have progressed by eight centuries in fifty years.'

Nevertheless, events have forced change in this key element of communist ideology. The opinion poll cited earlier revealed that only 1 per cent of delegates approved of the actions of Stalin, and the party now likes to believe that it is completely free of Stalinist influences and practices (even if in early 1995 the likeable new national secretary of the PCF, Robert Hue, could admit that they had been slow to reach the correct analysis of Stalinism). So, for example, Marchais felt able to locate Stalin within the Russian tradition of autocratic government going back to Ivan the Terrible, whilst in 1989 his colleague, Jean-Claude Gayssot, characterized Stalinism as 'dogmatism, authoritarianism and lying raised to the level of a system'. It was because of this that it constituted a 'monstrous perversion of socialism and of the communist ideal' (Gayssot, 1989, pp. 62–3).

Another casualty has been the endorsement of the dictatorship of the proletariat as the appropriate route to socialism. Denoting an acceptance of the use of violence for the seizure and maintenance of power and a disregard for parliamentary democracy, it was dumped unceremoniously (and with virtually no debate) at the PCF's 22nd Congress in February 1976 (Marchais, 1976, pp. 44–51). The argument was that if such a dictatorship had been 'necessary' in Russia in 1917, it was no longer 'appropriate' to the reality of a modern France, where 'revolutionary transformation' could be achieved by other means – a half-way position that did little either to please the party's old guard or to reassure those with doubts about the sincerity of the PCF's commitment to parliamentary practices.

Less quickly displaced was the key Bolshevik organizational principle of democratic centralism: indeed it was only formally abandoned at the Party's 28th Congress in January 1994, and even then there were critics from within the movement who argued that it was still much in evidence. Long the subject of controversy and dispute by such dissidents as Henri Fiszbin (1984), Pierre Juquin (1985), and latterly Charles Fiterman and party philosopher Lucien Sève, the party leadership had traditionally characterized this practice not as a means of suppressing dissent and discussion (as its critics claimed) but rather as a source of strength and unity. If abuses had occurred during the Stalinist period, the view was that considerable progress had been made in extending the democratic life of the party and that it was now typified by extended debate and the absence of secrecy. 'What characterizes the functioning of the Communist Party', Marchais wrote, 'is not centralism but the fact that it is democratic, the fact that the party belongs to its members' (1990a, p. 285). Nevertheless, he remained opposed to the formation of 'tendencies' or factions within the party, believing them to be a threat to internal democracy, and in September of that same year he responded to dissent from members of the Party's Central Committee by arguing that the party's functioning sought correctly not to foment 'division' and 'confrontation', but rather to secure 'the collective discovery through discussion of an agreed text representing the views of all communists'. The minority, in other words, could have their say, but then they had to toe the party line or depart, as many (including former government minister Charles Fiterman) have done over the last decade. The 1994 changes in the party's statutes do little to prove that the culture of obedience has come to an end or that, as is now proclaimed, 'a communist party of a new type' has come into existence.

Far more problematic has been the whole issue of the 'Soviet model' and the charge that French communism is inspired by an 'exterior' ideal. Any speech on the subject made by a PCF leader over the last decade or more would produce the same inventory of criticisms made of the Soviet Union and the same list of divergences with the Communist Party (CPSU): from 1968 onwards – and in books such as *L'URSS et nous* (Adler *et al.*, 1979) – the PCF has voiced its opinion that the USSR has never completely succeeded in freeing itself of the incubus of its Stalinist past and that, as we have already seen, what the PCF itself now proposes is a vision of socialism that is specifically French. Yet it is interesting to note the nature of the critique of the Soviet model that was being proposed. Invariably it was accompanied by a set of references to attenuating circumstances which served to explain the relative failure of the Bolshevik project, and, until 1991, there was the expectation that these problems would be overcome. Speaking to the Fête de L'Humanité in 1989, for example, Marchais provided the standard litany of recent censure before concluding: 'we have been worried, but we have never lost faith in the socialist societies, in their capacity to find in themselves the forces which will allow them to overcome the obstacles which prevent them from realising all their potential' (Marchais, 1989a). The USSR, for example, was credited with moving towards 'a complete realization of the rights of man' (Milhau, 1989, p. 63). The faults, in other words, derived from circumstances and the perversions of Stalinism and not from the original goal and objective. So was Stalinism already present in Lenin? Even after the collapse of the USSR the response was an even-handed 'yes and no'. 'Yes,' wrote Francis Cohen (1994, p. 110), 'in the sense that there was no new revolution, society remained set upon the same path; a series of economic, social and cultural changes that had already been begun and prepared were put into practice. Stalin was not a contrary and complete opposite of Lenin. No, because in the conceptions, goals and practices that determined policy there was a complete rupture. Stalin continued and betrayed Lenin.'

But to these difficulties of analysis and perspective were added, in the final years of the USSR, the need to articulate a coherent reaction to the rise and fall of Mikhail Gorbachev and to the politics of *perestroika*. The suspicion – voiced frequently in the press and by its opponents – was that French communism was never entirely happy with Gorbachev, a suspicion that despite considerable effort it was never able completely to dispel (Marchais, 1988, 1989b, 1991a). The official line was that the transformation being undertaken in the USSR constituted a 'second revolution': the economy was being freed from rigid state control and bureaucracy, priority was being given to improving services and con-sumption patterns, artistic and cultural freedoms were being restored, and political liberties extended. Four years into the experiment this was the nature of the assessment:

> We are not simple spectators of this movement. No one can be because the repercussions of *perestroika* are of world-wide significance. French communists approve of it and support it because the renovation of socialism that it articulates recalls many of the characteristics of the democratic, self-managing socialism that they wish to establish, because its success improves the image and influence of socialism, and because it stands for peace, the new international order and cooperation between peoples.
>
> (Cohen, 1989, p. 88)

As the USSR's problems mounted – and especially as the Soviet bloc disintegrated, giving rise to renewed fears of a united Germany – the warmth of allegiance declined, leading ultimately to the fateful ambiguity that surrounded the PCF's response to the August 1991 coup (Marchais, 1991c; Plissonier, 1991; Gremetz, 1991).

That coup threw party activists into disarray, but beyond reference to the 'unacceptable' methods used to depose Gorbachev it is clear that the initial reaction of the leadership was to suggest that Gorbachev was seriously at fault. If the crisis owed something to 'the structures and patterns of behaviour inherited from the past', the weight of the blame was attributed to:

> the errors committed most notably in economic affairs, the discontent and discouragement aroused by promises not kept, the rise of nationalisms [which] have led to the present situation of worsening poverty, social inequalities, corruption, disorientation, and social and interethnic conflict.
>
> (*L'Humanité*, 1991b)

Gorbachev's achievement, in this view, was to bring about the demise of the Soviet Union and with it the hopes and dreams of millions of communists, leaving only 'the ultra-liberal capitalist option' of Boris Yeltsin (Leyrac, 1994, p. 107). All was not lost, however, because as the red flag was lowered over the Kremlin there remained the tricolour, the other half of French communism's ideological identity (Plissonier, 1993).

The Tricolour

Most obviously French communism is a Marxist ideology, and no opportunity is lost to emphasize Marxism's continued relevance, be it on the centenary of Marx's death (*L'Humanité*, 1983) or in the post-Soviet era when Robert Hue spoke of the importance of 'the spirit rather than the letter of Marx' (Hue, 1996). Thus, if beyond capitalism there lies the promise of a revolutionary utopia, it is the capitalist system – in its present phase described as that of 'state-monopoly capitalism' – that is the cause of society's ills and problems. France is perpetually described as a country in profound crisis and one in which the situation of the people is becoming progressively worse. Capitalism means the growth of profits at the expense of personal consumption, decline in productive capacity, the export of capital, inflation, monetary instability, the ever-increasing exploitation of labour, uncontrolled urbanization and the abandonment of the countryside. It signifies austerity, unemployment, the failure to meet needs, wasteful and unplanned production, inequalities between regions, poor communications and transport, and the rape of nature. The majority of the world's population are condemned to poverty, disease and misery. So too militarism and the arms race are a necessary part of capitalism's workings, a political necessity as well as a source of huge profits. And, inescapably, capitalism is the cause of domination by the bourgeoisie, with its 'immense wealth' and 'enormous privileges'. Here is a class with a clear sense of its own interests and of its right to exercise power.[4]

Certain of the accuracy of this analysis and undaunted by the recent challenges to this vision of the world, Robert Hue could therefore assure delegates to the 1994 Party Congress that French society had simply entered 'a new phase of the crisis' (Hue, 1994, p. 25). Detailed in the party programme were its novel features: illiteracy, violence, racism, intolerance, drug addiction, corruption, AIDS, a worldwide refugee problem, mounting exploitation of women and the young, the concentration of power in ever fewer hands. Capitalism's response – in the shape of the 'baneful' Edouard Balladur – was to put the social and democratic rights of the French people under threat. A vast programme of privatizations plus the dismantling of public services were to be combined with an assault upon 'everything that assures that France is France': its schools, its hospitals, its social security system, and its 'capacity to integrate foreigners'. All of this conformed to a 'logic of capitalism' which recognized only 'the powers of money' (*Cahiers du communisme*, 1994).

French communism's reply, from the decisive moment of the 22nd Congress in 1976 onwards, has been to argue for what it defines as a programme of economic, social and political democracy, which it has characterized as 'the French style of democratic socialism and workers' self-management' (Marchais, 1982, p. 22). Spelt out by Jacques Chambaz (1990, p. 26), a member of the party's Central Committee, its 'central idea' amounted to this: 'to make the development of man and of his capacities the object and means of a new efficiency and to this end to tie social progress, economic progress and democratic progress inseparably together'. It was not to be confused, he went on, with a socialism reduced solely to the collectivization of the means of production and exchange, 'the socialism of the barracks'. The key word '*autogestionnaire*' – one of the buzz words that came out of the protests of May '68, one which socialists interpreted as 'workers' control' – was given imprecise definition. Described by Georges Marchais, for example, it featured as 'the systematic encouragement of the participation of the people – and especially the working class – in the running of affairs, in the factory, in the *commune*, throughout social life and at all levels of the State' (1991b, p. 40).

Given therefore that capitalism's crisis was structural and global, how could this *socialisme à la française* be brought about, and what are its constituent parts? The first point to stress is that if France itself is seen as 'the country of liberty', then the PCF is perceived very much as the party of liberty. Rationalism, the critical spirit, individualism and the love of life, we are told, have made their mark upon the consciences and aspirations of the French and, as 'the sons and daughters of this people', it is their struggles for liberty that are now being continued by the PCF. Recalling their 'complete condemnation' of Stalinism, proof of that commitment to liberty is demonstrated by reference to their opposition to colonial wars, the condemnation of the Munich accords of 1938 (although no mention is ever made of the Nazi–Soviet pact of 1939), participation in the Resistance, and the heroic and selfless sacrifice of the lives of countless communists in defence of their homeland. 'Every time,' Marchais told delegates to the 24th Congress, 'whether it be at local or national level that democracy is violated, diminished or threatened you, communists, are seen in the front line defending the liberty of our citizens, supported by the entire party' (1982, p. 36). By liberty is meant not the narrow liberal conception of the absence of formal restraint – 'what is the liberty', it is asked, 'of the unemployed worker anguished by his situation and deprived of his salary?' – but something which is tied to an altogether different vision of a just society.

At a purely political level, this now means endorsement of a set of liberties normally associated with the bourgeois democratic process and previously anathema to Marxist-Leninist parties. The PCF accepts the verdict of the ballot box and from 1963 onwards has rejected the Bolshevik concept of a one-party state. Regular, democratic elections based upon universal suffrage should be held for all tiers of government, with the results decided upon the basis of proportional representation, 'the only electoral system capable of assuring the accurate representation of electors'. Recommended also is an 'authentic decentralization' at local, departmental and regional levels. Unlike its former Soviet counterpart, the PCF recognizes the rightful independence of trade unions as well as the right to strike and the exercise of rights within the workplace. To this are added a whole series of rights associated with the individual: the rights to privacy, security, free expression, conscience and association; and, more generally, 'freedom of scientific, literary and artistic creation ... and publication'. Considerable emphasis is also placed upon freedom of information and upon what are described as the virtues of cultural diversity and pluralism. These rights in particular feature as part of what is seen as an indispensable process, which will allow individual workers and citizens to liberate themselves from the distortions of a capitalist and state-controlled media.

It should come as no surprise that the PCF has opposed the institutions of the Fifth Republic from 1958 onwards. Characterized as a system of 'personal power', de Gaulle's republic is portrayed as 'authoritarian' and 'anti-democratic' and condemned for its 'monarchical tendencies'. Excessive power is in the hands of the executive, whilst its electoral system, it is argued, is designed solely to operate in the interests of the bourgeoisie (Lajoinie, 1989). In these senses it constitutes a threat to political liberty.

It is interesting, however, to take one step back in order to address the deeper ideological perspectives that inform this reasoning. The ultimate grounds of this rejection of the Fifth Republic lay in a conception of the sovereignty of the people that has its origins in the French Revolution, and especially in the Constitution of 1793. Shortly we will say more about the PCF's attitude towards 1789, but at this stage it is sufficient to recognize that in the eyes of French communism there was a fundamental contradiction between the Revolution's original proclamation of rights and liberties (in the *Déclaration des droits de l'homme et du citoyen*, for example) and the manner in which its economic liberalism demanded that these liberties be subordinated to the claims of property and business. It was Robespierre's constitution that first brought together the exercise of popular sovereignty and a recognition of 'fundamental social rights', the most basic of which was a guarantee of the means to life for all members of society. The subsequent establishment of 'bourgeois hegemony', typified by the institutions of the Third Republic, saw not only an abandonment of this concern with the social dimension of rights but also a methodical attempt to limit the powers of popular sovereignty. This hegemony, it is argued, has since been dislodged only once, in 1946, when sovereignty was deemed to reside in a popularly elected National Assembly, and when the Constitution of the Fourth Republic institutionalized such important social rights as the right to work. It is in this way, as former presidential candidate André Lajoinie argued, that 'the Constitution of the Fifth Republic, by adapting institutions to the necessities of state-monopoly capitalism, represents a decisive return to the past by limiting the sovereignty of the

people' (1989, p. 83). And so beyond such narrow institutional demands as the restoration of the primacy of a single legislative assembly,
a reduction of the functions of the president, and criticism of the
'government of judges' exercised by the Conseil Constitutionnel, there
lies the call for the people to exercise their full sovereignty by combining the ideals of liberty, equality and fraternity with 'the storming of the
new bastilles of money and inequality'.

This itself takes us to the heart of the question of what French
communism properly understands by the concept of rights, an issue
which in turn is intimately connected to its assessment of the significance of the Revolution of 1789. Historically the Marxist tradition
has been hostile to talk of the rights of humankind, following Marx in
believing that such rights served simply to mask bourgeois egoism.
When therefore Jacques Milhau (1989, p. 61) writes that 'liberal-
conservative thought' has 'a mutilated, atrophied and restricted conception of the rights of man', it is this perspective that is being echoed.
It is in the interests of the capitalist system and of its dominant class to
evacuate these rights of any significant content and to deny the legitimacy of speaking about 'economic, social and cultural rights'. To that
extent, if any statement of rights receives communist approval it is the
Universal Declaration of the Rights of Man formulated by the United
Nations in 1949, rather than France's own historic declaration of 1789.
What is emphasized is the right to housing, education, good health,
employment, leisure and a decent wage, rather than civil and political
rights. Translated into the rhetoric of the PCF this produces the slogan
'La Justice d'abord . . . La Liberté ensuite' – 'Justice first, liberty second'
(Lajoinie, 1990, p. 20).

French communism's assessment of the Revolution of 1789 fits into
this ideological perspective. Clearly this was a subject that of necessity
had to be addressed during the bicentenary celebrations of 1989, and
which is no mere historical debate. All interpretations of the Revolution
are of political significance, and of late it has been the liberal reading
associated with François Furet and the Institut Raymond Aron that has
been in the ascendant. On this view the Revolution was essentially
derailed, the moderate demands for constitutional reform of the summer of 1789 being submerged by calls for social equality that ultimately
led to the Reign of Terror and Robespierre's Committee of Public
Safety in 1793. The official bicentenary celebrations effectively followed
this line, concentrating their attention upon the supposed universal
and timeless significance of the *Déclaration des droits de l'homme et du
citoyen*, and turning their back upon such unsavoury aspects as the

execution of the royal family. To combat this interpretation was clearly of great importance for the PCF. As Marxist historian Robert Bourderon (Bicocchi, 1989, pp. 100–1) commented: 'To emasculate 1789 and the whole revolutionary process by reducing it simply to a form of political conquest ... has as its principal object the denial of social movements as the cause of social, political and economic gains.'

Viewed simply, for Marxists the French Revolution is a bourgeois revolution, marking the passage from feudalism to capitalism. And yet, following the great socialist leader Jean Jaurès, there has also been a recognition that it had the potential to effect the transformation not just to political democracy but beyond to social democracy. And this was the theme repeated by Georges Marchais (1989c, p. 8) during the bicentenary year. 'Through the increasing intervention of popular forces inspired by demands for radical changes,' he told communists in Paris's 14th *arrondissement*, 'the manner in which France effected its transition from the old society to the new did not occur, as it did in other countries of the world, in a conservative manner.' What it demonstrated (through such figures as Gracchus Babeuf) was that society could be based upon relations of peace, equity and fraternity. Thus the Revolution's message was that civil and political rights could not be divorced from demands for social rights, liberty could not be separated from equality. It was this central idea that defined the actuality and continued relevance of the Revolution in today's world.

But the PCF's reflections upon the significance of the French Revolution had another theme, and one that takes us closer to the tricolour flag of the homeland. If 1789 disclosed in embryo the seeds of a future society based upon social democracy and equality, then it also represented the moment when France first constituted itself as a nation, 'one and indivisible'. Giving this significance is the vitally important idea that the interests of the working class are identical to those of the national interest, and therefore that a threat to either the identity or independence of the nation is a direct threat to the French proletariat. This, in fact, has been a key communist belief since the 1930s (Lazar, 1990, pp. 1080–3).

Frequently cited by communists themselves to prove the longevity of this identification of the working class with France are the words of their former leader, Maurice Thorez, who, at the time of the 150th anniversary of the Revolution in 1939, sanctified the revolutionary heritage of the French nation, thus 'uniting the red flag of the revolutionaries of the modern epoch with the tricolour flag of the revolutionaries of 1789' (Marchais, 1989c, p. 13). But a slightly earlier and more interesting example can be found in communist Jean Renoir's classic film of the Popular Front era, *La Marseillaise*. As the Marseille patriots march through France singing their patriotic battle hymn, what we witness on the screen is the birth of a nation from which only the *émigré* aristocrats (today's capitalists) are excluded. Even the Catholic clergy have their place.

This identification with the nation and, from 1937 onwards, this stated willingness to defend it prefigured communist participation in the Resistance, and then in the work of national reconstruction associated with the post-Liberation government. After 1947, and the beginning of the Cold War, this expressed itself strongly as anti-Americanism. America was perceived not just as an industrial threat to France but also as a military and cultural threat. It stood for Coca-Cola (consumerism), the English language (philistinism), the Marshall Plan (economic imperialism) and General Ridgway's germ warfare in Korea (barbarism). And so, for example, anti-Americanism lay behind the successive attempts of the PCF to foster a peace movement from the 1950s to the 1980s, as well as their criticisms of the foreign policies of Giscard d'Estaing and François Mitterrand as 'atlanticist' (both conveniently in line with Soviet interests). Today it still figures in such forms as the passionate defence of French science (Kahane, 1989), demands for protection of the French film industry, and the obvious refusal to see virtues in the American liberal 'model'. France is simply thought to be superior, 'more civilized' than the United States.

This overt Jacobinism also produces purple patches in praise of France of astonishing lyricism. Without hesitation it is proclaimed that France is one of the most beautiful countries in the world, rich in natural resources, enjoying a moderate climate and varied geography, with the intellectual and technological potential to take on and beat the rest. Equally there is pride in a specifically 'French conception of culture' made manifest in philosophy, music and literature as well as (not surprisingly) France's food and wine.[5] 'The modernity of France', Georges Marchais wrote, 'is this art of living, this style, this personality.'

Yet there is a keen awareness that the integrity and identity of France are under challenge. France is a beautiful country, but ... and the 'but' arises because of the numerous forces that are gradually diminishing its national sovereignty. Marchais (1976, pp. 30–1) therefore told his 1976 national conference that 'true to its traditions the French communist party fights and will fight with all its strength to preserve the independence and sovereignty of France'. Far from being outmoded, he went on, national independence remained of great importance and needed to be defended by 'all the patriots of our land'. And this is a message that has been repeated time and time again. In 1982, for example, delegates were told: 'we defend and will defend with absolute intransigence the independence and sovereignty of France' (Marchais, 1982, p. 55). Similarly, as the party prepared for its 27th Congress in 1990, Marchais (1990b, p. 20) told members: 'To consent to the enslavement of France and to its people being put under tutelage would mean no longer being communist, and our party would no longer merit its name if it did not fight with all its strength against this danger.' What this meant in practice was spelt out by the PCF's Central Committee prior to the European elections of the summer of 1989:

> The international politics of France should be based upon an active non-alignment. This presupposes that in every circumstance France should preserve its liberty and freedom of choice to decide both its internal and external policies and to engage in bilateral or multilateral cooperation with whatever country it likes.
>
> (*Cahiers du communisme*, 1989, p. 97)

The PCF is quick to deny that this fervent attachment to the independence of France could be confused with xenophobia, racism or simple chauvinism; the argument is that what is required is a new international order based upon cooperation and justice between equals. That international order, the PCF told electors prior to the 1993 legislative elections (*L'Humanité*, 1993), required the elimination of all nuclear weapons, concerted action against world hunger and underdevelopment, a solution to the world debt problem, and measures to prevent the UN from becoming the instrument of the 'superpowers', as it had been, for example, during the Gulf War (*L'Humanité*, 1991a). But beneath this lies the simple message that it is in Paris and not Washington, Tokyo or Bonn that decisions affecting France should be made. The French should not be subject to control by either financial speculators or multinationals, the IMF or NATO, the mark or the yen.

Of late, however, the principal target of the PCF's rhetorical abuse as a danger to national independence has been the European Union, and specifically the Maastricht treaty (Lajoinie, 1992; Wurtz, 1992). The argument in general is that the EU represents a new form of capitalist integration, a remodelling of the system that ensures the dominance of a free-market economy and a German-controlled supranational state. As for the Maastricht treaty, the following quotation from an article printed prior to the 1992 referendum gives a taste of the fierce opposition:

Maastricht is an instrument of war directed against the peoples [of Europe] which announces new sacrifices, new waste, serious challenges to rights, to liberties, and to national sovereignty. Maastricht is the Europe of economic war, of the law of the richest and strongest. It is a Europe of domination in total opposition to a Europe of cooperation.

(Ainardi, 1992, p. 19)

In every way it constituted a threat to France's national identity and sovereignty, be it in the form of a single currency, majority voting amongst the Council of Ministers, or any one of the innumerable measures promulgated by the bureaucrats of Brussels that diminished the authority of the French parliament (*Cahiers du communisme*, 1992, pp. 13–16). The PCF's own vision of Europe was, they believed, very different, and even managed to draw upon Gorbachev's concept of a 'common European home'. Restated in the report that accompanied the announcement that Robert Hue would be the PCF's candidate in the 1995 presidential elections, it was summarized as:

a democratic, pacific and sovereign Europe, a Europe of cooperation without domination, a Europe respectful of national sovereignties, a greater Europe stretching from the Atlantic to the Urals, without either discrimination or hierarchy, permitting the collective and peaceful solution to problems of common interest.

(*L'Humanité*, 1994)

Whatever else could be read into this it was certainly meant to be seen, in the words of Hue himself, as 'the refusal of France and its people to submit to the demands of Europe' (*L'Humanité*, 1994). And as such it was perfectly in line with the PCF's position that it would always defend 'the liberty of liberties', national sovereignty.

There is, finally, one further theme that illustrates French communism's attachment to the nation. Strategy, especially for a communist party, cannot be divorced from ideology, and therefore the PCF has laboured hard to define the best means of achieving its goals. For many years its conclusions were much influenced by the demands of the Soviet Union, but from the mid-1970s it pursued a more independent path, flirting with Eurocommunism and then adopting the policy of the 'Union of the Left'. The breakdown of this strategy in 1977 led to a reaffirmation of orthodoxy, only in 1981 for four communists to become ministers in the socialist-led government of Pierre Mauroy. This short-lived (and now much-regretted) experience gave rise not only to internal dissent and accelerated electoral decline, but to feverish attempts to rescue something from the wreckage of what was once France's largest political party and major ideological force. Juquin's *rénovateurs*, Poperen's *reconstructeurs* and Fiterman's *refondateurs* all grappled with the problem of changing and modernizing the culture of communism whilst avoiding the descent into social democracy. All have arguably failed. The party itself fell back upon old populist slogans: anti-Americanism, the crisis of capitalism, the abuses of the rich, and, latterly, the dictatorship of money. But holding it all together was the motif of *rassemblement*. If for the PCF the working class was adjudged to have a leading role in any process of social transformation, then it equally saw itself as the party which brought together all those who suffered exploitation. This was most famously demonstrated during the Popular Front era with Maurice Thorez's gesture of *la main tendue*, the hand held out to Catholics, but it is a stance that has reappeared on many occasions subsequently. Marchais (1976, p. 52), for example, told his party's 22nd Congress: 'We want to bring together all the active forces of the nation against the barons of capital; we want the union of the people of France.' The working class avant-garde were to find themselves besides peasants, intellectuals, all the social and economic categories that were disadvantaged and exploited by the bourgeois-dominated system. In the 1990s, with no possibility of or desire for an alliance with the leadership of the Socialist Party, this has again seemed the way forward. The aim, Robert Hue (1994, p. 29) told the 1994 conference, was 'to bring together all the components of our people, the world of work in its entirety, not forgetting those that society seeks to exclude'. This, he estimated, made up 90 per cent of the population, 'the millions and millions of men and women whose lives and hopes are crushed by the law of profit, who should unite and make themselves heard in order finally to bring into existence a politics that conforms to their interests'. The ultimate purpose of the PCF was precisely to represent these people, the people that made up the French nation.

But can this ideological rhetoric be taken seriously, and is there an audience that is prepared any longer to listen? François Furet (1995), a former communist himself, published a piece of sustained polemic masquerading as history in which the whole 'communist idea' was written off as an illusion. At best, according to Furet, it makes sense as a form of bourgeois self-mortification. Elsewhere the common theme is that we are now dealing with the end of Marxism and the disintegration of a tradition that has been of dubious benefit to France. A series of factors and indicators is marshalled – most importantly, the gradual disappearance of the traditional working class, the collapse of the Soviet bloc, and a percentage of the popular vote invariably in single figures – designed to prove the point that French communism has reached both a political and ideological dead end. And in truth it is hard to avoid this conclusion. A new leader and repeated denials that communism in France is dead do little to convince one that, since the partial departure of Georges Marchais, anything more than an attempt to provide a more friendly and accommodating image has taken place.

Conclusion

So, is communism now an irrelevance, and as an ideology can it ever be revivified? It will arguably continue to speak for those who feel themselves to be, and are described as, the excluded: the unemployed, immigrants, the old and the young. But the danger here is one of increasing marginalization. The strategy adopted in 1995 was one of *'ouverture'* and, more controversially, 'constructive opposition' to Chirac's presidency, but its chances of success were uncertain. Nor was it clear how much support it had within the party, especially amongst those who remained close to former leader Georges Marchais. There is the possibility of an opening towards the ecologists, but this has limited potential given that the PCF is still ultimately wedded to a productivist ethic. Historical enmity (and past party discipline) is such that it seems inconceivable that a reconciliation could be effected with the Trotskyist Lutte ouvrière led by Arlette Laguiller. Indeed, the latter's relative electoral success in the first round of the 1995 presidential election would seem, paradoxically, to have made this even less likely. As for social democracy, there is no desire to imitate the ideological vacuousness of the present Parti Socialiste. When, therefore, Robert Hue speaks of the need for a 'pacte unitaire pour le progrès', it is hard to know what it would look like.

A possible future is therefore perhaps only to be found, if at all, through a process of internal ideological renovation. This is to an extent found in the figure of Robert Hue, with all his undoubted gnome-like charm. His doctrinal statement, *Communisme: la mutation* (1995), not only buries the 'Soviet model' for good but also redefines communist ideology as 'a humanism of our time', with the full weight placed upon 'the affirmation of human dignity'. He, and those close to him, are, however, perhaps too groomed in the practices of the past. Beyond the humanistic rhetoric, there is little to suggest that serious thought has been given to the revision of either goals or the strategy for their implementation, even if it is reassuring to be told by Hue that

'French communists love their country'. But ideological renovation might emerge from the reflections of someone like Philippe Herzog, certainly one of the more intelligent and thoughtful current representatives of French communism (Herzog *et al.*, 1995).

Herzog's call for what he describes as a 'participatory democracy' continues many of the themes traditionally associated with communist ideology, but he gives them a new twist. On the EU, for example, there is a call for a more 'social' Europe and for the more effective representation of its peoples; but this is combined with a recognition that in this case 'membership of the Union would signify a form of divided sovereignty, not the giving up of freedoms but rather their extension'. With regard to the reform of the institutions of the state, the usual criticisms of the excessive concentration of executive power in the presidential Fifth Republic are accompanied by a commitment to decentralization that rests upon what seems a genuine endorsement of active citizenship. Yet the real ideological innovation lies in the outline of what is termed 'a culture of responsibility and solidarity' (Herzog *et al.*, 1995). Faced with the undeniable problems of an advanced capitalist economy that is a prey to ever-fiercer international competition, Herzog defends the idea of a new 'social contract' that will extend 'cooperation and interactivity in order to secure mutual development'. The vision is of a 'mixed economy' freed of excessive state control and the ruthless dictates of a free market, in which all citizens would play an active part in the decision making that affects every aspect of their lives.

To which, of course, critics can reply that it makes no sense to talk of a right to employment or a right to training, and that a reduction in working hours simply opens up the way to the increased incursions of foreign competition. But what in turn is their vision of the France of the future? Is it to be reduced to one part of a European superstate, vainly fighting off the challenges of Far Eastern economic competition, watching a diet of North American soaps, and fed on an ideological menu of lukewarm republicanism? French communism has many faults. It has remained silent before unpardonable sins. It has now seen one part of its vision vanish before its very eyes. It is easy, as so many former members and sympathizers now do from their semi-exile in the security and state of well-being of North American universities, to write it off as a terrible mistake. Yet it has served to represent and to praise those who have laboured and those who have sacrificed their lives for France. It has struggled for the causes of internationalism and peace. Can this combination of the tricolour and the red flag be so easily consigned to history?

Notes

1. See *L'Humanité* in the days following 20 August 1991.
2. Part of this opinion poll was published in *Le Monde*, 3 January 1991. Interestingly, the same poll showed that Solzhenitsyn received 0 per cent approval. As a whole this poll provides a fascinating insight into the attitudes of PCF activists.
3. For a general history of the PCF see Courtois and Lazar (1995). For the post-war period see Bell and Criddle (1994).
4. Such a description of capitalism is littered throughout communist literature, but can be found especially in the reports made to national congresses by party general secretaries.
5. Anyone doubting the PCF's commitment to the culinary delights of France should visit the annual Fête de L'Humanité, where, given a strong constitution, it is possible to sample the specialities of every region.

References

Adler, A., Cohen, F., Decaillot, M., Frioux, C. and Robel, L. (1979) *L'URSS et nous*. Paris: Editions Sociales.

Ainardi, S. (1992) 'Maastricht: c'est trop sérieux: la parole au peuple!'. *Cahiers du communisme* 5, 16–21.

Bell, D.S. and Criddle, B. (1994) *The French Communist Party in the Fifth Republic*. Oxford: Oxford University Press.

Bicocchi, F. (1989) 'La Révolution française vue en 1789'. *Cahiers du communisme* 4, 94–105.

Boutang, Y. (1992) *Louis Althusser*. Paris: Grasset.

Cahiers du communisme (1989) 'Comité central du PCF: la campagne du PCF pour les élections européennes'. 6, 90–8.

Cahiers du communisme (1992) 'Le Parti communiste s'adresse aux Français'. 7–8, 13–16.

Cahiers du communisme (1994) 'Le Manifeste'. 2–3, 188–226.

Chambaz, J. (1990) 'Une démarche moderne et positive'. *Cahiers du communisme* 2, 24–31.

Cohen, F. (1989) 'Le Perestroika a quatre ans'. *Cahiers du communisme* 5, 82–8.

Cohen, F. (1994) 'Faut-il abjurer Lénine 70 ans après sa mort?'. *Cahiers du communisme* 1, 108–14.

Courtois, S. and Lazar, M. (1995) *Histoire du Parti communiste français*. Paris: Presses Universitaires de France.

Desanti, D. (1975) *Les Staliniens*. Paris: Fayard.

Desjardins, R. (1988) *The Soviet Union through French Eyes, 1945–85*. London: Macmillan.

Fiszbin, H. (1984) *Appel à l'auto-subversion*. Paris: Robert Laffont.

Furet, F. (1995) *Le Passé d'une illusion: essai sur l'idée communiste au XXe siècle*. Paris: Robert Laffont/Calmann-Lévy.

Gayssot, J.-C. (1989) *Le Parti communiste français*. Paris: Editions Sociales.

Gremetz, M. (1991) 'Les Communistes français et les événements en URSS'. *Cahiers du communisme* 10, 22–35.

Herzog, P. (1991) *Tu imagines la politique*. Paris: Messidor.

Herzog, P., Kriegel, B., Roman, J. and Voynet, J. (1995) *Quelle Démocratie? Quelle Citoyenneté?* Paris: Editions de l'Atelier.

Hue, R. (1994) 'Rapport d'ouverture sur le projet de Manifeste'. *Cahiers du communisme* 2–3, 14–32.

Hue, R. (1995) *Communisme: la mutation*. Paris: Stock.

Hue, R. (1996) 'L'Esprit de Marx, plus que la lettre'. *Le Monde*, 12 April.

L'Humanité (1980) 'Huit Siècles en cinquante ans'. 22 January.

L'Humanité (1983) 'Marx vivant'. 16 March.

L'Humanité (1991a) 'L'Enseignement de la guerre du Golfe'. 13 January.

L'Humanité (1991b) 'Une déclaration du bureau politique'. 20 August.

L'Humanité (1993) 'Six Propositions pour la France'. 18 January.

L'Humanité (1994) 'Election présidentielle: les objectifs du Parti communiste français et la désignation de son candidat'. 7 November.

Juquin, P. (1985) *Autocritiques*. Paris: Grasset.

Kahane, J.-P. (1989) 'L'Appropriation collective de la connaissance: un objectif révolutionnaire'. *Cahiers du communisme* **7–8**, 91–9.

Kupferman, F. (1979) *Au pays des Soviets*. Paris: Gallimard.

Lajoinie, A. (1989) 'Pour le peuple souverain'. *Cahiers du communisme* **7–8**, 80–8.

Lajoinie, A. (1990) 'Le Parti de l'issue à la crise et du socialisme démocratique'. *Cahiers du communisme* **12**, 16–25.

Lajoinie, A. (1992) 'Après les élections gagner la bataille pour le référendum et le non à Maastricht'. *Cahiers du communisme* **5**, 5–12.

Lavau, G. (1981) *A quoi sert le Parti Communiste?* Paris: Fayard.

Lazar, M. (1990) 'Damné de la terre et homme de marbre: l'ouvrier dans l'imaginaire du PCF du milieu des années trente à la fin des années cinquante'. *Annales ESC* **45**, 1071–96.

Legendre, B. (1980) Le Stalinisme français: qui a dit quoi? (1944-1956). Paris: Seuil.

Leyrac, S. (1994) 'De l'URSS à la Russie'. *Cahiers du communisme* **1**, 100–7.

Marchais, G. (1976) 'Le Socialisme pour la France'. *Cahiers du communisme* **2–3**, 12–72.

Marchais, G. (1982) 'Rapport du Comité Central'. *Cahiers du communisme* **2–3**, 17–84.

Marchais, G. (1988) 'L'Avenir est au socialisme'. *L'Humanité*, 2 December.

Marchais, G. (1989a) 'L'Avenir appartient au socialisme pas au capitalisme'. *Cahiers du communisme* **10**, 7–14.

Marchais, G. (1989b) 'Pour un déploiement plus large et plus audacieux de notre politique'. *L'Humanité*, 13 October.

Marchais, G. (1989c) 'Le Parti communiste et la révolution française'. *Cahiers du communisme* **7–8**, 6–13.

Marchais, G. (1990a) *Démocratie*. Paris: Editions Sociales.

Marchais, G. (1990b) 'La Préparation du 27e congrès'. *Cahiers du communisme* **7–8**, 6–31.

Marchais, G. (1991a) 'Les Entretiens Gorbatchev-Marchais de septembre 1989'. *Cahiers du communisme* **10**, 50–66.

Marchais, G. (1991b) 'Rapport du Comité Central'. *Cahiers du communisme* **1–2**, 17–58.

Marchais, G. (1991c) 'La Raison d'être du PCF'. *L'Humanité*, 26 August.

Milhau, J. (1989) 'Le Sens et la portée de la déclaration universelle des droits de l'homme'. *Cahiers du communisme* **3**, 58–64.

Plissonier, G. (1991) 'Bataille de vérité'. *L'Humanité*, 7 September.

Plissonier, G. (1993) 'Identité communiste en France d'hier et d'aujourd'hui'. *Cahiers du communisme* **6**, 46–56.

SOFRES (1990) *Les Attitudes politiques des cadres du parti communiste interrogés au congrès de Saint-Ouen*. Paris: SOFRES.

Thomas, E. (1995) *Le Témoin compromis: mémoires*. Paris: Viviane Hamy.

Verdès-Leroux, J. (1983) *Au service du Parti: le parti communiste, les intellectuels et la culture (1944–56)*. Paris: Fayard.

Verdès-Leroux, J. (1987) *Le Réveil des somnambules*. Paris: Fayard.

Wurtz, F. (1992) 'Un nouveau projet européen'. *Cahiers du communisme* **6**, 5–11.

3

Gaullism and Liberalism

PETER FYSH

Introduction

Gaullist, liberal, right-wing, conservative, nationalist: for many years, a range of competing frames of reference in French right-wing political thought mirrored the right's fragmentation for the purposes of practical politics. Between the wars no less than six differently named right-wing parties sat in Parliament at one time or another. Only one kept the same name for the whole period. Something approaching the same situation occurred during the Fourth Republic, between 1946 and 1958. The reasons for this diversity of tradition – a sharp contrast with the British experience – are to be found in the French right's long hesitation in accepting as permanent the republican form of government and in the long-drawn-out war between church and state, as well as in the social conflicts arising from industrialization and economic modernization.

In the 1960s and 1970s, however, converging forces – crisis in the colonies, de Gaulle's prestige, the presidential regime inaugurated in 1962, changes in social structure – for a while compressed the conservative fragments into two major parties, the Gaullist Rassemblement pour la République (RPR) and the Giscardian Union pour la Démocratie Française (UDF), themselves condemned to apparently permanent collaboration. These parties or their ancestors shared power in 1962–81 and 1986–8, and have been in coalition again since 1993. At every parliamentary election except one (1978) they agreed on a common programme in order to avoid competing for the electorate's favour, stressing instead their common hostility to the left. They have generally adopted the same tactics even in European and local elections, when proportional representation eliminated the risk of letting in a left-wing opponent. As a result, the RPR and UDF have virtually identical electorates marked by classic conservative characteristics; their voters are more likely to be older and wealthier than voters for left-wing parties, and more likely to be managers, professionals and/or self-employed than workers. In short, conservatism has existed in France for over twenty years in all but name. Some prominent leaders on both sides have frankly wished that it could exist in name as well, following the lead of Edouard Balladur, who declared in March 1988 that, since there was now no longer any major ideological difference between the two parties, they ought to fuse into a single *grand parti conservateur*, the better to agree on a single candidate for presidential elections, the one forum where rivalry has repeatedly damaged their chances of success (*Le Monde*, 17 March 1988).

Should such a fusion ever take place, it would be all the more remarkable in that the two parties involved were founded on two quite distinct, often contradictory ideologies, neither of which bears much relation to what would normally be recognized as a conservative philosophy. One of these, Gaullism, is highly original, even idiosyncratic, distilled from the confrontation of one individual with the tumultuous history of the twentieth century. The other, which we may call Giscardism, was deliberately constructed in the 1970s to meet a specific and, as it turned out, transitory political conjuncture, and is clearly marked both by the task of refuting what it took to be a collectivist counter-ideology and by what can now be seen as excessive optimism engendered by the long post-war boom.

After a comparison of the core ideas of Gaullism and Giscardism, this chapter shows how, at the end of the 1970s and the beginning of the 1980s, the initiative in ideological production passed from parties to groups of intellectuals whose output subjected both Gaullists and Giscardians to the challenge of a reinvigorated and self-conscious liberalism. A third part of the chapter shows how liberalism in turn began to lose its appeal at the end of the 1980s, leaving room for a reassertion both of the importance of national sovereignty in a new international context and of the paternalistic 'social' component of Gaullism. The chapter concludes with some thoughts on the sources of ideology and the fragility of a French conservatism facing the challenge of the extreme right.

Two Systems of Thought

Although more practical politicians than political philosophers, both Charles de Gaulle and Valéry Giscard d'Estaing produced writings which can be treated as comprehensive belief systems.[1] De Gaulle summarized his life and writings as 'a system of thought, resolution and action ... a project of national renovation', of which the *raison d'être* was 'the service of France' (Charlot, 1992, p. 655). The Gaullism of de Gaulle was above all a variety of nationalism; the general's other ideas all involved projects which contributed to his central concern of guaranteeing national survival and the spread of French influence. These ideas – on the relations between French people ('participation' in place of class struggle), on the relations between French people and the state (parties and interest groups condemned as destructive of national unity), and especially on the system of government (a powerful head of state within a parliamentary system) – were developed by de Gaulle in greater or lesser detail in specific political contexts. Because for much of his life de Gaulle was effectively in opposition, nationalism and nationalist symbols became key mobilizing factors in the construction of Gaullism as a political movement.

Giscard, who came to office when the problem of the organization of power seemed to have been solved by the institutions of the Fifth Republic which de Gaulle had set up, is more concerned with the problems of society. While de Gaulle regally declined to define himself with reference to existing ideologies, Giscard is clearly in the liberal tradition, 'a determined liberal' (2F, p. 99), who sets himself the task of fusing two streams of (liberal and social) thought into a 'socially aware liberalism' or a 'liberal social conscience' (2F, p. 150). The cornerstone of his system is not France, but the full development of the individual (DF, pp. 15, 83–4). The two books in which his 'system' is mainly contained, *Démocratie française* (DF: 1978, first published in 1976) and *2 Français sur 3* (2F: 1985, first published in 1984), read more like sociological essays than political projects.

Continuity, Change and Agency

One of the great strengths of British Conservatism has been the exemplary continuity of the 'British' form of government, a constitutional monarchy modified only incrementally since 1688 and inspiring generations of Conservatives to defend, with Burke, the art of learning from the wisdom of ancestors, conserving by instinct what exists, resorting to change only after lengthy experience proves its necessity. France, by contrast, has known only upheaval – three monarchies, two empires, five republics and the odd dictatorship since 1789. In these circumstances, a political philosophy based on 'conserving' had no chance of taking root. To admit the desire to 'conserve' anything of what went before was to be branded a restorationist and banished to the extreme-right fringe of political life.

Both Gaullism and Giscardism, indeed, while unstinting in praise of past French achievements, are self-conscious forces of change. In his pre-war writings de Gaulle drew attention to the technical progress which required the organization of a professional army based on mobile armoured divisions. More than 30 years later, in a passage more reminiscent of Marx than of Burke, he explained how 'modern machine civilization' reduced citizens to powerlessness and a sense of alienation leading to disorders such as those that occurred in May '68 (Charlot, 1970, pp. 138–40). But he pooh-poohed the efforts of the students, contrasting their 'exhibitionism' with his own 'revolutionary' credentials, demonstrated:

> in starting the Resistance; in kicking out the Vichy regime; in giving the right to vote to women and to the Africans; when creating completely new social conditions at the Liberation by setting up works councils, by nationalizing, by setting up the social security system.
>
> (Charlot, 1970, p. 140)

Giscard has an equally strong sense of a 'tempest' of change, wrought by unprecedented economic growth, mass education and the 'exploding' media on existing structures such as family, school, university, church and social and moral habits (DF, p. 39). The job of the statesman, he believes, is not to repress or contain change, but to 'orient and guide' (2F, p. 51) what he expects to be an evolutionary process, 'the progressive adaptation of French society to future circumstances' (2F, p. 105). More modestly than de Gaulle, Giscard describes himself as a reforming traditionalist:

> Traditionalist because I think our history and our civilization have accumulated and moulded values which form the social and cultural 'foundation' of France; reforming, because I know that life is a renewal, a continual biological growth which it is our responsibility to accompany, and when obstacles get in the way, to facilitate and guide.
>
> (2F, p. 99)

We normally think of conservatism as a philosophy which looks to elites with strong roots in the existing society – monarchy, aristocracy, the church – to provide the political forces likely to carry the conservative project to fruition. By adopting a positive attitude to change, both de Gaulle and Giscard turned their backs on existing hierarchies. For de Gaulle their bankruptcy was confirmed by the isolation in which he found himself in 1940, when he waited in vain for 'imperial office-holders, a well-known politician, a famous general, a revered academician' to join him in rebellion in London (Charlot, 1970, p. 16). Ever afterwards he referred contemptuously to elites as, at best, 'coalitions of interests and privileges', at worst 'the so-called ruling class, that is to say the class comfortably provided with fame, fortune and jobs' (Touchard, 1978, p. 56). But it was in a text of 1927 that he had first sketched the portrait of the 'man of character', the model for a style of political leadership which he would proceed to act out in person.

> Everyday routine works to his disadvantage with his superiors . . . he is not tempted by the desire to please. The fact that he draws from himself, and not in the least from an order his decision and firmness, often holds him back from passive obedience . . . But when serious events occur, when danger threatens, when the safety of all suddenly demands initiative, daring, solidity . . . His advice is sought, his talent praised, his qualities relied on.
>
> (Charlot, 1970, pp. 10–11)

> In short, nothing can be achieved without the fortuitous combination of a man and a moment: the consent which allows laws to bear fruit often only appears, I know, in response to the echo of thunder . . . In politics as in strategy, in business as in love, you have to have the gift. You also need the opportunity.
>
> (Charlot, 1992, p. 665)

If de Gaulle rejected traditional elites because they had been tried and found wanting, Giscard relies on a sort of optimistic determinism which would not be out of place in the mouths of the communists who were his habitual targets:

> Is it utopian to expect the realization of a more united society? Not at all. The progressive elimination of class differences is one of the fundamental results of the historical evolution of Western-type societies.
>
> (DF, p. 67)

There is even a version of the vanguard class:

> The evolution under way is causing the expansion of an immense central group with ill-defined boundaries which, thanks to its exceptionally rapid numerical growth, its links with each of the other social groups, the ease

of access which its open character makes possible, and the modern values which it bears, is set to take over gradually and peacefully the whole of the rest of French society.

(DF, p. 68)

In 1976 Giscard claimed that the 'sociological centre' of the nation already accounted for more than half the population. In an argument heavily marked by his desire to refute contemporary theories of class struggle constructed in support of the Union of the Left then in vogue, he denied that this new middle class could be enrolled on one side or the other by communists or reactionaries. Instead it could itself gradually transform the whole of French society 'because the values it carries are already largely shared by the great majority of our society' (DF, pp. 69–70). If he avoids an excessive determinism by suggesting that 'the conscious action of men and the play of social forces' must work together (DF, p. 70), it is clear that the 'conscious action' Giscard is thinking of is not the action of a political movement but the reform programme of enlightened government officials, whose efforts in favour of the poor, the handicapped, 'the excluded' in general, are aimed at their incorporation into the 'immense central group' (DF, pp. 70–82). This failure to link himself with traditional elites – or with any other political constituency – has enabled Giscard's opponents to label him pejoratively and damagingly as a technocrat, an advocate of government by experts. When his goal of unification by social justice is threatened by 'problems' such as economic crisis, competition for resources, East–West tension, Giscard's reaction is to explain and justify his decisions by appealing to the 'intelligence' of the voters. (2F, pp. 85–6). As one might expect, 'intelligence' and 'problem solving' have had a much weaker impact as mobilizing slogans than the adulation of France declaimed by de Gaulle and his successors. As a result 'Giscardism' has failed to establish itself as a tradition of doctrine and action which could compare with Gaullism in solidity and emotional appeal.

Democracy and Representation

Both Gaullism and Giscardism accept the republican form of government and the principle of popular sovereignty, although differing radically on the form in which popular sovereignty can best be expressed. De Gaulle, mindful of 'our old Gallic tendency to divisions and quarrels', developed a deep antipathy to what he regarded as the futility of parliamentarism and the 'poisons and delights' of party rivalry, 'which too often obscures vital national interests'. At Bayeux in 1946 he described a set of institutions which 'compensate in themselves the effects of our perpetual political effervescence', a parliamentary system in which strong executive powers would be concentrated in a non-party head of state able to take unpopular decisions in crisis situations (MG3, pp. 526–8; ME1, pp. 9–15). Twelve years later the Algerian war and a new constitutional crisis enabled him to realize this vision in the institutions of the Fifth Republic.

The conception of democracy which animated this republic depended not on freedom of debate, on representation, or on the rights of the opposition, but rather on direct collaboration between the president and the people, a sort of personal rule legitimized by recourse to public opinion, as often as possible via referendum, 'the clearest, the most honest, the most democratic system possible', in de Gaulle's view (Touchard, 1978, p. 260). Endorsement of de Gaulle the leader was as important as endorsement of the issue of policy concerned; he frequently threatened to retire if a vote was negative, or even if the majority was 'weak, mediocre, unreliable' (Touchard, 1978, p. 260). The formal practice of democracy via the referendum was supplemented for Gaullists by informal methods: the television address and the provincial tour and walkabout among the crowds, from which the leader tried to gauge the 'reflection of the people's soul' (Touchard, 1978, p. 261). This was a style used to great effect by a later Gaullist leader, Jacques Chirac.

Such a personalized vision of democracy has little use for political parties, which de Gaulle execrated as defenders of 'particularist tendencies and the interests of one category or another' (Touchard, 1978, p. 256). When he set one up, in 1947, it was not called a party, but a 'gathering', the Rassemblement du Peuple Français, which all French people were invited to join, even if they were already members of other parties. Contesting elections but refusing to take part in government, the RPF's role was to exert such pressure on the politicians of the Fourth Republic that they would eventually throw in the towel and ask de Gaulle to take over. When this did not happen and de Gaulle was unable to prevent his followers joining in the political game, the RPF was wound up and he retired from public life (Charlot, 1983). Later, when he took charge of the Fifth Republic, he accepted the existence of a new Gaullist party, now called the UNR (Union pour la Nouvelle République), since there had to be a Parliament and a parliamentary majority, but he held no office in it and never referred to it by name in public (Touchard, 1978, p. 132; ME1, p. 12). The UNR had no democratic structures and no system for developing policy; its members willingly regarded themselves as the president's *godillots* (foot-sloggers), ready to carry out any order without question.

In de Gaulle's time the new presidential system and the authoritarian style of the 'man of character' combined to produce a species of enlightened despotism, in which the president's supporters claimed, against all the evidence, that the constitution granted him alone the right to make policy in the 'reserved domain' of defence and foreign affairs. De Gaulle himself even once claimed that the presidency was the source of all democratic legitimacy. Free elections were never interfered with, but television broadcasting was tightly controlled by the state in the interest of the ruling party, and the written press was subject to occasional random seizure and confiscation.

Giscard, who was de Gaulle's finance minister during much of this time, shares some of his views on the changeable and argumentative nature of the French people, and has welcomed the Fifth Republic as 'a political system adapted to the running of a modern state' (DF, pp. 40–1), which aimed to 'put an end to detestable former habits and to the permanent temptations arising from our national character' (PV2, p. 91). Nevertheless the central argument of *Démocratie française* is a complete refutation of the Gaullist style of government, which Giscard eventually condemned as the 'solitary exercise of power', going on to challenge and defeat the Gaullist candidate in the 1974 presidential election. If key words in the Gaullist lexicon are 'leader', 'people', 'honour', 'unity' and 'France' (Touchard, 1978, pp. 53–8), in Giscard's they are 'pluralism', 'participation', 'communication', 'autonomy', 'responsibility' and 'liberty' (DF, pp. 14–16, 47, 57, 83, 95–6, 109–10). He argues that the enormous economic, social and cultural changes of the post-war years have produced citizens who are better off than ever before, so with more time to devote to civic responsibilities, and better educated, so more equipped to carry them out: 'Man has the political and social capacity to give an opinion, frequently and in concrete terms, on the organization of the society in which he wants to live' (DF, p. 60).

Furthermore, the increasing role of press and television is bringing about what Giscard calls the 'society of communication', giving citizens a greater cultural awareness which will eventually make them unwilling to put up with the role of mere ratifiers of the leader's decisions. Whereas de Gaulle execrated organizations seeking to mediate between citizens and the state, Giscard's notions of pluralism and participation justify precisely the encouragement and empowerment of such organizations, which he wants to see getting involved in local government and in dialogue with the central administration (DF, pp. 96–113). His term of office (1974–81) did see some measures of political emancipation, such as votes at 18, the granting of administrative autonomy to Paris, and the right of deputies and senators to refer disputed legislation to the constitutional court. His tentative breakup of the state monopoly of television was the first step in what was to become an accelerating process of reform. He also called in rather vague terms for 'bold decentralization' of power from the centre to local government – but that reform had to wait for the socialist government which followed him in power.

Later, in the 1980s, when the atmosphere of crisis attending the inauguration of the Fifth Republic was becoming a distant memory, and when he had had time to reflect on his own experience in office, Giscard, among many others, developed doubts about the accumulation of so much power in the president's hands, and suggested a number of ways in which it could be shared with the prime minister and parliament (2F, pp. 154–64, 169–80). On the other hand – again in line with a swelling current of liberal theorizing – he came round to the idea of expanding the use, scope and popular control of the referendum, at one time viewed with suspicion as a weapon in the Gaullist panoply of direct democracy (2F, pp. 181–5).

Economy, Society and the State

Both de Gaulle and Giscard are interested by the problem of social inequality. De Gaulle proposed to deal with it by ensuring that capital and labour shared equally in the risks, profits and responsibilities of economic activity, an arrangement which he called 'association' or 'participation', while Giscard's 'social liberalism' looks to the more familiar remedies of taxation and transfer payments. For de Gaulle, the problem was one of class status and class privilege; for Giscard, the question is the distribution of goods. De Gaulle's reflection stemmed from his reaction to the 'mechanical' mass society which he encountered between the wars, when he was in his 30s, and which he could contrast with the more individualistic and apparently more humane society of pre-1914. Giscard grapples with a problem arising from one of the earliest axioms of liberalism: is the pursuit of private self-interest on its own enough to lead to the greater good of all?

The general's wartime speeches and messages necessarily dealt with the pooling of efforts by all classes in the struggle for national survival, but they also promised future radical action against a social and moral order which had failed the people, revealing a concern for the 'liberty', 'dignity' and 'security' of the 'salariat' (Charlot, 1992, p. 663). Later, in the speeches of 1947–53, the concepts of association and participation were regularly used to contrast with and condemn the waste of human talent arising from ownership by the few: 'Away with this absurd system in which the lowest possible wage buys the lowest possible effort, which produces the lowest possible collective result' (Charlot, 1992, p. 666). More than once de Gaulle evoked a vision of a society which was neither capitalist nor socialist, but somehow a 'third way' between the two:

> The human solution, the French, the practical solution is neither in the degradation of some (the salariat), nor in the servitude of all (under communism). It is in the dignified and fruitful association of those who would place in common, within the same enterprise, their work, their technical skills, their wealth, as the case may be, and who would then partake equally, openly and honestly as share-holders, the profits and the risks.

> (Charlot, 1992, p. 663)

In practice, attempts to convert de Gaulle's insight into a credible party policy and thence into law got bogged down in discussions about what participation actually meant, how it could be introduced and whether it should be voluntary or compulsory. 'Left' Gaullists would have liked not only to oblige employers to share their profits with their workers but also to establish a kind of trust fund which would eventually convert them all into shareholders; the best they could manage by the mid-sixties was to impose a measure of compulsory profit sharing on a small number of big firms. Other Gaullists condemned schemes which lost the support of the employers without winning that of the workers and, showing scant understanding of the kernel of de Gaulle's idea, argued in classic conservative fashion that the best way to improve the lot of the workers was to increase production (Charlot, 1983, p. 189). All were agreed, however, in rejecting anything which would infringe on the manager's right to manage; in de Gaulle's lapidary phrase, 'many people discuss; only one person acts' (Pickles, 1973, p. 400). De Gaulle himself produced his most radical and far-reaching definition of participation – too late – in response to the student demonstrations and the general strike of May–June 1968, promising that in the future, 'in all our activities', in universities as well as factories, 'everyone must be associated directly with the working, the results and the contribution to society of the concern in which he is involved. In a word, participation must become the rule and the inspiration of a new France' (Pickles, 1973, p. 400). It was doubtless no accident that de Gaulle veered furthest to the left only when political circumstances most required it; this and the scepticism of the employers and of succeeding Gaullist prime ministers Debré and Pompidou must explain why so little was done to put participation into practice. Other elements of the general's 'social' policy – the social security system, works councils, the Economic and Social Council, etc. – were genuine enough, but probably best seen as just another brick in the theoretical edifice which was de Gaulle's nationalism: social harmony for a stronger France.

For Valéry Giscard d'Estaing, the concept of class is defined by the reproduction of handicaps and privileges from one generation to the next (DF, p. 66); class exploitation is never mentioned; and unearned economic advantage, far from being structural in origin, arises from individual astuteness or malevolence, after the manner of the highwayman who in days gone by exacted his tribute from travellers at a strategic bridge or crossroads (DF, p. 45). There are also differences inherited from the past, such as sex discrimination and regional imbalance, and differences provoked by economic growth, such as unemployment or the marginalization of the old (DF, p. 45), which it is the government's task to reduce. On the other hand, Giscard approves of differences 'rewarding activity and talent' up to a point which he declines to specify, accepting any level which does not threaten social harmony. He asserts that 'there exists in a given society a "maximum social differentiation" ... varying over time beyond which the social fabric comes apart' (DF, p. 66). This is quite a different starting point from de Gaulle's ambition to 'change the condition of man within modern civilization', even if the result was arguably pretty much the same.

In choosing between rival 'systems' in the context of the Cold War, both de Gaulle and Giscard opted for free enterprise in preference to state control of the economy, which they think implies automatically the confiscation of political freedom. For de Gaulle, however, there was more involved than the most 'efficient' production of goods:

> although freedom remains an essential lever of economic activity, the latter is nonetheless collective, directly determines the fate of the nation and at all times affects social relations. That implies an impulsion, harmonization, rules which can only come from the state; in other words, *dirigisme*.
>
> (ME1, p. 163)

In practice this meant, as de Gaulle explained in his memoirs, 'first of all' an economic plan, which was to set objectives for private industry

and require the state to use taxation, credit and tariff policy to manipulate demand, to provide appropriate transport and housing infrastructure, develop the regions, organize energy production, stimulate
research and anticipate manpower needs (ME1, p. 164). This looks like
a programme which could be labelled social democratic or Keynesian.
But *dirigisme*, expounded in detail by Michel Debré, one of its chief
protagonists (Debré, 1972), did not make the redistribution of wealth
into a principle and went beyond the mere balancing of supply and
demand: the 'fate of the nation' required that medium-sized industrial
concerns be merged into units of a size able to take on British, German
or American giants in the world market; the government ought also to
decide which types of industry were strategically important, to be
expanded or developed and kept in French hands only (Debré, 1972;
Rassemblement pour la République, 1980). True to these ideas, in his
first spell of power in the 1940s de Gaulle nationalized credit and
utilities; in the 1960s, the Gaullists deliberately expanded manufacturing industry, brought about a number of important private sector
mergers, and excluded foreign capital from the computer, aerospace
and defence sectors.

While de Gaulle's conception of the relationship between state and
economy was shaped by the overriding aim of the greatness of France,
Giscard's is based on a compromise between individual and collective
needs and wishes. The overall tenor of his approach is liberal; French
society is based on 'individual growth and development' and its objective is to 'permit the development of every personality, let everyone
live his or her life' (DF, p. 83). This 'responds to the deep aspirations of
the French people and to what is most characteristic of our national
culture' (DF, p. 84). Conversely, Giscard is in principle against increasing the power or extent of the state administration, unjustified nationalizations, 'authoritarian' planning, anything which tends to suppress
initiative and competition (DF, p. 16). He approves in principle the
claim of 'classical liberalism' that the pursuit of individual self-interest
guarantees the good of all (DF, p. 57), but believes the unbridled
pursuit of economic advantage may require the state to intervene
against monopoly or restrictive practices (DF, p. 57), to regulate health
and safety matters, and to protect 'counter-powers' such as trade unions
and consumer organizations (DF, pp. 117–18). Furthermore, human
beings are motivated by qualities other than just self-interest. Of these,
the attachment to family life might require the state to organize a form
of family policy (DF, p. 93), while the defence of political pluralism
justifies subsidizing the press (DF, p. 113). But in the mid-seventies

Giscard went much further than all of this in a passage which seemed to negate the liberal inspiration of his project:

> Of course we cannot imagine confining the state in the narrowly defined sovereign functions of days gone by: defence, justice, money. All the great social questions – education, health, environment, industrial and agricultural development – require in one form or another a degree of intervention or participation by the state.
>
> (DF, p. 164)

This formulation brings Giscard much closer to de Gaulle on this question than he at first appears. He goes on to suggest that all state intervention should be in principle 'non-bureaucratic', 'supplementary', 'temporary' and 'indirect'.

In power, Giscard was not able to ensure that this was always the case. Not only did he have to deal with a policy community which was used to routine Gaullist interventions on interest rates and investment decisions, but his term of office also coincided with growing industrial failures and unemployment. To the preferential treatment of the 'national champions' inherited from de Gaulle and Pompidou was now added emergency aid to the 'lame ducks' left high and dry by the 1973 oil shock. The dirigiste de Gaulle and the liberal Giscard adopted much the same interventionist recipes in practice.

Republic, Nation, France and the World

The UK is accustomed to the association of nationalism with conservatism and the defence of empire, while the rights of small countries and internationalism are associated with liberals and the left. In France two nationalisms and two theories of the nation have traditionally confronted each other ever since the great revolution of 1789. For the revolutionaries, and the left-wing tradition which they inspired, any individual, of no matter what origin or race, could become a French citizen by accepting the ideals contained in the Declaration of Human Rights, making the nation the result of personal choice, a social pact between reasoning individuals. For the right, the nation is an 'ethnic' entity, predating the individuals who compose it, the product of a long common history and shared memories, something subconscious and instinctive. Defending this tradition, a whole section of the right – Catholic, nationalist, antisemitic – led by Charles Maurras and the Action Française, condemned democracy and the republic as 'anti-France', and was in turn regarded as counter-revolutionary right down to 1940.

De Gaulle's 'idea of France' was developed while growing up in a traditionalist, Catholic, fairly poor family in the 1890s and 1900s. All his life was marked by his idea of a France 'from the depths of time' (ME1, p. 9), which had been promised an 'eminent and exceptional destiny', and which was not really itself unless it was in the front rank (MG1, p. 5). Moved by stories of past French misfortunes, deeply saddened by contemporary 'social conflicts, religious discords ... national divisions' (MG1, p. 6), early on he formed the conviction, tirelessly repeated thereafter, that only unity and the gathering together of all French people could guarantee national greatness (Touchard, 1978, pp. 28, 42, 55, 88, 302). In the dire circumstances of 1940 the French people had once more to make a choice: Pétain and Germany or de Gaulle and France. While Pétain and the Action Française blamed the sin of republicanism for France's degeneration and defeat, de Gaulle insisted that there was only one French history; using national symbols taken from different periods of that history (Joan of Arc, Danton and Clemenceau are his three most cited heroes), he appealed to all French people, whatever their ideology, faith or social situation, to join him in rebellion. De Gaulle's originality was therefore to construct a doctrine transcending the left–right cleavage, a nationalism, as Charlot puts it, 'purged of revolutionary or counter-revolutionary connotations', based on both origins and personal commitment, a nationalism of both instinct and choice, feeling and reason, which would ultimately become a nationalism of both tradition and modernity. It was 'in essence and by necessity all-embracing [*rassembleur*]' (Charlot, 1992, p. 659).

For de Gaulle, furthermore, the unity of the French nation was more important than the form of the regime; he admired the *ancien régime* of the seventeenth century because its achievement of French unity resulted in 'brilliant military success' (Touchard, 1978, p. 42); even when inaugurating his own Fifth Republic he remarked that the *ancien régime* had lasted as long as it managed to maintain unity, indicating that republics should be judged by the same criterion. During the war he adopted the theme of the republic for the first time only in 1942, 'a theme to which de Gaulle is not hostile, but which is not immediately natural to him, and which he adopts because circumstances require it' (Touchard, 1978, p. 63).

The foreign policy de Gaulle devised from his nationalist doctrine is his best-known legacy. As early as 1951 he made the principled objection to the organization of NATO which later inspired his withdrawal of French forces from the command structure: 'We can never agree to stop being ourselves, to drown our security, our policy, our independence, in organisms called "collective" but in fact run by other people' (Touchard, 1978, p. 112).

Europe, for de Gaulle, was a collection of sovereign states situated within certain geographic boundaries; 'Europe from the Atlantic to the Urals', a phrase which he used for the first time in 1950 and many times thereafter, included Russia but excluded the island nation, the UK, and forcibly also the USA (Touchard, 1978, p. 211). In the 1940s he began to argue for a kind of collective organization of Europe, a 'Europe of States', which he referred to interchangeably as a federation or a confederation, but which in today's language we would say was a vision of an intergovernmental union from which any hint of supranational authority was rigorously excluded (Touchard, 1978, pp. 112–13). In the 1950s this led him to campaign passionately against the idea of integrated defence enshrined in Monnet's proposed European Defence Community, this 'stateless organism in the hands of a top American general', for 'the basis of the defence of the people is the people . . . War is waged with the souls and the blood of men. Neither the defence of Europe nor the defence of the Atlantic can be built on anything but realities, which means national realities' (Touchard, 1978, p. 115). In the 1960s, he attempted, via the 'Fouchet Plan', to liquidate the elements of supranationalism built into the nascent Europe of the Six, a grouping of which 'France has the honour and duty of being the centre and the leader' (Touchard, 1978, p. 113). When this failed he blocked the Community's functioning for several months in protest at the supranational claims of the Commission, that 'portentous, stateless, technocratic irresponsible assembly' (Touchard, 1978, p. 218).

De Gaulle's nationalism was constant but not impervious to context. By 1950, Adenauer's efforts to create a democratic Germany linked to the West persuaded de Gaulle to abandon his campaign for permanent dismemberment of the former Reich and to pursue instead Franco-German partnership, formalized by treaty in 1963. The road to decolonization was a painful retreat from cherished convictions in the face of force of circumstance. But with the Algerian war barely over, Gaullism astonishingly began to enjoy a new lease of life as the general toured the world with his message that all medium-sized and small nations were in the same position in relation to the 'double hegemony' of the two superpowers. In Latin America, Cambodia, Quebec and Poland, he denounced both 'the Soviet obedience and American hegemony'; he recognized Red China, declared that the American onslaught on Vietnam had turned that war into one of 'national resistance', and told Ceauşescu in Romania that 'it is nations, each one with its own body and

soul, which ultimately constitute the basic building-blocks, the necessary inspiration of universal life ... Our two peoples are setting the
example' (Touchard, 1978, p. 210). At the most dramatic moments of
superpower confrontation, however, de Gaulle could not maintain this
balancing act. Events like the construction of the Berlin wall (1961) or
the Cuban missile crisis (1962) led him to speak of 'the totalitarian
yoke', 'the Soviet empire', and their opposition to 'the free world' with
which he was in total solidarity (Touchard, 1978, pp. 198–211).

Nationalism plays a very limited role in Giscard's doctrine; although he
lists among his objectives 'confirming and assuring the place and role of
France in the world' (DF, p. 176) the chapter of *Démocratie française*
devoted to this subject is not bound to the rest of the book by any
particular logic. He can turn out phrases on France, the 'homeland of
universal ideas ... a people who have spread our language and our culture
around the world', concluding that 'democratic France will not turn in on
herself' (DF, p. 181), and admits to breaking down in tears in response to
feats of French arms (PV1, p. 257). During his term of office he was careful
to maintain French influence in Africa, frequently by military means. He
justifies these interventions neither in terms of France's 'universal ideas'
nor by reference to the rights of the small nations involved, but purely and
simply by the need to keep them within the 'Western' sphere of influence
(PV1, p. 226). The inspiration of his foreign policy has therefore justly
been described as more Atlanticist than nationalist.

The biggest contrast between Giscard and de Gaulle concerns their
attitudes to Europe. In the 1970s Giscard considered it a 'necessity' for
the nations of *Western* Europe (my emphasis), 'similar in their way of
life, civilization and political institutions', to unite amongst themselves,
a necessity deduced from the existence of superpowers and from the
emergence elsewhere of other groupings of states such as OPEC, the
non-aligned countries, etc. (DF, p. 178). Faithful to 'European' convictions since the early 1970s (PV2, p. 56), Giscard has steadfastly favoured
economic and monetary union and strengthening the supranational
character of Community institutions and decision making (DF, p. 179).
When in power, he worked to set up the first version of the European
Monetary System (EMS), helped institutionalize regular meetings of
the heads of government, and gave French approval for the first direct
elections to the European Parliament. His memoirs are littered with
references to his close collaboration with West German chancellor
Helmut Schmidt.

In the 1980s Giscard produced a more particular argument in
support of his Europeanism: the task of reversing the 'historic deca-

dence' of Europe. This was a decline relative to the rest of the world measured in terms of power and population, but also a moral decadence, illustrated by citizens' overriding concern with individual material needs at the expense of the fate of the community, by the tendency to avoid risk and enterprise, and by indifference to the Soviet threat. One concrete deduction from this is the need for an integrated 'European defence personality'; less consecutively, but perhaps in order to make possible defence integration, Giscard wants to break down barriers which prevent the emergence of a European consciousness, by steps such as the direct election of the president of the European Council by all the citizens of the Community (2F, pp. 107–40). In 1992, a decade after losing power and much of his influence in France, Giscard mounted the hustings once more to play a major role, along with his UDF colleagues, in securing French ratification of the Maastricht treaty on European Union.

Gaullism and Giscardism: Cross-over and Convergence

However distinct as systems of ideas, the translation of Gaullism and Giscardism into French political culture by followers of each tradition who were also major political actors in their own right inevitably blurred the boundary between them. During the 1970s the Gaullist heritage was given quite different emphases by some of the general's former collaborators. The Cassandra-like figure of Michel Debré (prime minister 1959–62) remained not only the gloomiest predictor of French demise in the 'international economic war', but also the stubbornest and most orthodox exponent of the Jacobin Gaullism of the 1960s, defending the state's mission to 'guide' the economy and resisting the surrender of sovereignty to Europe (Debré, 1972, 1982). In contrast, Jacques Chaban Delmas (mayor of Bordeaux since 1947 and prime minister 1969–72) anticipated Giscard's ideas about the open, participating society. His investiture speech of 1969 evoked a 'new' society which would be 'prosperous, young, generous and liberated', and promised both to reform state control of broadcasting and to devolve 'real autonomy' to local government, the universities and the nationalized industries (Bunel and Meunier, 1972, pp. 258–62).

Georges Pompidou, perhaps regretting that he had chosen Chaban as his prime minister, found all this dangerously left-wing; like Thatcher after him, he might have maintained: 'There is no such thing as society. There are only individuals and France' (Knapp, 1994, p. 372). He believed fervently that the strong political executive was de Gaulle's most important legacy to France (Peyrefitte, 1976, p. 199). Like Debré, he harnessed the state to drive forward rapid industrialization, but his philosophy, dubbed Pompidolisme, gave more attention than his predecessors did to the need for firms to make a profit: 'It is only upon these profits that we can develop a social policy ... The State must therefore diminish its hold over the economy instead of perpetually seeking to direct and control it' (Knapp, 1994, p. 425). On this point Pompidou occupied the same ground as Chaban, whose 'New Society' programme included an attack on 'tentacular and inefficient' state intervention too often directing subsidies in support of unprofitable activities (Bunel and Meunier, 1972, p. 254). Together they encouraged business and unions to develop a corporatist style of problem solving instead of waiting for state regulation.

An even more striking example of the intertwining of Gaullism and Giscardism is offered by the career of Alain Peyrefitte, seven times minister under de Gaulle and Pompidou, a prolific author, and political editor of the conservative daily *Le Figaro* since the early 1980s. Despite his Gaullist credentials, Peyrefitte's most celebrated book, *Le Mal français* (1976), identifies the cardinal vice of French society, arising from its Catholic culture, as dictatorial tendencies at the top and the centre, frequently mirrored by cravenness and lack of imagination at the base and the periphery. His attack on the arrogance and complacency of Paris-based civil servants, encountered via his work as mayor and constituency MP, and his proposal to devolve as many decisions as possible to the level of the *département*, are typical Giscardian themes (Peyrefitte, 1976, pp. 233–65, 476–7). Indeed if Giscard is said to have admitted his intellectual debt to Peyrefitte, Peyrefitte was not alone in recognizing Giscard as the inheritor of some aspects of the Gaullist tradition. In 1979, when official relations between the RPR and UDF were at an all-time low, with RPR leader Jacques Chirac making daily attacks on Giscard, Peyrefitte led a group of serving Gaullist ministers in public defence of the sitting president, arguing that his protection of the institutions of the Fifth Republic amounted to a satisfactory Gaullist credential (Fysh, 1990, p. 123). It was perhaps natural that different Gaullists chose their own favourites among the general's compendious stock of attitudes and insights. More bewilderingly for non-Gaullists, the party leader since 1976, Jacques Chirac, has varied his own interpretations over time. Reforming Giscardian prime minister in 1974, he was arch-defender of *dirigiste* and nationalist orthodoxy in 1979/80, only to become a kind of Thatcherite liberal in 1981, before swinging round again in the 1990s to a rediscovery of Gaullism's role as guardian of social cohesion (Chirac, 1978, 1994; Desjardins, 1983; Giesbert, 1987).

Giscard's followers are just as ideologically disparate as the Gaullists. Jean-Pierre Soisson, founding secretary-general of the Parti Républicain (PR) in 1977, made some attempt to repeat the general line of argument of *Démocratie française* in his own words, without hiding his sympathy with other currents such as radicalism and Gaullism (Soisson, 1978, 1990). But the literature of other Giscardian heavyweights reveals a range of attitudes mixing Gaullist and authoritarian reflexes (Poniatowski, 1978; Deniau, 1994) and a sort of vacuous moralism (Léotard, 1987). Furthermore, the UDF which Giscard founded in 1978 was a federation, not a unitary party. While the PR might be expected to promote his ideas to some extent, this was not the case for the other major component of the federation, the Centre des Démocrates Sociaux (CDS), the source of whose inspiration was quite distinct. An extensive survey of younger members of the RPR, PR and CDS showed that they too shared a range of attitudes to concepts and values such as nation, state, family, religion, unions, strikes, social security, crime, punishment, etc., which crossed over party boundaries (Frémontier, 1984). Likewise, when the Front National (FN) made its breakthrough in French politics after 1983, a few prominent members of both the RPR and UDF denounced the FN's racist policies and refused any political collaboration with it, but both parties also contained spokesmen who either advocated or practised collaboration with Le Pen and his henchmen.

The Liberal Challenge

If the personal interpretations of different members of the Gaullist and Giscardian camps contributed to blurring the boundary between the two systems in practice, a quite different type of convergence became apparent in the first half of the 1980s. The two wings of conservatism seemed to merge into a reinvigorated liberalism, stressing the importance of freedom of enterprise in wealth creation and the restriction of state activity to certain 'essential' functions. The impetus for this reorientation came from two rapidly succeeding events: Ronald Reagan's election to the US presidency in 1980, on a programme which blended free-market ideology with religious fundamentalism; and the victory of the socialist–communist coalition in France the following year. But the form in which Gaullists and Giscardians recast their ideas owed a great deal to the activities of two distinct and self-conscious intellectual 'movements' which had appeared in the 1970s: the Nouvelle Droite, to which we turn in a moment, and a group of academics calling themselves the New Economists.

The New Economists deliberately launched themselves in the media a few months before the 1978 parliamentary elections, with advertisements in the press and on television trailing the appearance of a clutch of works summarizing their liberal theories (Rosa and Aftalion, 1977; Lepage, 1978; Roy, 1978; Claassen and Salin, 1978). Their message was relayed by what became the annual New Economics summer schools held at the University of Aix-Marseille, and by the seminars and publications of the Association pour la Liberté Economique et le Progrès Social, founded by the summer school's host, Jacques Garello. Another of the group, Pascal Salin, founded the Institut Economique de Paris to publish the works of revered liberal ancestors such as Bastiat and von Mises, while Florin Aftalion used his position at the Presses Universitaires de France to publish Hayek (Garello, 1984). As well as reviving academic interest in classical liberal theory, the group set itself the task of bringing to the attention of the French public the 'discoveries' of the US Chicago School, including James M. Buchanan's public choice theory, which explains that state bureaucracies exist not for the public good but in order to maximize the private advantages of their own members, and Milton Friedman's attack on minimum wage and social security regulations, which allegedly induce a 'dependence mentality' of demoralization and laziness among citizens (Lepage, 1982 trans., pp. 82–139; Friedman and Friedman, 1980, pp. 227–90). The discoveries also included Gary Becker's iconoclastic vindication of classical theory's premise concerning rational and maximizing 'economic man': with more disposable income (says Becker), individuals will expand consumption of everything, including that of esteem through donations to charity, therefore tax cuts which lead to a shortfall in public solidarity will be made up by private charity (Lepage, 1982 trans., pp. 161–84). In policy terms, all these attempts to rehabilitate and extend the scope of classical liberalism pointed in the same direction; the need to cut welfare, cut taxes to stimulate the spirit of enterprise, and 'roll back' state activity generally.

If the New Economists contributed to the reorientation of French conservatism by 'rescuing' classical economics from the discredit in which it had languished since the great crash of 1929, other apologists of Reaganism were on hand to extol the political coalition which had brought the revived doctrine to power. Guy Sorman's *La Révolution conservatrice américaine* was devoted to celebrating 'the extraordinary democratic and religious vitality of the American people' (Sorman, 1983, p. 128), via interviews which revealed the likes and dislikes of the conservative activists who had worked for Reagan's victory (the right to life, prayers at school and the death penalty fell into the former category; taxes, feminism, atheism, the left-wing bias of the media and the 'secular humanist' bias of school books into the latter). Sorman also offered a liberal blueprint for the problems of French society, deduced from the best practice of America, Britain, Japan and Spain. It contained what had become familiar Thatcherite and Reaganite recipes such as privatization, the substitution of private insurance for public welfare, education vouchers, and tax cuts for the rich. But Sorman included two ideas which had a particular resonance on the French right. One, inspired by Japanese practice which had spread to the USA and the UK, was the 'workplace charter', in which the workers would consent to a 50 per cent wage cut (the rest made up by bonuses when the firm made a profit) in exchange for 'participation' in job organization and the promise of a job for life. This found favour with those Gaullists who were still interested in the theme of shared responsibility at work (Fysh, 1990, pp. 364–5). The second of Sorman's ideas, Swiss- or Californian-style direct democracy, which would allow citizens to take the initiative in changing laws by referendum, later also became particularly popular with the Gaullists (Sorman, 1984, pp. 179–89, 243–9).

The 1980s provided many examples of the influence of revived liberalism among French conservatives. The first was Jacques Chirac's 1981 presidential campaign platform. Distancing himself from traditional Gaullist *dirigisme*, Chirac adopted two main themes: unemployment and the growth of state expenditure as a share of GNP. For both problems he had a single package of solutions: cut taxes and social charges, balance the budget by reducing the number of state employees and ending the subsidization of unproductive activities, and firms will automatically expand their activities, taking on more workers in the process. In short, as his full-page newspaper advertisements repeated, 'By looking after fewer things the state will look after them better' (*Le Monde*, 4 March 1981).

Chirac's colleagues proved to be willing converts. Many were regular visitors to the Aix summer school or went on study visits to the USA, making contact among others with the Californians whose 'citizens' initiative' to cut taxes for the middle class in their own state was one of the founding references for the 'Reagan revolution' (Fysh, 1990, pp. 325–38). A series of party discussions led to the publication in 1984 of a

new programme, *Libres et responsables*, which revolutionized the traditional interventionist approach to the economy. There was no mention
whatever of planning, state ownership was to be rolled back via a
privatization programme, and state-directed industrial policy was abandoned in favour of a focus on individual firms as the carriers of French
hopes of economic success: 'it is only the periphery and not the centre,
the base and not the summit, the firm and not the state which can tap
the information emanating from the market place in order to make the
ten thousand daily decisions required by economic activity' (Rassemblement pour la République, 1984, p. 27).

Within a few years, Gaullist politicians produced a flood of books
putting their own gloss on the new liberalism. Some contented themselves with piling up any and every piece of evidence or analysis which
would condemn the socialists (Peyrefitte, 1983, 1985); some pragmat-
ically suggested that a residual role for the state might still be necessary
to correct market failures (Juppé, 1983; Auberger, 1984); some criticized in retrospect Gaullist and Pompidolist *dirigisme*, which had cut
France off from foreign capital, and argued that the knock-down sale of
shares to the workers in privatized firms was a continuation of de
Gaulle's *participation* (Balladur, 1987, 1989); others eulogized the free
market and the firm (Chalandon, 1986); and yet others gave free reign
to their imaginations, not only applying the new liberalism to industry
and trade but also proposing the breakup and decentralization of the
national education system, along with a battery of measures to implement direct democracy (Noir, 1984, 1989).

Faced with rivals who were now more Giscardian than himself,
Giscard made an adjustment to his doctrine in the preface to the
paperback edition of *2 Français sur 3*, which appeared in 1985. Abandoning his previous concern with 'correcting' certain social inequalities
by means of state action, he now wrote of the virtues of 'authentic
economic liberalism', which he opposed to 'a pastel-pink coloured
liberalism' (2F, pp. 21–2), explaining, in terms which evoke both
Becker's 'private charity' notions and Sorman's enthusiasm for
Japanese-style personnel management: 'Instead of seeking to "introduce" this social conscience from the outside by administrative interventions or by regulations, it will be found more and more directly in
the game plans of all those with important responsibilities, thanks to
the development of the social conscience of the whole group' (2F,
p. 23).

If the themes of personal freedom and personal responsibility dis-
seminated by the New Economists and their friends found a ready

audience among Giscardians and younger Gaullists, who reached maturity in a post-war world very different from that which had structured de Gaulle's philosophy, the same could not be true of earlier generations of Gaullists, who were more in tune with the general's attachment to order, authority and the state. That they also came to embrace the new liberalism is in part attributable to the influence of the so-called Nouvelle Droite. One wing of this movement, the Groupement de Recherche et d'Etudes pour la Civilisation Européenne (GRECE), eschewed conventional politics in favour of manufacturing ideology in its review *Eléments*, and of spreading it through the positions which its members managed to win in the mass-circulation weekly *Figaro-magazine*. GRECE was elitist, anti-egalitarian, possibly racist and very definitely a movement of the extreme right. Its influence on the mainstream was fairly slight and seemed to reach its zenith around 1979, after which it went into decline, partly because it broke with *Figaro-magazine*'s editor, refusing to share his enthusiasm for Reaganism, among other things (Vaughan, 1982; Duranton-Crabol, 1988).

Another wing of the Nouvelle Droite, the Club de l'Horloge, was founded in 1974 by a small group of young graduates of the elite civil service training schools, the Ecole Nationale d'Administration and the Ecole Polytechnique. Like GRECE, in which most of them had already been active, they devoted themselves to the production of ideology, but made more direct efforts to infiltrate conventional politics according to a deliberate division of labour, some joining the FN, some the RPR and some the UDF. The most influential individual was probably the Club's honorary life president, Yvan Blot, who from 1978 to 1984 held a key post in the RPR leadership as *directeur de cabinet* of successive general secretaries, and from 1984 until 1989 – when he left to join the FN – was on the staff of Charles Pasqua, for twenty years a top RPR leader. In their publications and in regular symposia, attended by the right-wing fringes of the RPR and UDF as well as like-thinking business and civil service elites, the Club members worked variations on the core of Nouvelle Droite ideology: the need to maintain the historic and essential separation between the 'three functions' in society, the sovereign (the political), the military and the economic. This separation was seen as uniquely characteristic of European societies since pre-Christian times; its abandonment, that is the 'confusion' of functions, was synonymous with deviant social development – fascism resulted from the confusion of the military and the political functions, while Keynesianism was denounced as the confusion of the political and the economic. The political function should at all times be sovereign, the Club believed, commanding the other two, and preferably incarnated in a charismatic leader drawing his inspiration from the heroic deeds of ancestors and presiding over a society united by hierarchy, duty and tradition (Le Gallou and Club de l'Horloge, 1977).

From this it is clear that Nouvelle Droite ideology provided a conceptual framework in which the notion of 'rolling back' the welfare state would not be out of place, even though the Club had little sympathy with the notion of personal freedom. During the 1970s, indeed, both GRECE and the Club deplored liberalism, which they blamed for imperialism and the extinction of a variety of ancient cultures by the tide of industrialization which it unleashed (de Benoist, 1979; Le Gallou, 1977, pp. 154–5). But after the political watershed of 1980–1, in an effort to concentrate fire against the socialist enemy, Yvan Blot threw open the pages of the Club's review, *Contrepoint*, to representatives of the New Economists and the American conservatives, as well as to RPR spokespeople and colleagues from the RPR's own Club '89, which devoted itself to drawing up policies deduced rather haphazardly from the ideology propagated by the New Economists and the Nouvelle Droite (*Contrepoint* 41, 23–33; Blot, 1985, p. 234; Fysh, 1990, pp. 353–8). In the next few years Blot and his friends revised a large part of their doctrine. In 1977 they had advocated a minimum wage to offset the downward pressure on manual wages which they attributed to immigration (Le Gallou, 1977, p. 175); in the 1980s they abandoned this in favour of the means-tested 'safety net' proposed by the liberals (Blot, 1985, pp. 48–9). The Club had at first denounced money-obsessed American society and United States imperialism (Le Gallou, 1977, pp. 69, 249) but in the mid-1980s Blot personally translated four contributions from three Republican standard-bearers, including two by Congressman Jack Kemp which regretted the loss of American influence in the third world and looked forward to a new era of self-confident leadership (*Contrepoint* 47, 15–25, 27–31, 61–9, 71–8). In 1977 the Club had dismissed direct democracy as a 'Rousseauist fiction' (Le Gallou, 1977, p. 50), but in 1985, after following Kemp's lead in examining the Swiss system, Blot allowed that French citizens might use referenda to veto laws but not to propose them, at least not until after a trial period (Blot, 1985, pp. 167–89, 227–31). By 1989 Blot had become an active advocate of direct democracy, through a new association founded by himself (interview with the author, 28 February 1989).

By the mid-1980s the streams of liberal ideas emanating from different sources were flowing into a single, ever-widening channel. In preparation for the 1986 elections, RPR and UDF leaders duly prepared a common programme of government containing a number of policy measures deduced from the new orthodoxy. Once in power, however, they soon ran into difficulty. Students struck against selection; train drivers and public utility workers struck against the introduction of merit payments into wage scales traditionally based on seniority; public opinion remained obstinately attached to the idea of the welfare state; and the stock exchange crashed in 1987 before the privatization programme could be completed. A second successive defeat in the 1988 presidential contest was therefore the signal for a new phase in the development of conservative ideology.

Revenge of the Nation State

A new cycle of convergence and divergence between Gaullist and liberal ideology became apparent in the 1990s, in the wake of a new double watershed. The 1988 election defeat rapidly converted many Gaullists into enthusiastic supporters of constitutional reform; it also impelled both parties to look again at the liberal adventure, rehabilitating the role of the state in society and the economy. The collapse of Stalinism and the end of the Cold War forced the Gaullists to re-examine the strategic assumptions linked to their traditional nationalism.

Faced with another seven years in opposition, the Gaullists became acutely aware of the undemocratic features of the Fifth Republic's constitution, the maintenance of which they had in better times made a determinant of their party's identity. The principle of referendum by citizen initiative is clearly a modification of the Gaullian doctrine of direct democracy, in which the referendum serves to give the leader *carte blanche* to do as he or she pleases. Nevertheless in 1989 the RPR officially adopted the principle, which had become a favourite among enthusiasts of the Reagan revolution. Furthermore, all the Gaullist leaders weighed in with suggestions to reduce the length of the presidential mandate, increase the power of parliament and protect the independence of the judiciary, which the 1958 text had somehow overlooked (*Le Monde*, 14 December 1989, 24 and 31 October 1991; Balladur, 1992, pp. 61–74; Chirac, 1994, pp. 73–6; Fysh, 1993).

The 1988 defeat was also a signal for a long-overdue critical re-appraisal of the liberalomania of the previous few years. Jean-Louis Bourlanges's *Droite année zéro* drew on Raymond Aron to remind readers that freedom was not incompatible with welfare, and went back over a hundred years to recall that Guizot, one of the fathers of French liberalism, had believed that liberal principles neither forbade state initiatives nor prescribed a given level of state activity – a judgement which was to be left to traditional conservative pragmatism (Bourlanges, 1988, pp. 255–8). But Bourlanges was no more than an RPR councillor who was shortly to cross over into the ranks of the UDF, and his book did not cause much of a stir. Nevertheless, the overall thrust of his analysis was shared by a number of Gaullists, who alleged that the government had paid too much attention to economics and not enough to social problems (Fysh, 1988); though these mutterings, directed against the person of ex-finance minister Edouard Balladur, were only later converted into doctrinal form in the context of epochal changes on the world stage.

With the arrival of the supposed New World Order the Gaullists have been faced with a number of dilemmas. They did violence to their own tradition by supporting the deployment of French troops in the Gulf under American command, with only a handful of die-hards protesting. They agreed to reorient resources away from the nuclear deterrent, seen since its inception as the ultimate guarantee of French independence, towards conventional forces configured to deal with a possible future version of Iraqi adventurism rather than the moribund Soviet threat (Howorth, 1991). Back in power in 1993, they announced that French representatives would in future take part in NATO committees when French interests required it (Fysh, 1996). A lot of Gaullist ink has been spilled on these questions, but they are matters of strategy rather than of ideology. If the pattern of future NATO decision making is intergovernmental rather than American-dominated, then no violence is done to de Gaulle's doctrine of national independence.

The strife caused by the debate over the Maastricht treaty on European Union was different, and the fall-out was not confined to the Gaullists. The measures agreed in the draft Treaty of European Union – single currency, common defence and security policies, more majority voting – flew in the face of de Gaulle's refusal to surrender French sovereignty and his insistence on intergovernmental decision making. The RPR leaders (Chirac, Juppé and Balladur) nevertheless swallowed their misgivings about these issues, for fear of damaging the domestic coalition with the UDF and the long-standing Franco-German leadership role in the Community, and campaigned for ratification along with Giscard. For the first time the Giscardians found themselves split over a European issue, when a PR deputy from a semi-rural constituency in the west campaigned against the treaty in 1992 and ran an anti-Maastricht list in the European elections two years later. Philippe de Villiers's ideology, close to that of the extreme right, seemed to be an incoherent amalgam of nationalism, nostalgia for authoritarian and family values, anti-immigrant rhetoric, and exploitation of the fears of his petty-bourgeois electorate concerning the unbridled competition promised by a frontierless Europe (de Villiers, 1994).

In the RPR, on the other hand, two party heavyweights, Charles Pasqua and Philippe Séguin, appeared during 1992–4 to be trying to reinvent the Gaullist tradition – progressively abandoned during the 1980s – by opposing Maastricht in the name of the loss of sovereignty, and by linking this to demands for a new social policy and a big programme of state-led investment in the regions, all in the name of the prized Gaullist goal of social cohesion. Séguin's speech in Parliament, which led nearly half the Gaullist deputies to vote against the bill ratifying the treaty, amounted to a full-scale restatement of Gaullist nationalism of a kind which had not been heard since Chirac himself led the opposition to Community enlargement in 1979. Attacking the notion of European citizenship and reciprocal voting rights in local and European elections, he declared that 'citizenship cannot be decreed . . . For there to be a European citizenship there would have to be a European nation . . . Well, nations can't be invented, any more than sovereignty can be. National "identity" imposes itself by itself without anyone being able to decide otherwise' (Séguin, 1992, p. 36). Like de Gaulle before him, he extolled the role of nations in world history, both as the emancipators of peoples from oppressive empires and (in the shape of Great Britain) as the last rampart of defence against totalitarian aggression (Séguin, 1992, pp. 73–8). Both he and Pasqua protested, in the name of de Gaulle's 'Europe from the Atlantic to the Urals', against the abandonment of the new democracies in central Europe which was implied by the obsession with ever-closer union of the existing members (Séguin, 1992, pp. 78–80; *Le Monde*, 4 January 1990, 14 November 1990).

In contrast, their social policy was somewhat eclectic. Pasqua dismissed de Gaulle's 'third way' as illusory (Pasqua, 1992, pp. 94–6), and they offered a number of other recipes – wages linked to merit, education vouchers, private health care provided by American-style 'health maintenance organizations' – which dovetail with the pre-1988 liberal thinking (Pasqua, 1992, pp. 113–14; Pasqua and Séguin, 1992, pp. 18, 71–9, 83, 130–6). As for the role of the state in regional development, Pasqua's approach smacks of political opportunism rather than ideological consistency. In 1985, in conformity with the spirit of the times, he had attacked the state 'which neglects its duties, gets mixed up in things which don't concern it ... It secretes a mass of regulations, norms and controls which give birth to a dreadful monster called bureaucracy' (Pasqua, 1985, p. 107). In 1993 he believed:

> France being what she is – a very old country forged by the will of the state ... over perpetually recurring divisions, nothing decisive can be accomplished here without the state ... The state should use all the means conferred by the institutions of the Fifth Republic to re-establish with the utmost urgency a true policy of investment, organization and equipment in the regions.
>
> (Pasqua and Séguin, 1993, p. 33)

Séguin's discourse throughout the 1980s was more consistent. In 1985 he stood aloof from the liberal fervour, developing instead an impeccably Gaullist analysis tracing the dysfunctions of the French political system to its persistent left–right cleavage and the demagogic behaviour of politicians, who, by making themselves the spokespeople for rival groups instead of the French people as a whole, had turned Parliament into a polarized battleground (Séguin, 1985). Everything he has done since then has been consistent with maintaining the heterogeneity and the all-class appeal of the Gaullist movement, a theme he has frequently defended at party meetings (Séguin, 1989, pp. 143–65). Some of his ideas, such as calls for employment policy changes to be decided by referendum and for the abolition of the GATT, excited accusations of demagogy, but others were borrowed by party leader Jacques Chirac for his 1995 presidential platform (Chirac, 1994). Séguin remains an enigmatic and influential figure, perhaps the last Gaullist in the conservative ranks.

Conclusion

Séguin apart, the picture that emerges from this survey of conservative ideology in France is not an encouraging one. Subject to outbreaks of internecine warfare, the conservative coalition has been held together, or periodically patched up, over the last twenty years, thanks to electoral interest rather than a strong ideological focus. The UDF is a disparate coalition, which almost fell apart in 1988–9, whose leaders have often preferred throwing in their lot with a rival from the RPR to the difficult task of forging a common identity. The RPR has frequently been riven by internal conflict and presented two rival candidates in the 1995 presidential election. In the production of ideology, French conservatives have seemed to lurch from one enthusiasm to another in response to changing electoral fortunes and university fashions, a habit which could leave their electors prey to rival offers from the extremist fringe.

Note

1. Here we are following Charlot's (1992) persuasive account. Touchard, in contrast, tends to emphasize the 'accidental' events which made possible the construction of Gaullism. He also tells us that de Gaulle's ideas are 'absolutely not an original corpus of doctrine' (1978, p. 313). It seems to me that no ideology – unless it were the most utopian of utopias – can be completely free of derivation. Identifying the components of de Gaulle's thought and tracing their origin to the spirit of the times of his formative years does not seem to invalidate the originality of their combination.

References

References to works by Charles de Gaulle are abbreviated as follows:

ME1 (1980) *Mémoires d'espoir*, Vol. 1, *Le Renouveau, 1958–62*. Paris: Plon.
MG1 (1954) *Mémoires de guerre*, Vol. 1, *L'Appel, 1940–42*. Paris: Plon.
MG3 (1980) *Mémoires de guerre*, Vol. 3, *Le Salut, 1944–46*. Paris: Plon.

References to works by Valéry Giscard d'Estaing are as follows:

2F (1985) *2 Français sur 3*. Paris: Livre de Poche.
DF (1978) *Démocratie française*. Paris: Livre de Poche.
PV1 (1988) *Le Pouvoir et la vie*, Vol. 1, *La Rencontre*. Paris: Compagnie 12.
PV2 (1992) *Le Pouvoir et la vie*, Vol. 2, *L'Affrontement*. Paris: Livre de Poche.

Auberger, P. (1984) *L'Allergie fiscale*. Paris: Calmann-Lévy.
Balladur, E. (1987) *Je crois en l'homme plus qu'en l'Etat*. Paris: Flammarion.
Balladur, E. (1989) *Passion et longueur de temps*. Paris: Fayard.
Balladur, E. (1992) *Douze Lettres aux Français trop tranquilles*. Paris: Livre de Poche.
Benoist, A. de (1979) 'L'Erreur du libéralisme'. *Eléments* 28/9, 21–3.
Blot, Y. (1985) *Les Racines de la liberté*. Paris: Albin Michel.
Bourlanges, J.-L. (1988) *Droite, année zéro*. Paris: Flammarion.
Bunel, J. and Meunier, P. (1972) *Chaban Delmas*. Paris: Stock.
Chalandon, A. (1986) *Quitte ou double*. Paris: Grasset.
Charlot, J. (1970) *Le Gaullisme*. Paris: Armand Colin.
Charlot, J. (1983) *Le Gaullisme d'opposition 1946–58*. Paris: Fayard.
Charlot, J. (1992) 'Le Gaullisme', in J.-F. Sirinelli (ed.) *Histoire des droites en France*, Vol. 1. Paris: Gallimard, pp. 653–89.
Chirac, J. (1978) *Discours pour la France à l'heure du choix* and *La Lueur de l'espérance*. Paris: Stock.
Chirac, J. (1994) *Une nouvelle France*. Paris: Nil.
Claassen, E. and Salin, P. (1978) *L'Occident en désarroi*. Paris: Dunod.
Debré, M. (1972) *Une certaine idée de la France*. Paris: Fayard.
Debré, M. (1982) *Peut-on lutter contre le chômage?* Paris: Fayard.
Deniau, J.-F. (1994) *Ce que je crois*. Paris: Livre de Poche.
Desjardins, T. (1983) *Un inconnu nommé Chirac*. Paris: La Table Ronde.
Duranton-Crabol, A.-M. (1988) *Visages de la Nouvelle Droite, le GRECE et son histoire*. Paris: Presses de la Fondation Nationale des Sciences Politiques.
Frémontier, J. (1984) *Les Cadets de la droite*. Paris: Seuil.
Friedman, R. and Friedman, M. (1980) *Free to Choose*. London: Pelican.
Fysh, P. (1988) 'Defeat and Reconstruction, the RPR in 1988'. *Modern and Contemporary France* 35, 15–25.

Fysh, P. (1990) 'Gaullism and the Liberal Challenge'. Unpublished PhD thesis, University of London.

Fysh, P. (1993) 'Gaullism Today'. *Parliamentary Affairs* **46** (3), 399–414.

Fysh, P. (1996) 'Gaullism and the New World Order', in T. Chafer and B. Jenkins (eds) *France from the Cold War to the New World Order.* Basingstoke: Macmillan, pp. 181–92.

Garello, J. (1984) 'Une détermination libérale'. *Contrepoint* **48**, 155–61.

Giesbert, F.-O. (1987) *Jacques Chirac.* Paris: Seuil.

Howorth, J. (1991) 'France and the Gulf War'. *Modern and Contemporary France* **46**, 3–16.

Juppé, A. (1983) *La Double Rupture.* Paris: Economica.

Knapp, A. (1994) *Gaullism since de Gaulle.* Aldershot: Dartmouth.

Le Gallou, J.-Y. and Club de l'Horloge (1977) *Les Racines du futur.* Paris: Albatros.

Léotard, F. (1987) *A mots découverts.* Paris: Grasset.

Lepage, H. (1978) *Demain le capitalisme.* Paris: Livre de Poche. Trans. S.C. Ogilvie (1982) as *Tomorrow Capitalism.* La Salle, IL: Open Court.

Noir, M. (1984) *1988, Le Grand Rendez-vous.* Paris: J.-C. Lattès.

Noir, M. (1989) *La Chasse au mammouth.* Paris: Robert Laffont.

Pasqua, C. (1985) *Une ardeur nouvelle.* Paris: Albin Michel.

Pasqua, C. (1992) *Que demande le peuple . . . ?* Paris: Albin Michel.

Pasqua, C. and Séguin, P. (1992) *La Priorité sociale.* Paris: Demain la France.

Pasqua, C. and Séguin, P. (1993) *La Reconquête du territoire.* Paris: Demain la France.

Peyrefitte, A. (1976) *Le Mal français.* Paris: Plon.

Peyrefitte, A. (1983) *Quand la rose se fanera.* Paris: Plon.

Peyrefitte, A. (1985) *Encore un effort Monsieur le Président.* Paris: J.-C. Lattès.

Pickles, D. (1973) *The Government and Politics of France,* Vol. 2. London: Methuen.

Poniatowski, M. (1978) *L'Avenir n'est écrit nulle part.* Paris: Albin Michel.

Rassemblement pour la République (1980) *Atout France.* Paris: Roudil.

Rassemblement pour la République (1984) *Libres et responsables.* Paris: Flammarion.

Rosa, J.-J. and Aftalion, F. (eds) (1977) *L'Economie retrouvée, vieilles critiques et nouvelles analyses.* Paris: Economica.

Roy, M. (1978) *Vive le capitalisme.* Paris: Plon.

Séguin, P. (1985) *Réussir l'alternance, contre l'esprit de revanche.* Paris: Robert Laffont.

Séguin, P. (1989) *La Force de convaincre.* Paris: Payot.

Séguin, P. (1992) *Discours pour la France.* Paris: Grasset.

Soisson, J.-P. (1978) *La Victoire sur l'hiver.* Paris: Fayard.

Soisson, J.-P. (1990) *Mémoires d'ouverture.* Paris: Belfond.

Sorman, G. (1983) *La Révolution conservatrice américaine.* Paris: Fayard.

Sorman, G. (1984) *La Solution libérale.* Paris: Fayard.

Touchard, J. (1978) *Le Gaullisme 1940–1969.* Paris: Seuil.

Vaughan, M. (1982) ' "Nouvelle Droite": Cultural Power and Political Influence', in D.S. Bell (ed.) *Contemporary French Political Parties.* London: Croom Helm, pp. 52–66.

Villiers, P. de (1994) La Société de Connivence. Paris: Dunod.

4

National Populism

CHRISTOPHER FLOOD

Introduction

The label of national populism is applied to a contemporary right-wing
ideology which is nationalist in the sense that it gives priority to
defending the independence and the integrity of the nation. It is
populist in so far as it seeks to mobilize support by claiming to speak on
behalf of the mass of ordinary, decent people against a corrupt,
degenerate ruling elite. It is not exclusive to France, but in the context
of French politics the label is widely used to refer to the ideological
stance of the Front National (FN). It is not the only ideological current
on the French extreme right at present, but it is by far the most
important by virtue of its connection with the FN. Apart from the short-
lived success of the Poujadist movement in the mid-1950s, the FN is the
only party of the hard right to have made a real impact in France since
the collapse of Marshal Pétain's Vichy regime in 1944. Of negligible
importance from the time of its inception in 1972 until the early 1980s,
the FN survived under the leadership of Jean-Marie Le Pen to become
a significant force in national politics (Camus, 1989; Hainsworth, 1992;
Perrineau, 1994; Marcus, 1995). From the mid-1980s to the mid-1990s,
despite setbacks, the party's national electoral support consolidated in
the 10-15 per cent band, with opinion polls indicating sympathy for its
policy positions well in excess of its electoral scores. It forced serious
dilemmas of policy and tactics on other parties. Even if it does not
continue to gain support, the FN will still have had a powerful influence
on French political life. One of the major reasons for this has been the
ideological self-confidence which allowed it to take advantage of a
climate of political and economic uncertainty to force the concerns of
the hard right to the forefront of public debate.

Influenced by the arguments of New Right theorists concerning the importance of ideological struggle and the need for thorough renewal of right-wing political culture, the FN has devoted enormous effort to production and dissemination of ideology (on the New Right, see Duranton-Crabol, 1988; Piccone, 1994; Taguieff, 1994). In this respect it is also following the earlier example of the Action Française (AF) movement, as it developed in its heyday before and after World War I. Under the intellectual leadership of Charles Maurras, the AF had published a daily newspaper, produced or influenced a number of political and cultural magazines in Paris or the provinces, controlled more than one publishing house, and run series of lectures and conferences at its own educational institute (see Weber, 1962).

For its part, the FN has created increasingly sophisticated organizational structures for developing and communicating its ideology (on party organization, see Birenbaum, 1992; Institut de Formation Nationale, 1991; Marcus, 1995). Since 1988 this area of the party's activity has been coordinated by the Délégué Général and his staff. The Délégation Générale includes a number of different sections. The propaganda section produces posters, tracts, leaflets, audio and video cassettes, etc. There is a section responsible for organizing major demonstrations, commemorations, festivals, public meetings, and so forth. A training section runs the Institut de Formation Nationale (IFN) to educate activists and organize conferences, series of evening lectures, etc. The study section produces reports and brochures to provide arguments for use by the president and the movement. The communication section deals with press releases and monitors the media. It is also responsible for producing the magazine, *La Lettre de Jean-Marie Le Pen*. There is a section devoted to spreading the FN's intellectual influence. This includes the Conseil Scientifique, which brings together the party's leading intellectuals. It produced the theoretical journal *Identité* from 1989 to 1994, followed by a two-year break pending relaunch in 1996. The journal has served as a laboratory and showcase of ideas which can subsequently be distilled into the party's manifestos. That was the case, for example, in *300 mesures pour la France* (FN, 1993), a glossy, 429-page book published for the 1993 parliamentary elections. Besides the communication apparatus directly attached to the party, there are daily (*Présent, Le Français*) or weekly (*National hebdo, Minute, Rivarol*) newspapers, and other periodicals (*Le Choc du mois, Monde et vie, Itinéraires, Militant*, for example), which support the FN and in some cases reflect the particular orientation of one of its internal currents. It is worth adding that the party has its own twenty-four-hour, seven-days-a-week radio station, and the FN was ahead of other French parties in establishing a substantial site on the Internet.

Like the Communist Party in its better days, the FN has attracted a significant number of intellectuals, many of them from the New Right think-tanks, the Groupement de Recherche et d'Etudes pour la Civilisation Européenne (GRECE) (for example, Pierre Vial, Jean-Claude Bardet, Pierre de Meuse, Jean Haudry and Jean Varenne) or the Club de l'Horloge (Jean-Yves Le Gallou, Yvan Blot and Bruno Mégret, among others). The editorial advisory board of *Identité*, numbering 20–25 members at any given time, has always had a majority of university teachers, albeit not from the *grandes écoles*. Le Pen himself is a tireless publicist who has authored many books, articles, prefaces and pamphlets. His editorials introduce issues of *Identité*, and he normally plays a prominent role in the annual lecture series organized by the IFN.

National populism is a synthesis of elements deriving from almost every major current of French extreme right-wing thought. It provides common ground between the party's different ideological families. Christophe Bourseiller (1991, pp. 73–95) distinguishes six of these groupings: revolutionary nationalists/neo-fascists, classical nationalists, royalists, Catholic traditionalists, national conservatives and the New Right, with its subdivision between the anti-liberal GRECE grouping and the national liberal Club de l'Horloge. It has been alleged that there are elements around the fringe with neo-Nazi beliefs (Camus, 1995). Whatever the case, the FN tolerates a considerable degree of internal diversity, subject to the prohibition of organized factionalism such as exists in the Parti Socialiste (PS). At the same time, the FN has set out its common programme in numerous publications and has underpinned it with theoretical arguments developed in books and articles by the party's intellectuals. For the purposes of this chapter, I will concentrate for the most part on what unites the FN rather than dealing with differences between internal currents.

Issues of Identification and Self-Representation

In identifying its own ideological position, the FN does not deny that it has its roots in the intellectual traditions of what it calls 'the national right' or simply 'the right' (for standard histories of the traditions, see Rémond, 1982; Chebel d'Appollonia, 1988; Sirinelli, 1992; Winock, 1994). On the contrary, it is proud to present its own ideology as being consistent with the fundamental values and goals of the national right in the past. Its publications often eulogize earlier extreme right-wing thinkers. For example, *Identité* regularly carries articles and book reviews concerning writers such as Rivarol, Taine, Maurras, Barrès, La Varende, Bonnard, Montherlant, Céline or Jünger. The whole of the 1989–90 series of eighteen evening lectures run by the IFN was devoted to the theme of 'national thought'. With the exception of neo-Nazism, it covered theorists representing all of the main strands of extreme right-wing thought since the time of the French Revolution – from counter-revolutionary traditionalists and theocrats (notably Joseph de Maistre and Louis de Bonald) to theorists of national identity (such as Hyppolite Taine, Ernest Renan and Maurice Barrès, who merited an entire lecture to himself), theorists of elitism (such as Gustave Le Bon or Wilfredo Pareto), populist nationalists (from General Boulanger to Colonel de la Rocque), reactionary social Catholics (Louis Veuillot, René de La Tour du Pin and Xavier Vallat, among others), neo-traditionalists and neo-monarchists (Charles Maurras and his school of thought) and assorted fascists (Robert Brasillach, Pierre Drieu La Rochelle and Julius Evola) to a range of national liberals, or theorists of the political applications of ethology. The FN located itself as part of that broad lineage by launching the series with a talk by Le Pen entitled 'National Thought and Political Struggle', and ending the series with Bruno Mégret on 'The Renewal of National Thought in the 1980s'.

However, as the title of Mégret's lecture suggested, the FN purports to offer something more than a mere reassertion of earlier ideas. It presents itself as a creative ideological force which harmoniously blends the best of the old with new ideas adapted to the circumstances of the present. The way in which it wishes to be perceived is described by Jean-Claude Bardet as follows:

> The Front National can be viewed in two ways. On the one hand, it embodies the philosophy of the eternal right – and in this respect it can be said to be restoring the right's legitimate access to the French political scene. On the other hand, because the issues and the ideological contours have changed, its nature is innovative and it achieves an original political synthesis which cannot be reduced to the old frameworks of thought.
>
> (1994, p. 6)

Yet, while it claims to represent the true right as distinct from parties which merely pass for right-wing, the FN does not accept the label of extreme right for itself. It argues that the label is not merely an ideologically neutral classification in terms of relative distance from the notional centre at any given period in the history of the political system. The FN maintains that those who label it an extreme right-wing party are doing so in the knowledge that the label has historical connotations of extremism, violence, racism and authoritarian hatred of democracy. Their aim is to marginalize the party by implying that it is neo-fascist or neo-Vichyite, while ignoring the features – notably, its rejection of racism and anti-semitism, as well as its positive commitment to republican democracy – which make the party different, dynamic and new (for example, Le Pen, 1995c, 1996; and see Marcus, 1995, pp. 129–30). The FN, the newspaper *Présent* and the Club de l'Horloge have all brought successful court cases to force a right of reply when described as extreme right-wing in the press, with the predictable result that large numbers of journalists, politicians, intellectuals and academic analysts have lined up to assert their right to use the label (for extensive discussion and responses, see *Le Monde*, 9–10 June 1996; *Libération*, 11 and 19 June 1996; *Le Nouvel Observateur*, 20–26 June 1996; *National hebdo*, 27 June–3 July 1996).

Still, the FN's disclaimer has to be treated with caution. The official policies of any party are normally a compromise between the positions of its different internal currents, depending on the balance of power in the party and on the political environment in which it is operating. Parties which undertake ideological renewal for purposes of adaptation to changing political contexts do so with varying degrees of conviction and of internal division. Clearly, there can be a distinction between the party's official line on a given issue and the views of particular factions or individual activists. There can be a difference between what is said in private gatherings and what is said to wider publics. In any case, it is not always necessary to spell out chapter and verse: a discourse can be framed so that it carries different connotations for different sections of a single audience (compare Billig, 1979, pp. 124–90, on the National Front in Britain during the 1970s).

In the FN's case, to declare loyalty to the ideological traditions of the extreme right, while asserting that new times require new positions, leaves plenty of scope for ambiguity (Rollat, 1985; Milza, 1992). Numerous exposés have shown that there are members of the party who hold racist, anti-semitic, Holocaust-denialist and/or other opinions which would be classed as extremist in relation to the norms of the French political mainstream (for example, Plenel and Rollat, 1984; Etchegoin, 1987; Tristan, 1987; Taguieff, 1989; Assouline and Bellet, 1990; Bresson and Lionet, 1994; Collectif, 1995; Marcus, 1995). There are undoubtedly members who could be described as authoritarian traditionalists in the Vichyite lineage, and others who could be labelled as neo-fascist. When extremist opinions are aired publicly, they can offer ammunition to the FN's enemies, but there is clearly a margin of tolerance in relation to writings and other public statements which do not appear directly under the auspices of the party. As Guy Birenbaum (1992, pp. 252–77) points out, newspapers and magazines which are notionally independent of the FN, but which serve the party, often have a more extremist tone than the official organs.

In terms of the current topography of the French party system the FN is on the extreme right, even though there are micro-parties further to the right. Furthermore, the content of its ideology owes much to precursors who are normally classified as belonging to the extreme right, even if the FN itself does not choose to label them in that way. On the other hand, rather than constantly looking for tell-tale lapses which might cast doubt on the sincerity of the official line, it is more productive for present purposes to analyse the salient features of the national populist synthesis itself. As they stand, the positions elaborated in the FN's official publications and in other writings by its leading theorists constitute a modernized nationalist discourse which includes a sweeping critique of the values, the practices and the institutions of contemporary French society, coupled with an extensive range of alleged solutions to the problems.

Persecuted for Defending the People

The discourse of the FN operates on the basis of a classic binary scheme of us/them = right/wrong = good/evil. It supposes that good is always forced to defend itself against aggression by the coordinated forces of evil. 'We are the people against the Establishment', runs the heading of one of the sections in *Militer au Front*, a manual for FN activists (Institut de Formation Nationale, 1991, p. 43). The FN does not like the connotations of the term 'populist', but it describes itself as 'popular' in the sense of being for and of the people. The FN claims that France is undergoing a crisis of values and identity, amid a host of urgent social, economic and political problems. The blame for this state of affairs is placed squarely on the mainstream parties which are defined as the Establishment – that is to say, the Parti Socialiste (PS), the Parti Communiste Français (PCF), the centre-right Union pour la Démocratie Française (UDF) and the Gaullist Rassemblement pour la République (RPR). 'Destabilize the Establishment' was the title adopted by Le Pen for his editorial in the issue of *Identité* devoted to attacking the oligarchy of 'new masters' ruling over French society (Le Pen, 1990).

The preoccupation with decadence and the tendency to explain national decay as a consequence of conspiracy have been recurrent features of extreme right-wing thinking since the time of the French Revolution (Chebel d'Appollonia, 1988; Winock, 1990). Under the Third Republic, right-wing polemics against the regime had habitually included denunciations of the corruption and duplicity of the politicians who operated the parliamentary system. Nationalist writers such as Maurras and Barrès – the precursors most widely quoted by FN intellectuals – had been in the habit of presenting politicians as a single, self-interested group colluding together to maintain their power and privileges. The nation was being subjected to a massive confidence trick, they argued, as politicians formed a parasitic class trading in words, peddling influence, selling their services to the highest bidder, plotting and scheming behind the façade of irreconcilable party differences which hid their common aim of exploiting the people. The parliamentarians were also presented as being in league with powerful economic interests, Jewish finance, Freemasons and other sinister, anti-national forces.

In a similar way the FN habitually presents the mainstream parties, 'the Gang of Four', as all being equally statist, incompetent, devoid of idealism, indifferent to the interests of the nation and often corrupt. The suggestion is that there is objective collusion between the mainstream parties as they manipulate France's institutions for their own benefit (for instance, in Le Pen, 1985; Constans, 1990a; Lefranc, 1990a; Sirgue, 1994). Thus, although the FN professes to differ from the old extreme right because it accepts democratic, republican principles, its vilification of the mainstream parties provides a substitute for the extreme right's traditional distrust of parliamentary democracy as such. The FN also voices claims made familiar by its nationalist precursors when it assumes that the circle of collusion extends to the media, trade unions, state bureaucrats, 'moral authorities' (notably the soft-left clergy who dominate the church), pressure groups and lobbies that share common interests and values as members of the privileged elite. Notwithstanding the FN's professed rejection of anti-semitism, the denunciations of these groups sometimes echo the extreme right's eternal obsession with Jewish and Masonic machinations to exercise a hidden control over the levers of power. For example, Grégoire Legrand announces:

> Above all there is the 'antiracist' nebula, the conglomerate of Jewish, Masonic or Christian associations, often at the heart of important economic interests, which have experienced the maintenance of the

national idea, the idea of French France, as a threat to the minorities and the lobbies.

(1989, p. 11)

It should be added that the alleged conspiracy extends beyond France. As always, the enemy within is linked to an enemy without. It is true that the role of the PCF as the fifth column for world communism ceased to be a particular focus for denunciation after the collapse of the Soviet bloc from the end of the 1980s to the early 1990s. But the other parties, along with the various special interest groups, the 'lobbies', are now seen to be locked into the emergent global system of political and economic power relations centred on the US, with the United Nations as its surrogate and the European Union as its Trojan horse (Blot, 1992a; FN, 1993; Gannat, 1994). Although hostility to the US as a political, socioeconomic and cultural model never had the same force as hatred of the Soviet regime, the French extreme right has had a long history of distaste for American society as a multi-ethnic mishmash characterized by acquisitive individualism, compulsive consumerism and a debased mass culture. The emergence of the US in the 1990s as the only surviving superpower was greeted with deep ambivalence (de Meuse, 1990a; Blot, 1991b). It is accused of promoting international collusion between power elites to create a New World Order of homogenized societies, stripped of all particularity or sense of identity which could obstruct the global oligarchy and its clients.

The instrumental value of positing the existence of a pervasive state of decadence and accounting for it in terms of conspiracy is not only that it reduces complex processes to simplicity. It also supports the FN's claim to be the only true force of national renewal in opposition to the agents of decay. Whereas the parties of the Establishment are supposedly formed by self-interested careerists, the FN claims to be a movement of activists driven purely by a reforming ideal. And whereas the mainstream parties represent particular sectional interests, the FN asserts that it alone invites the whole nation – or at least its healthy elements – to join together. The FN thereby makes a virtue of political marginality. Serving the FN is construed as a vocation requiring courage and self-abnegation. The acceptance of personal sacrifice for the higher cause is echoed, for example, in *La Flamme* by Bruno Mégret, when he confides that he had renounced a potentially successful career in the RPR and had rejected the shabby compromises that went with it (1990a, p. 12). According to the FN, because the party represents the aspirations of the people against the self-interest of the Establishment, it naturally suffers unrelenting persecution. The themes of victimization, moral superiority and heroic struggle in the face of systematic attack recur constantly in FN literature. For example, a November 1994 issue of *La Lettre de Jean-Marie Le Pen* is entitled ' "They" Attack Him Because He Defends You', and the tone is captured well in the article 'The Pride and Honour of Pariahs' by Carl Lang in the same issue, where it is followed by a lengthy list of physical attacks on FN members (compare Gaucher, 1991).

In keeping with its heroic self-image, the FN has a stock of political myths. By this I do not mean that the accounts of events are necessarily false, but that they are ideologically marked in their selection and interpretation of events. *Militer au Front* offers useful examples. It contains a brief history of the movement, presented as a secular redemption story in which the party learns how to fulfil its mission through a process of trials and obstacles surmounted (see Bariller and Timmermans, 1993, for the party's official history). Thus, the first phase is entitled '1972–1982 the Necessary Foundations', which contains subsections with titles which speak for themselves: 'The Front National: Structuring the National Right', 'An Original Creation', 'The Crossing of the Wilderness', 'Maturing', 'The Martyrs' and 'The Pointers towards Emergence' (Institut de Formation Nationale, 1991, pp. 13–16). The second phase has the overarching title, '1983–1989 the Emergence of the Le Pen Phenomenon', with its subsections 'The First Successes', 'Entering Parliament', 'The Presidential Elections of 88' and 'Second Wind' (pp. 16–18). The claim is that despite the endless litany of false accusations and other dirty tricks by its enemies, 'nothing makes any difference, the FN continues to shake up French political life, which is taking on new shape because of it' (p. 18): soon the party will be ready for government, it proclaims.

Perpetuating the personality cult of Le Pen promoted in the FN's publications, *Militer* also contains a hagiographic sketch of the leader's life, woven around the themes of 'the man of the open sea', evoking his Breton roots, and 'the man of faith', representing Le Pen as the embodiment of firm convictions and, above all, absolute belief in France at a time when others have lost their sense of national identity. The March/April 1995 issue of the *Lettre de Jean-Marie Le Pen*, published during the presidential election campaign, made an interesting addition to the hagiographic literature with a strip cartoon autobiography of Le Pen under the title of 'Passionately French'. It opens with the arrival of a letter announcing his fisherman father's death in 1942 after hitting a German mine. The words of Le Pen's mother to her son are: 'Now my little lad, you're the one who is head of the family' (p. 3). The 14-year-old boy's precocious assumption of authority sets the tone for the entire story, through to its conclusion with Le Pen announcing to serried ranks of FN members that he will run in the 1995 presidential election to lead France to the Sixth Republic.

Ideology, Identity and Immigration

In keeping with its discursive technique of treating the mainstream parties as a single block, the FN habitually reduces the differences of values, policies and practice between them to mere gradations. In the 1970s and 1980s, the vilest source of ideological evil was the Marxism represented by the PCF, itself linked to the totalitarian tyranny of the Soviet Union. The PS was assimilated to the PCF as the vehicle of a watered-down version of the same pernicious, statist ideology. The mainstream right-wing parties, in turn, were assimilated to the left. In his book *La France est de retour*, Le Pen asks a rhetorical question as to whether any one political programme could win the support of a majority of the people. He replies:

> I think so, on one condition as far as the Front National is concerned – that the programme includes an explicit determination to break with socialism. Not only with the socialism of the left, but also with the socialism practised before 1981 by the governments of Barre, Chirac and Giscard.
>
> (1985, p. 283)

By the early 1990s the FN had modified aspects of its analysis, while maintaining the binary contrast between itself and the other parties. Its publicists argued that there had been a profound ideological change as the doctrinal oppositions of the post-war decades had been replaced by a new configuration. On the one hand, FN writers could gloat that the erosion of support for the Marxism of the PCF in the 1970s and 1980s had been cemented by the collapse of the Soviet bloc. They could equally point out that this had been paralleled by the disintegration of reformist socialism, as evidenced in France by the PS's progressive abandonment of its former goals while in government during the 1980s and early 1990s. Cherished notions of class struggle, redistribution of wealth and state ownership had withered under the disastrous consequences of attempting to put them into practice. However, ideological conflict was by no means over, and again the FN depicted it in terms which linked domestic agents of France's national decay with the international coalition of forces pursuing world domination. According to the FN's interpretation, the left-wing Establishment, followed meekly by the centre-right, had needed to find a new ideological vehicle to save itself from gradual extinction. The ingredients of the new amalgam were social democracy, human rights, cosmopolitanism and globalism (Bardet, 1989; Rousseau, 1989; FN, 1993, pp. 15–16). Social democracy amounted to an uneasy blend of old-style statism with a leavening of economic liberalism, which gave particular emphasis to the globalist, free-trade dimension in keeping with the demands of European Union technocrats in cahoots with the United States. In terms of its influence on the ideological climate, as interpreted by the FN, America's triumph in the Cold War had enormously boosted the receptiveness of France's Establishment parties to the influence of the degraded American brand of consumerist economic liberalism, with its self-serving globalist advocacy of free trade and its utopian vision of a New World Order underpinned by American power (Gannat, 1994). In the FN's apocalyptic rhetoric, the practical application of this cosmopolitan ideology would mean world government over an undifferentiated, borderless, ethnic melting-pot extending to the whole planet, endlessly traversed by migratory flows of people following the vicissitudes of employment markets. Le Pen sums up the matter in terms of titanic conflict:

> In fact, what needs to be understood here, is that it is always a struggle between the same forces, a battle by those who have no loyalty to a country and care only about establishing and maintaining a system which allows them economic domination of the world against those who reject woolly-minded ideologies in favour of common sense, attachment to traditions and bonds with the land. In this gigantic, global struggle the Front national is an essential pole of resistance to the decadence all around. That is what I meant when I once parodied our enemies by shouting loudly and clearly: 'Nationalists of all countries, unite.'
>
> (1995b)

One line of the FN's attack on its enemies within France focuses on the way in which the social democratic left, followed by the centre-right, has paraded the creed of human and civil rights inherited from the Enlightenment and the Revolution in support of a voluntaristic, contractual conception of citizenship, which the FN takes to be undermining national identity. The reference to the Enlightenment and the Revolution is important, and it gained particular topicality for a time by virtue of the bicentenary celebration of the Revolution in 1989. Ideologically, the roots of the contemporary extreme right in France can be traced back to the late eighteenth and early nineteenth centuries, to counter-revolutionary theorists, such as Joseph de Maistre and Louis de Bonald, who wrote against the spirit of rationalism, humanism, liberalism and constitutionalism passed down from the Enlightenment to fuel the French Revolution's destruction of the organic, hierarchical society of the *ancien régime*. The reactionary current of thought had continued down the nineteenth century among Catholic traditionalists. By the end of the century it had been enriched by the arguments of positivistic thinkers, such as Taine, Renan and Maurras, who claimed that systematic, empirical study of the historical evidence demonstrated the disastrous long-term consequences of the Revolution down to the present. The counter-revolutionary current has remained in existence since that time. Indeed, the FN's Catholic integrist wing remains within the pure reactionary tradition. It commemorated the bicentenary by devoting its annual conference to the theme of '1789, the Terrorist Dawn', sympathetically described by one FN reporter as a gathering where 'thousands of people were able to benefit from moral support in an entirely counter-revolutionary atmosphere' (Castagne, 1989, p. 31).

However, since the later nineteenth century the nationalist right has also encompassed a more pragmatic, modernizing current of thought, often labelled 'neo-Bonapartist' by analogy with the ideas and practices of Napoleon I and Napoleon III. Representatives of this current – in the lineage of Maurice Barrès and Paul Déroulède – have tended to have a more nuanced view of the Revolution and its legacy. They might condemn its radical excesses, but they have tended to accept its historical importance as a spur to social, economic and political modernization. The emancipation of the masses could be recognized as a necessary component of nationhood, so long as the pursuit of liberty and of civil or political rights was counterbalanced by a proper degree of social order and political authority. Today, Le Pen himself embodies a similar outlook (Taguieff, 1989, pp. 195–203; Marcus, 1995, pp. 102–4).

Still, theorists in *Identité* have often drawn heavily on the old counter-revolutionary themes in support of their own ethnic model of national community, and against the civic model of legal-political community passed down from the Revolution as an important element of the republican tradition (for example, Legrand, 1989; Blot, 1991a, 1992b; Salvisberg, 1992). They argue that the Establishment parties of today have inherited an impoverished notion of citizenship which is rationalistic, legalistic and individualistic. Citizenship is conceived in purely voluntaristic, contractual terms, whereas the core of national identity and the true basis of citizenship are shared ethnicity and participation in a common culture. The PS, in particular, is accused of having promoted this conception from the early 1980s onwards in support of its demagogic claim to be the protector of equal human rights against all forms of social exclusion. By the same token, FN writers again echo counter-revolutionary themes when they castigate the Revolution for inaugurating a quasi-religious cult of rights without concomitant duties, with the result that the pursuit of individual rights, or the rights of particular groups, takes precedence over recognition of obligations and attention to the good of the nation as a whole.

The FN expounds the necessity of cultural homogeneity and rootedness, the need for a sense of national history and for sustaining a spirit of national community. Pointing to the rise of nationalist parties in other countries of Western and Eastern Europe, the FN represents itself as the harbinger of an international wave of renewal of identitarian feelings (Brys, 1989; de Meuse, 1989; Le Chevallier, 1994). Threatening though they are, anti-Western movements in the Middle East and elsewhere can be interpreted as variants of the same identitarian drive. This is taken by the FN to mean that its own ideological moment is only just beginning, because it is entirely suited to the new historical situation. Its concern with restoring national identity can be presented in part as an extension of the ideology of rootedness inherited from Barrès (Sanders, 1990), but it is fused with the discourse of cultural identity and difference propagated by the New Right in place of the older, less publicly acceptable discourses of pseudo-scientific racial inequality (Taguieff, 1988, 1994, pp. 64–106; Adler, 1995). Indeed, whatever the racist undertones of many of its publicists' discussions of immigration-related issues, it is perfectly possible for FN theorists to dismiss racism explicitly as a scientifically and ideologically outdated creed, but to defend the principle of excluding alien elements from any organic or social body as a law of nature (Lefranc, 1990c; Gregor, 1990; de Meuse, 1993).

The discourse of identity and difference is articulated, for example, by the university teacher Pierre Vial, one of the founders of GRECE, a leading figure on the FN's Conseil Scientifique, and head of an association named Terre et Peuple, established in June 1995 to organize visits to historic sites and to run seminars on what Vial describes as 'the theme of rooted cultural identity' (Chombeau, 1995). Vial contributes a regular historical column entitled 'Notre Mémoire' in *National hebdo*. He has written pieces for *Identité* (1993b, 1994a, 1994b) on the ethno-history and culture of different French provinces with the intention of celebrating the ways in which each one makes a distinctive contribution to French national identity. He is an enthusiast of explorations into Indo-European and Nordic cultures – the contemporary, culturological counterpart of Aryanism (for example, in Vial and Mabire, 1975; and see Moissonnier, 1995, for an attack on the fascistic implications of some of Vial's writings). He shares this interest with other leading intellectuals in the FN, such as Jean Haudry, author of a book on the Indo-Europeans in the popular 'Que sais-je?' series (1981; and see Sergent, 1982, for a critique of its racist implications), or Bernard Lugan, with whom Vial runs the Centre d'Etudes Indo-Européennes at Lyon III university.

Against those who claim that France has derived its culture from the diversity of ethnic groups which have settled its territory over the centuries, FN writers emphasize that until the influx of non-European immigrants since the 1950s, France's ethnic structure had not been significantly modified since the early Middle Ages. Culturally, too, France was the product of a line of development which stemmed from the Celtic, Roman and Germanic descendants of the Indo-Europeans, enriched and refined over the course of time by the penetration of Christianity. According to Jean-Claude Bardet, 'French culture is in a sense the concentrate and the epitome of Europe's different cultures. That is probably why it has wrongly appeared less national and more universal. Wrongly so, because the "universal" quality imputed to it corresponds solely to European values and not to those of others' (1991, p. 14).

The FN portrays the defence of this heritage as *the* challenge to be faced in the future. It feeds directly into the immigration issue, which the FN, like other national populist parties in Europe, has used as a centrepiece of its attack on the forces allegedly threatening French society (for example, in Le Gallou and Club de l'Horloge, 1985; Le Chevallier, 1989; Milloz, 1990a, 1990b; Le Gallou and Olivier, 1992; FN, 1993; and on national populism in Western Europe, Betz, 1994). According to the FN's reading, the gospel of human rights and the denunciation of all forms of social exclusion have served as smoke-screens for the inability of successive governments to deal effectively with the problem of mass, non-European immigration into France. In practice, one FN writer claims, the creed of human rights means allowing anyone 'to live in France, enjoy the facilities of the welfare state, to acquire our nationality without constraint and to vote here' (Legrand, 1989, p. 11). French national identity is obscured in the name of a purely abstract, juridical conception of nationality based on mere presence on French soil and obtaining the right document.

As interpreted by FN publicists, the political Establishment is using an unscrupulous, demagogic tactic when it calls for struggle against racism. The ploy allows the Establishment to brand the FN as racist, which it is not (Peltier, 1996a; Roberto, 1996; Roy, 1996b), and to trump up charges against it under unjust laws (Constans, 1990c; de Meuse, 1990b). At the same time, the issue of racism serves as a useful distraction from governmental failure to deal with major social and economic problems, such as unemployment, rampant crime, the declining birth rate, or massive budgetary deficits. Reversing the arguments of its detractors, the FN designates the conspiracy by defenders of non-European immigration to crode France's ethnocultural identity as anti-French racism (for example, in Le Gallou, 1988; Madiran *et al.*, 1995).

Governments of both right and left are accused of having colluded in a double lie to the effect that immigration has virtually been halted since the early 1970s and that the immigrants already resident in France would be integrated into French society (FN, 1993, pp. 25–35; Mottin, 1993). When FN publicists are arguing in melodramatic mode, the impression is conveyed that there has been an unarmed invasion, which is the preface to even greater inundations in the future as demographic pressures build in Africa. It is not surprising that the latest edition of Jean Raspail's *Le Camp des saints* (1985), an apocalyptic novel of the arrival of a massive armada of immigrant ships on the south coast of France, has been marketed through *National hebdo*, and its author given a forum in *Identité* (Raspail, 1990).

In less hysterical vein, FN writers acknowledge that legal immigration by adult males did slow massively, but they focus on the large numbers of dependants who have continued to enter the country, alongside asylum seekers – most of them bogus claimants – and illegal immigrants. The FN's constant refrain is that immigrants are a major cause of unemployment among the native French population because they are rivals for jobs (Milloz, 1991; Mottin, 1991). The presence of large concentrations of non-European immigrants in or around major cities is blamed for rising crime, civil unrest, urban decay, the swamping and deterioration of schools, alien religious and cultural practices (such as polygamy or female circumcision), plus the imposition of colossal burdens on the welfare system, hence on taxation. Thanks to the power of sympathetic pressure groups within the Establishment, immigrants often benefit from privileged access to state benefits and services which are denied to native French people. Thus, positive discrimination in favour of immigrants means negative discrimination against the French population. Furthermore, whereas European immigrants can be integrated over relatively short periods of time because they share kindred cultures, those who have come from non-European, third world cultures cannot be assimilated in the same way (Lefranc, 1991a; Le Gallou, 1991; Vilmin, 1992). Therefore, given their numbers, immigrants can be presented as a significant threat to French identity, and this is all the more true because so many of them are Muslims. In keeping with the habitual positions of the New Right, it is not argued that the immigrants should renounce their own cultures or their original national identities – on the contrary, FN theorists claim to defend the right of all peoples to their own identity – but rather that they should cherish their own identities in their own countries, not in France.

Following its usual practice of assuming conscious or unconscious collusion between sets of domestic and foreign enemies, the FN links non-European immigrants with the French Establishment, on the one hand, and with the expanding force of Islamic fundamentalism, on the other. A substantial part of the immigrant community – often represented as if it were the whole of the immigrant community – is perceived, in effect, as a fifth column serving Islamic expansionism in the geocultural and potentially geopolitical struggle which is developing between the South and the North (Vial, 1990; Cabantous, 1990; Le Gallou, 1990). Islam is France's second religion, the size of the Muslim community in France is constantly increasing, mosques and Koranic schools are proliferating. The FN attacks those who justify the presence of these people by claiming that, except in its aggressive, fundamentalist version, Islam can be integrated because it is inherently tolerant. According to the FN, history shows that it is not a case of an aggressive version of Islam being cherished by an extremist minority while the true, tolerant version is held by the majority. Islam is double-faced – tolerant when it is not in a position of strength, but intolerant and aggressive when it is in an expansionist period. It has a theocratic, totalitarian worldview which bases the political and personal spheres on the religious. Consequently it is entirely incompatible with secular European culture. In explosive demographic conditions from Morocco to Azerbaijan it is undergoing a huge cultural and religious revival. It is a threat to Europe, and it has its external bases for terrorism and subversion on French soil. Le Pen claims that the field of French foreign policy starts in the immigrant suburbs of France's own cities, which have been exterritorialized to such a degree that the government no longer has sufficient control to prevent the formation of 'networks which can be used for any form of war' (Le Pen, 1995b).

Over the years, the FN has developed an increasingly elaborate range of radical and repressive proposals for dealing with the immigration issue (compare Le Pen/Front National, 1985, with FN, 1993). They start from the principle that it is legitimate and necessary for any society to protect its identity by excluding foreigners whose numbers and/or culture make them unassimilable. The proposed measures include, for example, a ban on new immigration; a ban on family regrouping; expulsion of unemployed immigrants; expulsion of immigrants convicted of criminal offences; further reform of the Nationality Code to make naturalization more difficult; restricted access to welfare, housing, etc.; quotas in schools; immigrants to be last in and first out in employment. Le Pen's 1995 election platform included the extraordinary claim that 3 million immigrants could be compulsorily repatriated in the course of a single seven-year presidential term, opening more jobs and better welfare benefits for French people (Le Pen, 1995a; Mégret, 1995). The principle of systematic privilege for French citizens over foreign residents would be enshrined in the Constitution itself by the addition to Title I, Article 2, Paragraph 1, of the words: 'It [the French Republic] applies the principle of National Preference in relations between citizens and foreigners' (Le Pen, 1995a, p. 4). However, it should be said that the FN's policy platform is not entirely focused on repression. It also includes proposals for establishing bilateral arrangements to channel aid and investment to states which cooperate with arrangements to repatriate their nationals. More generally, despite their differences on other aspects of the matter, the party shares the view held by the European Commission and other international bodies that the issue of migration needs to be tackled at source by concerted action to help the countries of origin to mitigate the causes of emigration.

Restoring Social Cohesion

Not all FN publicists are religious devotees, but from Catholic traditionalists to neo-pagans of the New Right they can make common cause in condemning the reign of hedonistic values and lamenting the decline of the sacred in French national life. Since the time of the Revolution, many Catholic traditionalists have seen secularism and dechristianization as scourges of a society which deserted its God-given vocation as Eldest Daughter of the Church. They were joined from the later nineteenth century onwards by thinkers in the manner of Taine, Maurras and Barrès, who took an instrumental view of religion as a necessary counter to the baser drives in human nature. This fitted with the moralism which has been such a constant feature of extreme right-wing thinking in France, even at the fascist end of the spectrum with its 'righteous indignation at all it deemed decadent and its zealous determination to root out sinfulness (e.g. weakness) wherever it was found' (Soucy, 1966, p. 55).

Like many of their predecessors, FN writers have blamed the philosophy of the Enlightenment for opening the ideological path towards an era of hedonistic individualism justified in the name of rights (Vial, 1991; Salvisberg, 1992). France and other Western societies are accused of treating the idea of sacredness as an archaic category of thought which has been superseded. The dominant worldview equates historical progress with the triumph of scientific and technical reason over emotion and religious superstition. The religious societies of the Middle East, Africa and Asia are regarded with disdain. Yet, argue FN writers, Western societies have reached a dead end, where material advance is matched by a vacuum of spiritual and moral values.

Echoing the eternal charges of traditionalists against the contamination of modernism within religion, harsh criticism can be directed at the church itself on the grounds that it has largely evacuated the sacred in its attempts to appease contemporary taste by updating its rites and watering down its doctrine (de Meuse and de Meuse, 1991). In the absence of a coherent set of shared moral imperatives, the decay allegedly extends to other institutions which ought to be defending the values of national community against the obsessive pursuit of individual self-gratification. Given that the family rather than the individual is the fundamental cell of the social body – to use an organic metaphor dear to the FN and its predecessors – it is seen as a disaster for France that the family has been undermined by laws encouraging abortion, divorce or cohabitation, as well as by inadequate tax and welfare provisions, with the result that the declining birth rate is preparing the way for a demographic winter (Mégret and Comités d'Action Républicaine, 1986; de Rostolan, 1987; FN, 1993; Cochet and Robinson, 1995).

Similarly, the state school system is said by the FN to be in crisis, staggering under the weight of bureaucracy and perpetrating colossal wastage of funds, undermined by politicized teachers' unions, neglecting essential skills of literacy and numeracy. Extending an earlier conspiracy theory popularized in Barrès's novel *Les Déracinés* (1988 [1897]), it is even claimed that the endless series of supposed reforms adopted by successive ministers, regardless of the political colour of the government in power, have been deliberately aimed not at improving the communication of knowledge, but at modifying pupils' values, attitudes and behaviour, while actively purveying a shapeless, multi-culturalist mishmash of 'politically correct' pseudo-knowledge to the detriment of the pupils' sense of national identity (Vial, 1993a; Gannat, 1993). The aim is to strip the pupils of their national culture and to reduce the masses to a state of mindless ignorance which makes them infinitely susceptible to manipulation. The process is therefore no less attractive to the false-right elite than it is to the left. As is often the case, the more paranoid versions of this conspiracy theory represent what is happening in France as an extension of international collusion in the creation of a 'new worldwide educational order', fostered by UNESCO, the UN, the OECD, the Council of Europe, the European Commission and other bodies committed to globalism (Pichon, 1993; Bernardin, 1996a, 1996b; Roy, 1996a).

Outside education the malaise extends to architecture, the arts and entertainment (analysed, for example, in Le Gallou, 1991). Although state budgets and those of local government bodies have never been higher for supporting the arts, the problem perceived by the FN is summarized in its 1993 manifesto under the claim that 'culture which is rooted and situated in French history' has been replaced by 'global, mass culture' (FN, 1993, p. 88). Again, it is a case of quasi-conspiracy through the misuse of bureaucratic selection processes and patronage to exclude works which reflect national values and traditions, so that authentically French culture is reduced to the status of a historical curio found in heritage sites.

The question of law and order follows similar lines. Having posited the existence of a general climate of moral decay, the FN has an underlying explanation for the terrifying crime statistics which it con-stantly brandishes at the public (for instance, in FN, 1993, pp. 277–82). The populist line is that while the discourse of human and civil rights reigns supreme, the real rights of respectable citizens are violated, often violently, by thugs. At the same time, it is claimed, the powers of the judiciary and the police are systematically undermined, as they are given neither the resources nor the laws to be able to act effectively but are subjected to constant political interference. The rise of violence in the cities and suburbs as gangs of youths roam the streets makes a particularly potent symbol of social disintegration, and the fact that the pro-FN press focuses relentlessly on 'ethnic gangs' drawn from minorities allows it to convey the impression that social breakdown is primarily due to the activity of unassimilable, non-European immi-grants. In keeping with its claim that many French immigrant suburbs have become no-go areas for the French authorities, the FN has even argued that immigrant crime is a threat to national security. It should therefore be covered by defence policy. Thus, Hervé Morvan argues:

> The deliberate refusal to consider the potential problems arising from the presence of large, organized, non-indigenous populations in terms of defence is a danger, not only to the security of individuals, but also to the state's ability to exercise full sovereignty on its national soil. In time of crisis, public order is a defence issue.
>
> (1991, p. 14)

The FN's policy response to all of these evils is muscularly conservative with an authoritarian edge (Le Pen/Front National, 1985; Institut de Formation Nationale, 1991; FN, 1993; Le Pen, 1995a; and the series of interviews by spokespersons in *National hebdo* during the early months of 1995). The assumption is that there is a need to restore strong codes of behaviour, clear social duties, and firm social bonds underpinned by effective laws. Restoration of traditional morality and the integrity of the patriarchal family are to be encouraged by fiscal measures and an income for mothers of large families who choose to stay at home. Abortion would be banned and relentless struggle against AIDS would express the war against moral depravity. The activities of militant 'right-to-life' activists in the US are frequently reported with approval in *Présent* and other periodicals controlled by the Catholic traditionalist wing of the FN.

Support for private Catholic schooling and for the principle of parental choice, operated through a system of education vouchers, also figures prominently in FN programmes. For state education, the stress is on restoration of discipline, competitive ranking of pupils, return to grammar and basic skills, coupled with teaching of France's national history and national values. Likewise, in the arts and entertainment, financial support from central and local government would be for work which was identifiably rooted in French traditions, work which cele-brated French history, and work which reflected the particularities of the different regions of the country. Measures relating to art teaching, the restoration of the purity of the French language, the promotion of French folk culture, the renaming of streets, or the institution of new public holidays on major historical anniversaries all tend in the direc-tion of cultural nationalism.

As for the field of public security, the FN has a vast, and extremely expensive, array of measures. The general principle is that law and order would be restored, with ruthless suppression of violent crime, stiffer prison terms, modernization of penal facilities and restoration of the death penalty for many categories of murder, terrorism, serious drug dealing or international racketeering. The judiciary and the police would receive additional manpower and other resources, as well as better conditions of service. Aside from other measures to reduce the presence and the geographical concentrations of immigrants, the perception of the threat to civil order as a defence issue also leads to arguments for a dense network of military reserve units to support the gendarmerie (as well as providing armed resistance in the event of foreign invasion) (Verdier, 1991).

Social Well-being, Prosperity and Sustainability

The critique of contemporary values extends to the FN's attack on the deficiencies of France's economic system. It is not merely an issue of success and efficiency, as measured in terms of indicators such as GDP or rates of growth. Here, as in other areas, the FN has remained broadly consistent with earlier incarnations of the extreme right, albeit with some modification. From the time when the pace of industrialization began to increase in the mid-nineteenth century, the various currents of the extreme right habitually reserved their harshest attacks for those who preached socialism or communism. Nevertheless, Catholic traditionalists, neo-Bonapartist nationalists and eventually fascists had their own, somewhat equivocal versions of anti-capitalism. Publicists of the extreme right voiced concern for the lack of moral conscience, the social divisiveness and the alienation fostered by unbridled liberal capitalism, especially when plutocracy could be linked to international finance, which it often associated with Jews. They protested on behalf of the small people – the small businessmen, the shopkeepers, the artisans, the peasant farmers and the labourers – who were marginalized, uprooted, expropriated or treated as mere tools of production. The extreme right was proud to describe its ideology as social, in the sense of being concerned by the problems of the lower middle and working classes under modern capitalism. Some elements even used the label 'socialist', although this did not mean a commitment to egalitarian redistribution of wealth or collective ownership. Private ownership of the means of production, distribution and exchange remained sacrosanct, but the extreme right tended in varying degrees to favour a corporatist 'third way' between socialism and free-market capitalism.

Nowadays, although there are still currents in the party which favour the latter approach, the FN's official line is somewhat different. It pays homage to the spirit of pioneering nineteenth-century social theorists and campaigners such as René de La Tour du Pin, Frédéric Le Play and Albert de Mun. It applauds the Action Française theorists of corporatism and the attempt to put those ideas into practice under the Vichy regime. But it takes the Vichy experiment as a demonstration of the dangers of technocracy inherent in corporatism, and no longer puts it forward as a viable solution for the future (Gannat, 1990). From the late 1970s to the late 1980s the FN was quick to catch the ideological tide of neo-liberalism sweeping across from the US and Britain. It incessantly attacked the technocratic, statist economic policies of the left and the soft right on the grounds that they were destroying the economy by means of a political, regulatory and fiscal straitjacket on businesses and returns. It proclaimed the virtues of free-market economics: enterprise, dynamism, risk taking, individual initiative, free competition, wholesale privatization of nationalized industries and services, deregulation, lower taxes and contributions (especially for large families), reduction of public spending, budgetary rigour, promotion of private health insurance and pensions – these were the watchwords (for the party's economic programme at that time, see Le Pen/Front National, 1985, pp. 61–96). The moralistic side of the party's thinking was not entirely absent, however, and it centred on one of the most durable of all conservative beliefs – namely, that possession of property encourages habits of social responsibility, provident behaviour and saving. The extension of property ownership was to be achieved, on the one hand, by the sale of social housing to tenants at preferential prices in the manner of the Thatcher government's policy in Britain. On the other hand, the privatization of public sector firms would not be a straightforward sale of public assets, but would involve distribution of 70 per cent of the shares free of charge to French families in proportion to the number of members in each case – part of the intention being to reward those who had shown their commitment to the nation's future by producing children.

As Hans-Georg Betz (1994, pp. 127–9) points out, the FN's position was modified during the early 1990s in the light of the party's concerns regarding the erosion of national solidarity. In fact, Le Pen (1989b, pp. 127–8) had already been arguing in the late 1980s that government should correct the effects of the free market when they threatened social cohesion. In their denunciations of moral decay in contemporary society, FN writers have matched their attacks on left-wing statism with a critique of the soulless destructiveness of American-style, speculative capitalism (Lefranc, 1991b, 1992; Gannat, 1992). They lament the fact that economic considerations are given precedence over all others, imposing the logic of profit as a universal yardstick, so that society itself is reduced to a market. Social bonds dissolve amid enormous disillusionment as everything and everyone is rated in economic terms. From the philosophical standpoint, it is argued that the economy needs to be restored to its proper function of serving society in subordination to higher political and social goals, not the other way round. Nevertheless, the counter-examples of the Soviet bloc and of statist, social democratic France can be taken to show that the economic sphere has its own laws which must be respected. No prosperous economy can exist without the right to property, free enterprise, free markets and the profit incentive. Just as the political sphere must be freed from the economic, the economy must be freed from the stranglehold of the state in order to work effectively.

Therefore, the FN claims to balance the necessity for political oversight with rejection of the statist approach (FN, 1993; Le Pen, 1995b). The party still stands for giving maximal autonomy within the public sector, reducing bureaucracy and waste, denationalizing firms in the competitive sectors (still including distribution of free shares to French families), deregulating the economy, and limiting the role of trade unions. Popular capitalism and extension of home ownership would be promoted. Small businesses and small farms are given particular prominence in the FN's policies, since they are defined both in economic terms as essential to the nation's prosperity, and in a traditionalist social perspective as ethnically rooted communities of work. Hence, besides the channelling of state and local government financial aid to small and medium-sized producers, rather than to the large conglomerates which undercut them, the party argues for a range of measures such as tax concessions, and a system for increasing access to investment capital and to loans at favourable rates of interest. The ubiquitous solution of reducing the immigrant population and restricting immigrants' access to welfare benefits is presented as a key to lower unemployment, financing improved access for French families to low-cost housing, and allowing increases in welfare benefits and state pensions for French citizens. By reducing the burden of immigration and unemployment carried by the state, the consequent reduction in charges levied on employers would allow the minimum wage to be raised for the benefit of the low paid. The elimination of damaging competition by immigrants for France's economic resources will be matched by protectionist policies to reconquer domestic markets which have been lost to foreign imports (discussed later in this chapter).

Since the later 1980s, in keeping with its claim to reconcile a restoration of civilized moral and social values with improvements in economic efficiency, the FN has adopted a modern-looking approach to environmental issues. It ties in with the thinking of the New Right, makes an appeal to the young, and offers possible opportunities for extending influence through contact with environmentalist groups. At the same time the FN claims that environmentalism, correctly understood, is essentially conservative (Le Pen, 1989b; Constans, 1990b). The party's standpoint on the question evokes the Barresian emphasis on cultural and territorial rootedness. It also fits with the FN's stance on protection of French agriculture (FN, 1993, pp. 194–211; Martinez, 1995), especially the peasant smallholding and the rural way of life which the traditionalist right has always regarded as a repository of time-honoured values such as hard work, continuity and stewardship – themes which had been endlessly reworked in nineteenth-century writings against the effects of the industrial revolution, and which had later formed central planks of the Vichy regime's reactionary vision of National Revolution.

The FN's position is that the political debate about protection of nature has been falsely reduced to two extremes: on one side, the virtuous greens, with their ideal of ending progress and returning to a state of nature; on the other side, the heartless predators who want technological and economic progress at any price. The dichotomy is false, it is argued (Mégret, 1990b). The greens have an ideology based on a retrograde, romantic conception of nature borrowed from Rousseau, which confuses science with utopian fantasy. This must be opposed with a lucid view which acknowledges that man necessarily imposes his mark on nature because he is a creator of culture. However, man needs to be aware of his place as part of the natural order. This requires a determined effort to restore balances and move away from unbridled productivism. To face the technocrats, the statist socialists, the urban developers, the big business lobbies, and all those who indiscriminately disfigure the natural or human environment, it is essential to rediscover an ethics and aesthetics of life, and a long-term perspective, allowing the individual to rediscover his roots and his identity as a member of a community bonded to a particular site (Chossat, 1990).

In policy terms this means, for example, favouring alternative, renewable energy sources. It means promoting modern public transport systems to reduce dependence on motor vehicles in cities. It entails strict controls on air, water and land pollution, as well as stricter protection of fauna, flora, waterways, shorelines and sites of natural beauty. Polluters will be made to pay and new legislation will bring a range of offences under the criminal code. It requires tighter planning controls enforced by a new inspectorate with real powers. It demands wider public consultation on urban schemes and infrastructure projects. None of this is especially controversial, but it is not impossible that the pseudo-scientific racism formerly preached by the extreme right, including the New Right in the 1970s, still lingers under the surface. For example, in *Identité* 7 (1990), which was devoted to ecology, three of the four substantive articles, as well as Le Pen's editorial, cited Dr Alexis Carrel, winner of the Nobel Prize for Medicine in 1912, as one of their intellectual precursors in this area. Although there was no direct reference to the fact, the writers were presumably aware that Carrel's views on the ecology of the nation had included the application of eugenics (as well as euthanasia for serious criminals) as a means of maintaining the quality of the stock and creating a hereditary biological aristocracy (Bonnafé and Tort, 1992; Cambier, 1995). There is something a little sinister even in the FN's 1993 manifesto, when its authors blithely declare: 'We are attached to our identity and our country, we are the defenders of our patrimony in the broadest sense of the term: biological, cultural and natural' (1993, p. 111).

Towards the Sixth Republic

In matters of government, the extreme right has a history of authoritarianism and elitism. It has been contemptuous of parliamentary democracy, especially when the political system allowed Parliament to dominate government at the expense of the head of state, as was the case under the Third and Fourth Republics. Some currents of thought have been hostile to any form of electoral democracy, on the grounds that the future of the state should not be at the mercy of a primitive numerical calculation of majority opinion among the ill-informed masses. From the time of the Revolution onwards, the traditionalist current held up an idealized and purified vision of monarchy as a model for France if only the country would free itself of the aberrant legacy of the Revolution. It was assumed that the legislative as well as the executive functions of government should be centred on the monarch, whose duty it was to take appropriate advice from individuals or from bodies of counsellors and to consult with intermediary bodies –

professional, religious, cultural and other associations. In that sense the monarch would be a dictator, as Maurras acknowledged, though it was the monarch's duty to respect the traditional rights, freedoms and customs of the people. Failing a restoration of the monarchy, tradition-alists would settle for an uncrowned head of state, as they did for Marshal Pétain in 1940. At the same time, many representatives of this current were hostile to the highly centralized administrative system which had been set in place during the Revolution and consolidated by Napoleon I. They believed that the power of the head of state as guardian of higher national interests should be counterbalanced by administrative decentralization, to restore a considerable degree of local autonomy in the provinces under their own assemblies. Among the many ironies associated with the Vichy regime was the fact that it was pledged to a Maurrassian conception of provincial decentralization, but as it evolved from authoritarian towards totalitarian rule it effected the very opposite.

Characteristically, the type of system favoured by the neo-Bonapartist current looked more modern, more pragmatic and more populist. But it was no less hostile to parliamentary rule, which it often represented as a confidence trick whereby the people – the mass of decent, patriotic citizens who constituted the real nation – were manipulated and deluded by professional politicians. It still required a strong head of state in control of the executive and legislative functions, but neo-Bonapartists could accommodate easily enough to the principle of a strong, elective presidency. Many also admired the Napoleonic practice of using popular consultations in the form of plebiscites to seek public ratification of constitutional changes. A Parliament, however elected, was not unacceptable as long as its powers were strictly limited in relation to those of the head of state and the government. At the authoritarian extreme, where neo-Bonapartism prefigured or shaded into fascism, it might imply little more than window dressing to mask dictatorship. At the more liberal end of the neo-Bonapartist continuum lay the type of conception which informed the institutions of the Fifth Republic, founded by Charles de Gaulle. Although some representa-tives of the neo-Bonapartist current, such as Barrès, favoured a greater or lesser degree of administrative decentralization, others did not see it as a matter of concern. Even if they felt a commitment to cultural regionalism and the idea of social *enracinement*, many were strongly attracted by the centralized, hierarchical Napoleonic state.

Operating under the Fifth Republic as it has developed since 1958, the FN has found itself in a very different political system from its nationalist predecessors under the Third and Fourth Republics. The primacy of the executive over the legislature has been maintained since de Gaulle's time. Directly elected since 1962, the presidency itself remains the principal seat of governmental power. Conversely, successive decentralization reforms since the early 1980s have produced a massive devolution of political, economic and other powers to local government institutions. This situation, added to the fact that the FN wishes to distance itself from the authoritarian, anti-democratic associations of its predecessors, has led the party to adopt a somewhat contorted ideological posture, which nevertheless enables it to claim that it is more, not less democratic than the mainstream parties. By the mid-1990s it was claiming to represent the march towards a new Sixth Republic.

We have already seen that the FN has retained the practice of vilifying the mainstream political parties and other sets of political actors presumed to be conniving with them at the nation's expense. The charge is summarized in the claim: 'The French People have been progressively deprived of their right of expression by the technocratic bureaucracy, the parties of the Gang of 4, the pressure groups and the media' (Le Pen, 1995a, p. 10). Governments are castigated for incompetence and for their willingness to delegate the execution of policies to a caste of civil servants who are unaccountable to the public. Parliament is condemned for failing to exercise its duty of vigilant surveillance of the executive and for failing to carry out effective scrutiny of national budgets. Similar charges of incompetence, irresponsibility and abuse of power are levelled at local government. The FN has denounced the practice whereby individual politicians are permitted to hold two or even three elective offices at the same time. The waves of corruption scandals which came to light in the early 1990s provided further ammunition for the FN in its claim to be the only clean party.

On the other hand, although it has argued that the present degree of executive dominance over the legislature is excessive, and although it has called in somewhat vague terms for revitalizing parliament in matters of budgetary scrutiny and fully restoring its ability to initiate legislation, the FN has made no fundamental critique of the principle and extensive powers of the directly elected presidency. To that extent it has remained faithful to the extreme right's allegiance to strong leadership. Indeed, it is striking that the internal organization of the FN itself operates on top-down, authoritarian lines, whatever the party's democratic pretensions for the political system of the country as a whole (Marcus, 1995). The charismatic, autocratic personality of Jean-Marie Le Pen has encouraged a leadership cult, and there is some evidence that many militants favour a dictatorship or a monarchy in preference to a republican system (Birenbaum, 1992, p. 324).

Be that as it may, democratic principle coincides with self-interest in the FN's long-standing demand for proportional representation in parliamentary elections – a system which brought enormous benefit to the party when it was used for the 1986 election, and corresponding disaster when it was replaced by the old system of single-member constituencies for the elections of 1988. Furthermore, harking back to a proposal which had figured in some conservative electoral pro-grammes under the Third Republic, such as that of the Fédération Républicaine in the 1930s, the FN advocates multiple votes for parents in proportion to the number of children in the family – family size being taken as an indicator of social responsibility and, no doubt, conservatism. On its populist platform, betting on the potential suscep-tibility of sufficient numbers of people to its own values and attitudes should the proposals ever be enacted, the party advocates not only extension of the use of referenda by presidential initiative, but also Swiss-style national and local referenda by popular demand, which it advertises as a means of giving the people a real voice in the face of the Establishment on matters such as taxation, immigration, abortion or the death penalty (Blot and Club de l'Horloge, 1989; FN, 1993; Le Pen, 1995a). Reduction in the number of layers of local government and in the length of local electoral mandates also ties into the demand for greater transparency and responsiveness in political processes.

A range of other measures are aimed at settling scores with particular sets of enemies. Closure of the Ecole Nationale d'Administration is intended to destroy one of the training grounds for future members of the cosy political/administrative Establishment. Legislation would be passed to curb the role of trade unions. The allocation of grants to pressure groups would be reviewed to eliminate those which did not clearly serve the public interest as the FN construes it. The Constitution would be amended to include provisions relating to radio and television – including the right of all political tendencies to fair allocation of broadcasting time and the right of immediate reply to attacks. The Pleven and Gayssot Laws against incitement to racial hatred and against denial of the Holocaust would be repealed, on the grounds that they infringed the principle of freedom of opinion and were used for 'the repression of national ideas' (FN, 1993, p. 403; see also Constans, 1990c; de Meuse, 1990b).

Resistance to Absorption and Eclipse

As we have seen, the FN presents itself as the force of national revitalization in response to the debilitation of the national community. Revitalization means the reassertion of control – control over what happens within France's confines, of course, but also over what enters from outside and over what leaves from within. The obsession with internal decay is matched by fears concerning the erosion of France's power as an international actor. However, in this area as in others, the FN's approach to foreign policy is not purely negative. It claims to offer strength and renewal. Interestingly, the historical exemplar to whom its theorists sometimes refer is none other than Charles de Gaulle, despite the extreme right's traditional resentment towards the general in the light of his 'sell-out' of French Algeria in 1962, as well as his earlier role in the destruction of the Vichy regime and the post-war purges of collaborators.

Not surprisingly, the FN has never supported the idea that France should become a component of a fully federated European superstate. But this is not to say that the party has been hostile to all forms of European organization. As the self-proclaimed defender of identities, it purports to stand for a European Europe, just as it does for a French France. Its intellectuals have persistently expounded the nobility of the common European heritage of culture and civilization, with France as its epitome (for example, Mégret, 1989; Bardet, 1991; Blot, 1993). Their elation at the collapse of the Soviet bloc was motivated partly by the hope that Europe as a whole, West and East, would at last discover its strength and forge a new collective role in the world once it was liberated from the tutelage of the two post-war superpowers (Morvan, 1990b; Lefranc, 1990b; anticipated in Le Pen, 1989a). But the party has always claimed that the supranationalist conception which underlies the progressive integration of what has now become the European Union is unacceptable in principle and damaging in practice. The FN conjures up the threat of homogenization in every sphere under a centralized governmental and administrative system that annihilates the specificities of the member states and dissolves the national identities of their citizens. Inevitably, the parties of the French Establishment are accused by the FN of selling out French sovereignty and French economic interests to Brussels. Brussels, in turn, is charged with selling out European interests to the United States. It is an aspect of the conspiracy to destroy the nation as part of the cosmopolitan, globalist project for the future (Martinez, 1989; Milloz, 1989; Morvan, 1990; Martin, 1993).

Thus, part of the complaint against the EU centres on the claim that it aims not only to abolish internal frontiers, but also to abandon meaningful external frontiers as well. In the economic sphere, as interpreted by the FN, the development of international free trade serves as a vehicle for American economic expansionism and for the development of the world as a single space traversed by flows of products, services and people under the surveillance of a universal superstate. FN publicists preached against the GATT agreement on the grounds that no state, or group of states, should have international free trade imposed on it against its interests. Just as the FN wants to protect French workers from immigrant competition on classical nationalist lines harking back to the late nineteenth century, so it also wants to protect French products and services by means of trade barriers. However, its central line is that the existence of the Single European Market means that these barriers now have to be around the EU as a whole. The notion of community preference at European level is intended to parallel the notion of national preference within the French nation state. Even so, although it is not official party policy, one of the FN's leading theorists, Jean-Yves Le Gallou (1993), has argued for a gradual introduction of protectionist measures at national level and for a shift towards bilateral trading agreements, which would imply withdrawal from the Single European Market.

As regards the political dimension of the EU, the FN argues for the primacy of cooperation over integration. It calls for a Europe of nations, with each nation remaining firmly rooted in its own culture. Nevertheless, the FN's preference for a loose confederation, which should eventually extend to Eastern as well as Western Europe, allows for coordination in the fields of defence, economic protection, anti-terrorism and, of course, barriers to third world immigrants. With the FN having ten Members of the European Parliament from 1984 onwards, statements made during the mid- and late-1980s were not always negative on the subject of European integration in particular fields, and were often equivocal on the question of how much sovereignty should be pooled or in what form. For example, the party's 1985 manifesto referred sweepingly to the need for a common currency, a common anti-terrorist police force and court, and a common foreign policy and defence capacity (LePen/Front National, 1985, p. 191; and see Le Pen, 1989a, 1989b). Later, under threat of being outflanked by anti-integrationist elements of the more orthodox right and sections of the left in the wake of the Maastricht and GATT debates, the discourse hardened (FN, 1993; Le Pen, 1995a). The emphasis was placed primarily on denouncing the technocratic power of the European Commission and calling for its abolition, pointing to the dangers arising from the Schengen agreement (allowing in huge flows of immigrants and criminals), and calling for the Maastricht treaty to be scrapped and for Europe to withdraw from the GATT agreements. The need for restoring France's national sovereignty by reasserting the primacy of French law over international law has likewise become a theme in the party's discourse.

In addition to other charges against the EU, the FN accuses it of betraying European security interests in pursuit of the perverse, globalist utopia of an integrated European defence community under American tutelage. Defence and security issues have always been a major preoccupation for French nationalists, given that their perception of international relations reflects a combination of social Darwinism and *Realpolitik*. Indeed, the emergence of nationalism as an identifiable right-wing phenomenon had been closely linked to a burning sense of humiliation in the wake of their country's catastrophic defeat in the Franco-Prussian War of 1870–1. The obsession with French military fragility in the face of foreign threats and with the ever-present risk of betrayal by fifth columnists has remained constant since that time.

The FN has sustained the tradition of scenting weakness and betrayal in the face of unprecedented dangers to France's international position. Prior to the collapse of the Soviet bloc, the FN was preoccupied with the threat from that direction. Behind the slogan, 'Neither red nor dead, but French and alive', it pointed relentlessly to the supposed inadequacies of France's military capability, while arguing that the European Community should take primary responsibility for its own defence by creating a unified command structure, developing its own nuclear and conventional strategy, and pooling national forces so that the Community would function as a distinct entity within NATO (Le Pen/Front National, 1985; Le Pen, 1989a, 1989b).

In the 1990s the FN has anticipated that threats might arise from the instability of Russia and Eastern Europe (including states with nuclear arms), but above all from the Islamic countries of North Africa and the Middle East (many with massive conventional arsenals and potential access to nuclear and/or chemical weapons) driven by religious fanaticism, economic deprivation and explosive demographic conditions. Meanwhile, in France's overseas territories and in former colonies within the French sphere of influence, the perceived danger is that internal subversion by native groups may play into the hands of foreign powers which have ambitions to absorb the territories into their own spheres of influence. FN writers conclude that France needs to obey what Bruno Mégret – sounding like a cross between de Gaulle and Nietzsche – has called 'the imperative of power' (1991, title of article). Yet successive French governments are deemed to have starved the defence budgets and failed to define a coherent role for the armed forces. The deficiencies of France's performance in the Gulf War of 1991 have been held up as testimony to the lack of adequate equipment or properly trained manpower (FN, 1993, pp. 306–7) – this, notwithstanding Le Pen's opposition to the war itself (Marcus, 1995, pp. 122–4; Hainsworth, 1996; and see Peltier, 1996b, for an account of Le Pen's protests against American aggression, the New World Order, etc., during a friendship visit to Saddam Hussein in May 1996).

Since the end of the Cold War the FN's anti-Americanism has led it to favour a European military alliance and Security Council outside, and in place of, NATO. The aim would be to remove Europe from American hegemony by collectively building the alliance's level of armaments to that of a superpower. Even so, the FN places particular stress on building up France's own military capability and on developing an assertively independent foreign policy (du Verdier, 1991; FN, 1993; Mégret, 1993). Among other things, this means pushing defence budgets to the equivalent of 4–5 per cent of GDP. It means developing and testing new, miniaturized nuclear weapons for anti-personnel use. It means creating a rapid reaction force for overseas operations. It means new aircraft carriers, new submarines, and a modernized airforce with at least 400 combat aircraft. It means improving radar cover along the Mediterranean and developing an anti-missile defence system. It means well-paid, professional armed forces in place of conscription. It means a new military organization for sealing France's frontiers against immigration. It means a coherent civil defence programme.

These and other measures would be the buttress for a foreign policy aimed, in effect, at restoring France's international influence by revitalizing relationships in all those parts of the world where it was a major actor in its days as an imperial power. Despite its eagerness to follow the New Right in attacking the ideological, economic and cultural neo-colonialism practised by the United States (Gannat, 1994; Lefranc, 1994), the FN has every wish to see France strengthen its own political, economic and cultural hold on its remaining overseas territories and to extract maximum advantage from their locations. For example, small though they are, the FN sees its islands in the South Pacific as vital strategic cards in the power game which will unfold there. Aside from their value as military and logistical bases, they also allow France a direct presence in the part of the world which is predicted to become the hub of economic and commercial activity for the future. The theory is that by re-establishing itself as a great power outside Europe, France will ensure its role as a great power within Europe.

Conclusion

As a producer and communicator of ideology, the FN has shown enormous vitality. The sheer volume of production is massive and the quality of argument is not conspicuously inferior to that of intellectuals belonging to different ideological families. As with any body of ideological writings, of course, there are plentiful contradictions between different elements within and between particular texts – not least, the clash between liberal, illiberal and anti-liberal components in the system of ideas. There are many areas in which the principles and the policies remain vague. The same is true of the FN's broad-brush attempts to explain how its proposals would be financed. For example, would the expulsion of 3 million immigrants in the space of seven years really prove an unalloyed economic blessing for the long term, let alone for the immediate period of transition? Yet the FN's effort to push its way towards the forefront of the French political stage has owed much of its energy to the fact that it could offer an apparently cogent analysis of the nation's problems, and an increasingly comprehensive range of solutions. The process has been dynamic, since political drive and ideological self-confidence feed on each other. At a time when other ideologies were crumbling or insufficiently attuned to the concerns of substantial sections of French society, the FN's brand of national populism could be presented as both traditional and modern, conservative and radical.

From any political standpoint to the left of it, the party's increasing appeal is a distressing symptom of profound malaise in French society, not a solution to France's problems. The FN's programmes cater to popular anxieties at a time of collective uncertainty. They single out particular groups as deliberate or unwitting instruments of damage to the nation's identity, cohesion and material well-being. They postulate the existence of conspiracies or at least objective collusion between domestic and external forces which are responsible for the nation's debasement. Their political mythology locates the present historical moment as the culmination of a period of decline, but they offer the promise of salvation. Of course, the promise is conditional. If the nation will recognize the validity of national populist answers to the questions which have to be asked, it will be capable of renewal. If it undergoes renewal, it will be able to accept the imperative of power. If the nation fails to do these things, catastrophe awaits in the form of disintegration, submersion and absorption.

It is a fact that the FN has made a successful effort to regenerate the ideological tradition of the extreme right, while remodelling it in ways which offer at least partial defence against those who wish to damn it by association with the failures and excesses of its predecessors. Short of a significant ideological renewal on the left, which appears unlikely in the short to medium term, the major threat to the FN would probably arise from further repositioning of the orthodox right to take up more of the party's ideological ground on issues such as immigration, direct democracy, reduction of unemployment, strong policies on law and order, and a forceful stance in the name of French national interests in foreign policy. The problem is that this type of strategy could easily backfire by giving further credibility to the FN itself. Whatever the case, the mainstream parties have yet to regain sufficient ideological vitality to be able to drive national populism back to the margins.

References

Adler, F. (1995) 'Racism, *Différence* and the Right in France'. *Modern and Contemporary France* NS 4 (3), 439–51.

Assouline, F. and Bellet, R. (1990) 'Pas antisémites? Voici ce qu'ils écrivent'. *L'Evénement du jeudi*, 17–23 May, pp. 18–19.

Bardet, J.-C. (1989) 'Le Totalitarisme larvé'. *Identité* 1, 18–21.

Bardet, J.-C. (1991) 'L'Identité française'. *Identité* 13, 9–14.

Bardet, J.-C. (1994) 'Un projet pour la nation'. *Identité* 21, 5–8, 34.

Bariller, D. and Timmermans, F. (1993) *20 ans au Front: l'histoire vraie du Front national*. Paris: Editions Nationales.

Barrès, M. (1988 [1897]) *Les Déracinés*. Paris: Gallimard/Folio.

Bernardin, P. (1996a) *Machiavel pédagogue*. Paris: Notre-Dame des Grâces.

Bernardin, P. (1996b) 'L'Ecole nulle, c'est fait exprès', interview with M.-C. Roy. *National hebdo*, 18–24 April.

Betz, H.-G. (1994) *Radical Right-Wing Populism in Western Europe*. Basingstoke: Macmillan.

Billig, M. (1979) *Fascists: A Social Psychological View of the National Front*. London: Harcourt Brace Jovanovich.

Birenbaum, G. (1992) *Le Front national en politique*. Paris: Balland.

Blot, Y. (1991a) 'Baroque et politique'. *Identité* 12, 28–32.

Blot, Y. (1991b) 'L'Imposture américaine'. *Identité* 14, 30–2, 34.

Blot, Y. (1992a) 'Contre la bureaucratie mondiale'. *Identité* 16, 9–12.

Blot, Y. (1992b) 'Gnose et orthodoxie'. *Identité* 17, 29–32.

Blot, Y. (1993) 'La France et l'Europe'. *Identité* 18, 15–18.

Blot, Y. and Club de l'Horloge (1989) *La Démocratie confisquée*. Paris: Jean Picollec.

Bonnafé, L. and Tort, P. (1992) *L'Homme, cet inconnu? Alexis Carrel, Jean-Marie Le Pen et les chambres à gaz.* Paris: Syllepse.

Bourseiller, C. (1991) *Extrême Droite. L'Enquête.* Paris: François Bourin.

Bresson, G. and Lionet, C. (1994) *Le Pen: biographie.* Paris: Seuil.

Brys, J. (1989) 'La Montée de la droite nationale en Europe'. *Identité* 1, 16–17.

Cabantous, M. (1990) 'Deux Cultures incompatibles'. *Identité* 6, 9–15.

Cambier, J.-P. (1995) 'Alexis Carrel: un médecin aux ordonnances tachées de brun', in Collectif *Lyon, capitale du négationnisme?* Villeurbanne: Golias, pp. 7–16.

Camus, J.-Y. (1989) 'Origine et formation du Front national (1972–1981)', in N. Mayer and P. Perrineau (eds) *Le Front national à découvert.* Paris: Presses de la Fondation Nationale des Sciences Politiques, pp. 17–36.

Camus, J.-Y. (1995) 'L'Internationale brune se municipalise'. *L'Evénement du jeudi,* 22–28 June, p. 22.

Castagne, B. (1989) 'IXèmes Journées d'Amitié française'. *Identité* 1, 31.

Chebel d'Appollonia, A. (1988) *L'Extrême-droite en France. De Maurras à Le Pen.* Brussels: Complexe.

Chombeau, C. (1995) 'Le FN veut s'appuyer sur des syndicats et des associations "amies" '. *Le Monde,* 28 December.

Chossat, B. (1990) 'L'Homme et la terre'. *Identité* 7, 19–22.

Cochet, J. and Robinson, C. (1995) 'Le Pen à Lyon: pour la famille'. *Présent,* 11 April.

Collectif [J.-P. Cambier *et al.*] (1995) *Lyon, capitale du négationnisme?.* Villeurbanne: Golias.

Constans, R. (1990a) 'La Nomenklatura politique'. *Identité* 5, 17–20.

Constans, R. (1990b) 'Le Matérialisme, ennemi de l'environnement'. *Identité* 7, 10–14.

Constans, R. (1990c) 'De l'antifascisme à l'antiracisme'. *Identité* 9, 10–14.

Duranton-Crabol, A.-M. (1988) *Visages de la Nouvelle Droite: le GRECE et son histoire.* Paris: Presses de la Fondation Nationale des Sciences Politiques.

Etchegoin, M.-F. (1987) 'Ceux qui ne désarment pas'. *Le Nouvel Observateur,* 25 September–1 October, pp. 38–9.

FN (Front National) (1993) *300 mesures pour la renaissance de la France. Programme de gouvernement.* Paris: Editions Nationales.

Gannat, P. (1990) 'La Tradition sociale de la droite'. *Identité* 10, 5–8.

Gannat, P. (1992) 'Ni libéralisme ni dirigisme'. *Identité* 17, 10–13.

Gannat, P. (1993) 'Pédagogie ou idéologie?'. *Identité* 19, 13–16.

Gannat, P. (1994) 'Le Nouveau Visage du colonialisme'. *Identité* 22, 18–21.

Gaucher, R. (ed.) (1991) *SOS-hystérie: les anti-Le Pen.* Supplement to *National hebdo.*

Gregor, C. (1990) 'L'Exclusion: une loi de la nature'. *Identité* 9, 20–2.

Hainsworth, P. (1992) 'The Extreme Right in Post-War France: The Emergence and Success of the Front National', in P. Hainsworth (ed.) *The Extreme Right in Europe and the USA.* New York: St Martin's Press, pp. 29–60.

Hainsworth, P. (1996) 'The Front National and the New World Order', in T. Chafer and B. Jenkins (eds) *France: From the Cold War to the New World Order.* Basingstoke: Macmillan, pp. 193–203.

Haudry, J. (1981) *Les Indo-Européens.* Paris: Presses Universitaires de France.

Institut de Formation Nationale (1991) *Militer au Front,* 2nd edn. Paris: Editions Nationales.

Le Chevallier, J.-M. (1989) *Immigration en Europe: attention, danger.* Paris: Groupe des Droites Européennes.

Le Chevallier, J.-M. (1994) 'Dans le sillage de l'histoire'. *Identité* 21, 13–16.

Lefranc, D. (1990a) 'La Notion d'établissement'. *Identité* 5, 5–9.

Lefranc, D. (1990b) 'Le Retour de l'Europe'. *Identité* 8, 19–23.

Lefranc, D. (1990c) 'Patriotisme = racisme?'. *Identité* 9, 5–9.

Lefranc, D. (1991a) 'La France désagrégée'. *Identité* 13, 15–19.

Lefranc, D. (1991b) 'La Dérive de l'Etat'. *Identité* 16, 5–8.

Lefranc, D. (1992) 'L'Hégémonisme économique'. *Identité* 17, 5–9.

Lefranc, D. (1994) 'Le Tiers Monde à libérer'. *Identité* 22, 13–17.

Le Gallou, J.-Y. (1988) *Le Racisme antifrançais.* Paris: G.C. Conseils.

Le Gallou, J.-Y. (1990) 'La Menace est au sud'. *Identité* **6**, 20–3.

Le Gallou, J.-Y. (1991) 'Préserver notre identité'. *Identité* **13**, 20–3.

Le Gallou, J.-Y. (1993) 'Actualité du protectionnisme'. *Identité* **20**, 17–20.

Le Gallou, J.-Y. and Club de l'Horloge (1985) *La Préférence nationale: réponse à l'immigration.* Paris: Albin Michel.

Le Gallou, J.-Y. and Olivier, P. (1992) *Immigration: le Front national fait le point.* Paris: Editions Nationales.

Legrand, G. (1989) 'La Mue socialiste'. *Identité* **4**, 9–13.

Le Pen, J.-M. (1985) *La France est de retour.* Paris: Carrère-Michel Lafon.

Le Pen, J.-M. (1989a) *L'Europe: discours et interventions, 1984–1989.* Paris: Groupe des Droites Européennes.

Le Pen, J.-M. (1989b) *L'Espoir. Entretien avec J.P. Gabriel et P. Gannat.* Paris: Albatros.

Le Pen, J.-M. (1990) 'Destabiliser l'établissement'. *Identité* **5**, 3.

Le Pen, J.-M. (1995a) *Les Priorités de Jean-Marie Le Pen,* supplement to *La Lettre de Jean-Marie Le Pen* **211**.

Le Pen, J.-M. (1995b) 'Le Pen: la nation est l'avenir de l'homme', interview with B. Racouchot and M. Plat. *National hebdo,* 26 October–1 November.

Le Pen, J.-M. (1995c) 'Le Front national récuse la qualification d'extrême droite'. *Le Monde,* 19–20 November.

Le Pen, J.-M. (1996) 'Droit de réponse'. *Le Monde,* 9–10 June 1996.

Le Pen, J.-M./Front National (1985) *Pour la France: programme du Front National.* Paris: Albatros.

Madiran, J., Wagner, G.-P. and Monnerot, J. (1995) *Le Soi-disant Antiracisme,* 4th edn, special issue of *Itinéraires.*

Marcus, J. (1995) *The National Front and French Politics.* Basingstoke: Macmillan.

Martin, T. (1993) 'Le Complot libre-échangiste'. *Identité* **20**, 5–8.

Martinez, J.-C. (1989) *Autant en emporte l'Europe.* Paris: Jean-Cyrille Godefroy.

Martinez, J.-C. (1995) 'Un million de paysans en 2002'. *National hebdo,* 9–15 March.

Mégret, B. (1989) 'L'Europe: identité et puissance'. *Identité* **1**, 12–15.

Mégret, B. (1990a) *La Flamme: les voies de la renaissance.* Paris: Robert Laffont.

Mégret, B. (1990b) 'L'Ecologisme contre l'écologie'. *Identité* **7**, 5–9.

Mégret, B. (1991) 'L'Impératif de puissance'. *Identité* **14**, 5–9.

Mégret, B. (1993) 'Une vision pour la France'. *Identité* **18**, 19–22.

Mégret, B. (1995) 'Rapatrier trois millions d'immigrés en douceur', interview with J. Roberto. *National hebdo,* 16–22 February.

Mégret, B. and Comités d'Action Républicaine (1986) *L'Impératif du renouveau: les enjeux de demain.* Paris: Albatros.

Meuse, P. de (1989) 'La Résurgence des identités'. *Identité* **4**, 14–17.

Meuse, P. de (1990a) 'Le Déclin des Etats-Unis'. *Identité* **8**, 15–18.

Meuse, P. de (1990b) 'De l'antiracisme à l'intolérance'. *Identité* **9**, 15–19.

Meuse, P. de (1993) 'Exclusion: le piège des mots'. *Identité* **20**, 21–4.

Meuse, P. de and Meuse, C. de (1991) 'L'Eglise désacralisée'. *Identité* **12**, 18–19.

Milloz, P. (1989) 'Les Pièges de l'harmonisation européenne'. *Identité* **1**, 6–9.

Milloz, P. (1990a) *Rapport Milloz: le coût de l'immigration.* Paris: Editions Nationales.

Milloz, P. (1990b) 'Le Coût de l'immigration étrangère'. *Identité* **7**, 23–6.

Milloz, P. (1991) *Les Etrangers et le chômage en France.* Paris: Editions Nationales.

Milza, P. (1992) 'Le Front national: droite extrême ou national-populisme?', in J.-F. Sirinelli (ed.) *Histoire des droites en France,* Vol. 1. Paris: Gallimard, pp. 691–732.

Moissonnier, M. (1995) 'Hommes veillez!', in Collectif *Lyon, capitale du négationnisme?* Villeurbanne: Golias, pp. 29–42.

Morvan, H. (1990) 'L'Eurocratie contre les peuples'. *Identité* **5**, 28–31.

Morvan, H. (1990b) 'La Fin de Yalta'. *Identité* **8**, 5–9.

Morvan, H. (1991) 'La Défense intérieure'. *Identité* **14**, 14–17.

Mottin, J. (1991) 'Immigration = chômage'. *Identité* 12, 23–4, 34.

Mottin, J. (1993) 'Immigration et naturalisations'. *Identité* 18, 23–5.

Peltier, M. (1996a) 'Pourquoi les "antiracistes" s'affolent'. *National hebdo*, 28 March–3 April.

Peltier, M. (1996b) 'Le Pen à Saddam: "En vous défendant contre l'agression US, c'est nous tous que vous défendez ... " '. *National hebdo*, 30 May–5 June.

Perrineau, P. (1994) 'Le Front national: 1972–1994', in M. Winock (ed.) *Histoire de l'extrême droite*. Paris: Seuil, pp. 243–99.

Piccone, P. (ed.) (1994) *The French New Right: New Right–New Left–New Paradigm?*, special double issue of *Telos* 98–9.

Pichon, O. (1993) 'Anatomie d'un monstre'. *Identité* 19, 9–12.

Plenel, E. and Rollat, A. (1984) *L'Effet Le Pen*. Paris: La Découverte/ *Le Monde*.

Raspail, J. (1985) *Le Camp des saints*, 3rd edn. Paris: Robert Laffont.

Raspail, J. (1990) 'A la recherche des peuples perdus: entretien avec Jean Raspail', interview with N. Manceaux. *Identité* 9, 26–8.

Rémond, R. (1982) *Les Droites en France*. Paris: Aubier.

Roberto, J. (1996) '*Seven*: esbroufe pour sept crimes prétendument racistes'. *National hebdo*, 28 March–3 April.

Rollat, A. (1985) *Les Hommes de l'extrême droite: Le Pen, Marie, Ortiz et les autres*. Paris: Calmann-Lévy.

Rostolan, M. de (1987) *Lettre à mon peuple qui meurt*. Paris: Fernand Lanore.

Rousseau, C. (1989) 'La Mort des vieilles idéologies'. *Identité* 4, 5–8.

Roy, M.-C. (1996a) 'Comment les "pédagogues" mondialistes déforment nos enfants aux frais du contribuable'. *National hebdo*, 25–31 January.

Roy, M.-C. (1996b) 'La Révolution des boubous'. *National hebdo*, 28 March–3 April.

Salvisberg, C. (1992) 'La Religion de la raison'. *Identité* 16, 29–32.

Sanders, A. (1990) 'Barrès, découvreur de l'identité'. *Identité* 6, 28–30.

Sergent, B. (1982) 'Penser – et mal penser – les Indo-Européens'. *Annales ESC* 37(4), 669–81.

Sirgue, P. (1994) 'Le Peuple contre les partis'. *Identité* 21, 9–12.

Sirinelli, J.-F. (ed.) (1992) *Histoire des droites en France*, Vol. 1. Paris: Gallimard.

Soucy, R. (1966) 'The Nature of Fascism in France'. *Journal of Contemporary History* 1 (1), 27–55.

Taguieff, P.-A. (1988) *La Force du préjugé: essai sur le racisme et ses doubles*. Paris: La Découverte.

Taguieff, P.-A. (1989) 'La Nouvelle Judéophobie: antisionisme, antiracisme, anti-impérialisme'. *Les Temps modernes* 520, 7–80.

Taguieff, P.-A. (1994) *Sur la Nouvelle Droite: jalons d'une analyse critique*. Paris: Descartes.

Tristan, A. (1987) *Au Front*. Paris: Gallimard.

Verdier, J. du (1991) *Eléments de réflexion sur la défense de la France*. Paris: Editions Nationales.

Vial, P. (1990) 'L'Islam contre l'Europe'. *Identité* 6, 5–8.

Vial, P. (1991) 'Le Pouvoir sans le sacré'. *Identité* 12, 10–14.

Vial, P. (1993a) 'Les Décombres'. *Identité* 19, 5–8.

Vial, P. (1993b) 'Identité française: la Normandie'. *Identité* 20, 29–32.

Vial, P. (1994a) 'Identité française: la Lorraine'. *Identité* 21, 29–32.

Vial, P. (1994b) 'Identité française: la Provence'. *Identité* 22, 29–32.

Vial, P. and Mabire, J. (1975) *Les Solstices: histoire et actualité*. Paris: GRECE.

Vilmin, F. (1992) 'Culture et immigration'. *Identité* 17, 23–5, 34.

Weber, E. (1962) *Action Française: Royalism and Reaction in Twentieth-century France*. Stanford: Stanford University Press.

Winock, M. (1990) *Nationalisme, antisémitisme et fascisme en France*. Paris: Seuil.

Winock, M. (ed.) (1994) *Histoire de l'extrême droite en France*. Paris: Seuil.

5

Ecologism

BRENDAN PRENDIVILLE

Introduction

French ecologism has certain specific ideological features, but it also represents a link in a planetary chain. The worldwide ecologist discourse which stretches from the 'limits to growth' period of the 1970s to the 'sustainable development' of the 1990s, for example, has influenced French ecologists in much the same way as it has other national movements. Similarly, the international philosophical debate concerning nature and society represents a fundamental premise to ecologist actions. Within the French context, however, the debate has a particular resonance. The question which has haunted certain intellectuals in France since the rise of ecologism concerns what is seen as a reversal of roles between nature and culture. Is concern for the natural environment the sign of a lack of concern for the social one (Ferry, 1992)? More worrying, given that Hitler liked animals, and that the most elaborate ecologist legislation this century came out of Nazi Germany, do those who share such concerns represent a 'fifth column' at the very heart of Western civilization, with ecologists ready to trade in their green shirts for black ones? Finally, is ecologism an ideological broadside aimed at the French humanistic tradition? To address these issues with particular reference to the largest green organization, Les Verts, I will focus on three aspects of ecologism: ideological sources, values and class.

Ideological Sources of Ecologism

Romanticism

The eighteenth-century English pre-romantics, and especially the romantics who followed them, gave an impetus to the English environmental tradition which is now being recognized (Bate, 1991). The work of the poet William Wordsworth in particular produced an association between romanticism and nature which had implications for the perception of conservationism, environmentalism and ecologism far beyond the field of literature.[1] In France, Jean-Jacques Rousseau was the principal defender of the environmental faith at this time, although his political and philosophical works are his major legacy. Both forms of romanticism were forged in a time of revolution; industrial revolution in England, political revolution in France. Yet men of progress had little time for the natural order. On the contrary, Descartes and Bacon had done their best to free humankind from the constraints of this natural order so that humanity could reach a higher social order. Within the context of the nature–culture debate, the effect of these major social changes was to relegate concern over nature to a hopelessly conservative position. Even if the literary forms created by the romantics in poetry, for example, were quite revolutionary, the interest in nature, the old order, gave them a somewhat reactionary flavour, and it stuck. When ecologists began to politicize nature in the 1970s, the knee-jerk reaction to such talk was a similar one on both sides of the Channel.

As a result, perhaps the most widely held image of ecologists is that of the straw-hat brigade whose principal life support is carrot juice and who live in candle-lit communes. This image of course stems from the commune movement of the 1970s. From Jean-Jacques Rousseau complaining that trees are made to stand to attention in French gardens to contemporary advertisements for environmental countryside holidays the theme of a romanticized, clean life away from the insalubrious town is one which is at the heart of the ecologist collective consciousness.[2] Indeed, it could be seen as the starting block of the ecologist movement via the different conservationist groups whose growth accompanied industrialization in the country (Vadrot, 1978).

Coupled to this outer cleanliness is an inner one that is considered by many to be equally important, if not more so. 'Fundamental change comes from within' could be the slogan that underpins a philosophical and religious tradition incarnated in the debate between idealism and materialism. Over the centuries, materialism, no doubt, won this debate, and the 'deep' side of the ecologist movement sees as one of its tasks the (re)incorporation of idealism and more especially spirituality into human action. The excesses of this approach are to be found in the belief that social change can be brought about by an aggregate of individual consciousness-raising based on the power of intuition:

> Each of us has within himself a spark of creative power, of universal energy which can change the inner and outer world. This power ... is the result of thought processes, not just intellectual ones but those which come from deep thought, from thought of the heart. (Les Verts, 1987)[3]

Humanism

At a time when some French intellectuals are beginning to have doubts as to the real nature of ecologism (see Ferry, 1992), the debate on ecologist humanism has taken on added importance. Within the French context, it can be traced back to two sources: Ivan Illich and Emmanuel Mounier. The former is a worldwide reference in ecologist literature and direct influence, whereas the second is a more indirect influence on French ecologism.

Without Illich, ecologism would not be ecologism. He has been an inspiration for the French ecologist elite and writers over the past twenty years, from Brice Lalonde to Serge Moscovici and from André Gorz to René Dumont. He is not as well known today among activists but his work on conviviality and the theory of watersheds remains a linchpin of ecologist theory.

Conviviality has become a very fashionable term in recent years. 'Sociable and lively' is one dictionary definition, and in computer language it is synonymous with 'user-friendly'. However, in the vocabulary of Illich, 'conviviality' has a more precise meaning within the context of social organization and human relationships:

> As an alternative to technocratic disaster, I propose the vision of a convivial society. A convivial society would be the result of social arrangements that guarantee for each member the most ample and free access to the tools of the community and limit this freedom only in favour of another member's equal freedom.
>
> (Illich, 1979, p. 25)

This perspective brings together three different strands of ecologist humanism. First is the political liberalism reminiscent of humanists such as John Locke and John Stuart Mill. Second is the struggle against technocracy. Technocrats, in ecologist vocabulary, are the people who to a large extent control the destiny of society. The capitalists are deemed to have lost much of their control to this new class, which controls knowledge and technology and uses it – all too often in the minds of ecologists – at the expense of human beings' welfare. The definition in the *Petit Robert* dictionary is instructive: 'Minister or upper technical functionary who tends to focus on the technical side of a problem at the expense of its social and human consequences'. This definition gives the full dimension of the philosophical nature of the ecologists' struggle against the dehumanization they consider to be present in the politics of technocracy, be they left or right.

The third strand is visible in Illich's notion of 'tools' and its accompanying concept of autonomy (see below). The term 'tool' covers the common-sense idea of an implement used for working on something (e.g. a hammer, etc.) or the wider notion of a system and/or organization (e.g. an educational, political or economic system). A convivial society is one in which people can control the tools: 'Defence of conviviality is possible only if undertaken by the people with tools they control' (Illich, 1979, p. 125). Autonomy is a linked notion in that convivial, human-scale tools allow individuals the autonomy necessary to participate in the running of society.

The Two Watersheds Theory is a corollary of Illich's ideas on conviviality. In it he describes the process by which an institution can pass through two watersheds; the first one of efficiency and conviviality, the second one of inefficiency and harm. In Illich's opinion, most industrial tools have passed or are passing these two watersheds, and are making individuals increasingly dependent on them in the process. One example is transport: 'It has taken almost a century to pass from an era served by motorized vehicles to the era in which society has been reduced to virtual enslavement to the car' (Illich, 1979, p. 20). The rehumanization of society is synonymous, therefore, with convivial reconstruction.

The second source of French ecologist humanism is Personalism. The term was first used by the philosopher Charles-Bernard Renouvier, but has become better known in connection with a school of thought whose principal exponent was Emmanuel Mounier (1905–50), co-founder of the famous revue *Esprit* in 1932. Mounier wished to create a movement based on a doctrine of social and moral humanism which would herald a new civilization. Such a form of revolutionary humanism, in Mounier's opinion, was necessary in the face of rampant materialism (East and West) that had the effect of producing either an individualistic form of social Darwinism or a faceless, bureaucratic collectivism.

Mounier was dismayed by the incapacity of the institutionalized left to imagine anything other than the utilitarian, consumerist tools of capitalism as a model for a future socialist society. In this respect, the ecologists have taken up, virtually verbatim, ideas which have a 50-year-old history: 'the greatest trial of the 20th century will no doubt be to avoid the dictatorship of the technocrats who, be they right-wing or left-wing, forget man under the organization' (Mounier, 1985, p. 115). These prophetic words reflected the Personalists' concern over the direction which Western industrial society had taken through a form of social mechanization. This social mechanization was held responsible by Mounier for the depersonalization taking place in Western society, which led to a form of individualistic atomism. It was not a question of refusing technological progress but rather of opposing its excesses, and this directly reflects another tenet of the ecologist paradigm: the watershed theory mentioned above.

The second parallel between ecologism and Personalism concerns their respective criticisms of individualism. For Mounier, individualism was the basis of bourgeois capitalism, which he loathed, whereas respect for the individual as a person in the midst of a bureaucratic, consumerist anonymity is a constant ecologist theme. More interestingly, however, the distinction that Mounier makes between Personalism and individualism is similar to that which ecologists make between autonomy and individualism.

The concept of autonomy in ecologist discourse can be vague and is perhaps best defined with regard to what it is not. It is not separatism, whereby an individual or a region in a country decides it needs nobody's help to survive. On the contrary, autonomy considers the individual unit, be it a person, a community or a region, to be a free entity within a superior whole of which it is an integral and necessary part. 'The nature of the whole is always different from the mere sum of its parts' (Capra, 1982, p. 287) sums up this idea of individual autonomy within a free association of responsible persons. In this respect, autonomy and solidarity are inseparable (see the section on values below).

Autonomy as a Personalist and ecologist concept is translated politically and strategically in similar fashion by independence from the political power blocks: 'Neither left nor right' (Mouvement d'Ecologie Politique, 1980) was already a popular ecologist slogan in the early 1980s. For Mounier this principle had also constituted a strategic way forward: 'At least in the beginning, independence from established parties and groups is necessary to fully measure new perspectives' (1985, p. 112). This suggestion of Mounier's that an independent political line is only necessary at the outset of a movement's existence is highly interesting, given the ongoing debate within ecologist circles concerning political alliances.

A final parallel that may be drawn between the Personalist movement of the 1930s and the ecologists of today is in the field of politics. The political and social themes put forward by Mounier in his defence of Personalism strongly resemble ecologist concerns, and three examples bear this out. First, Mounier was a fervent feminist: 'The vast problem concerning the condition of women . . . it is true that our social world is made by men for men and that humanity has not massively delved into the depths of the feminine being' (1985, p. 118). The ecologists remain equally attached to the feminist movement, even if the latter is no longer as strong as it was in the 1970s. Within Les Verts, however, men have predominated (see Table 5.1). In France, as elsewhere in the Western world, men are more politically active. Therefore the male majority is no surprise. However, the gender imbalance within the membership has had a bearing on ecologist discourse. The French ecologists gave less emphasis during the 1980s to feminism and eco-feminism than, for example, their German counterparts did, and this difference in emphasis is reflected in these figures.[4] More recently, the situation may have been changing within Les Verts following the departure of Antoine Waechter, the former spokesman of the party, in 1994. The ecologist candidate for the presidential elections of 1995 was a woman (Dominique Voynet), as is the only ecologist president of a regional council (Marie-Christine Blandin) at the time of writing.

Table 5.1 Gender divide within Les Verts

	1988 (%)	1989 (%)	1990 (%)
Men	74.6	70	72.6
Women	25.4	27	27.4
No response		3	
Total	100	100	100

Source: Prendiville, 1994

Second, Mounier considered that federalism was an answer to many of the world's problems in a similar way to ecologists' support for political decentralization. Finally, he took a firm stand, as do ecologists, against ethnocentrism and racism: 'equality amongst persons excludes, obviously, any form of racism and xenophobia ... there is not one culture next to which all other activity is ignorant but as many diverse cultures as there are activities' (1985, pp. 119, 124). Personalism, therefore, is very much a philosophical forerunner to the ecologist movement, and both ecologists and Personalists recognize as much (Allan Michaud, 1979, pp. 1013–15).

Authoritarianism

On a potentially more worrying note, the authoritarian undertones within ecologist discourse have been evident on various occasions:

> I await the arrival of a world government which can oppress populations in order to reduce pollution of all types as well as to change desires and behaviour by psychological manipulation.
>
> (Pronier and Le Seigneur, 1992, p. 191)

> ... insidiously a code of licence and amorality is being created, backed up by social security payments and benefits of various kinds ... This freedom which gives way to irresponsible licence, and this permissiveness which is encouraged by social security reimbursements for activities such as dangerous driving, abortion and dangerous sports, only pushes individuals into passionate and perverse excesses (e.g. drugs, homosexuality, adultery, abandoning of children, incest ...).
>
> (Pronier and Le Seigneur, 1992, p. 194)

The first quotation is from Jean Fréchaut and the second from Dr Gillard, the once tireless defender of alternative medicine at the AGMs of Les Verts. Both have been members of Les Verts and were active in the 'fundamentalist' tendency which reared its head in 1986 and 1990.

The doubts as to the real 'nature' of ecologism are linked to its attachment to things of the land. History has its precedents, and this fear was brutally summed up by Grosser:

> It is no accident if ecologism took off in Germany where nature – *die Natur* – is perceived very differently. The forest – *der Wald* – is a strong symbol ... In France this conservative tradition has less of a history, except perhaps for the one which stretches from Vichy to Jacques Tati in

Mon Oncle:[5] Long live that which is non-industrial and agricultural; the farmer, the tree and the plough.

(1992, p. 65)

This type of reactionary picture of ecologism has tainted its appeal for many a prospective activist and voter, even if the party political nature of certain attacks has sometimes been quite obvious. Pursuing this line of reasoning further, and from a purely theoretical point of view, there is a more worrying train of thought present in ecologism which could lead down a potentially dangerous path. This concerns the use and extension of the organic analogy to social structures.

The ecologist paradigm bases itself on an organic, systemic view of the social and natural world which fundamentally opposes Cartesian dualism. Human beings are no longer viewed as 'masters and possessors of nature' but as an integral part of it. Such a view is often reflected in organic metaphors. However, the potential danger of leaning on organic, biological analogies is that they take over. That is to say, they may lead to a form of 'biologism' or 'biological imperialism' by which the social order is perceived as being governed by biological principles. What is in question at this point is the concept of self-regulating systems to which ecologist writings sometimes refer. This concept, based on systems theory and cybernetics, assimilates a future environment-friendly society to an open system, similar to that of a living organism within which individual units (e.g. cells, individuals, towns, etc.) exist in a state of mutual interdependence. This means that each unit is dependent for its survival on the whole but retains a measure of autonomy, permitting it to evolve as it sees fit. The system as a whole is consequently self-regulating via a process of input/output and positive and negative feedback in much the same way as a cybernetic machine. This, at least, is the open-ended, optimistic interpretation of systems-cybernetic theory as applied to the social structure. A more pessimistic, restrictive version would be the kind of 'vision' outlined by Christiane Barrier-Lynn:

> Surely the image of a self-regulating system is likely to favour a form of status quo. Might not cybernetic policies simply give power to the scientists? And who is to say that they would not yield to the temptation of enlightened despotism?

(Barrier-Lynn, 1975, p. 191)

The possibility of extracting two radically different visions of the future from the same body of thought illustrates the ambiguous nature of the systemic approach when applied to social structure. In the same way as

Auguste Comte had hegemonic pretensions for his 'science of society', there is the risk that ecologism may also have delusions of grandeur; that is, the desire to become the total, global science to which all others are subjugated. The temptation to extrapolate from the sciences into the social and political worlds is ever present in the ecologist movement and is understandable when one considers the high proportion of scientists who have taken part in its history. It is reasonable to suggest that the majority of activists are now aware of this danger.

Utopianism

Outside the dominant centralizing tradition in socialism, there is a decentralizing, self-managing current embodied in the nineteenth-century utopian socialist movement. Themes such as a desire for a human-scale economy based on political and economic decentraliza-tion; for a labour-intensive, cooperative type of production as opposed to a capital-intensive, monopolistic system; for work which is socially useful in content and which leads to a more equitable distribution of wealth – these would all be supported by anarchists, democratic social-ists and ecologists worldwide. This historical and philosophical link between anarchism, socialism and ecologism has been referred to at various points during the ecologist movement's short life-span. Whether it is emphasized or not depends on the period in question. During the 1970s, one of the principal ecologist papers, *La Gueule ouverte*, boasted its anarchism when it called for 'the disappearance of parties, of the vote, of the delegation of power, of hierarchies and, therefore, of the State', and one well-known ecologist theorist, Denis de Rougemont, described himself as being 'completely Bakunian' (Allan Michaud, 1979, p. 850). Others consider that the ecologists have given a new lease of life to ideas which had gone out of fashion. For example, Dominique Simonnet argues that 'the old federalist and anarchist cause, tortured by history, has found a new lease of life with ecologism' (Simonnet, 1979, p. 83). And Lebreton observes: 'The most obvious analogy is to see the ecologists take up, one century later, what were usually called the benevolent utopias of the first socialists' (in Allan Michaud, 1979, p. 851).

This anarchist tradition should not be underestimated, as it explains certain attitudes and practices within the ecologist movement. With regard to attitudes, the reason for the scorn ecologists have at times poured on the communist movement can be seen as a reflection of the traditional enmity between anarchists and communists. It also explains why secondary political sympathies among ecologists have traditionally been closer to the anarchists than to the Trotskyist or Maoist movements on the extreme left. Similarly, it is no surprise to see that the ex-leader of the French 1968 student movement, Daniel Cohn-Bendit, subsequently decided to join the German Greens.

At least three ecologist practices can be explained by reference to this anarchist tradition. First, the favourite ecologist sport of 'head-chopping' could be seen against a background of reticence towards leaders in general. One northern green light, Guy Hascoët (1986), explained this tendency in the following terms: 'Having let the "mad head choppers" loose within the ecologist movement, all the leaders' heads which stuck out have been chopped off'. Second, the atmosphere of direct democracy at Les Verts' AGMs is also a measure of this tradition, even if they are now more organized. Finally, this tradition is visible in the political power of the regions within the governing body of Les Verts, the Conseil National Inter-Régional.

The ecologists of the 1980s and early 1990s made much less reference to the anarchist and democratic socialist ideals of their predecessors, because of their overwhelming desire to forge their own political identity and political culture. One potential problem with such a manoeuvre is the creation of a form of historical amnesia. Among the consequences of this 'start from scratch' tendency is the millenarian phenomenon which has always been latent within the ecologist movement. Millenarianism is a term which has been applied to those movements, principally religious, that await ultimate, collective and total salvation with the coming of a saviour, be it Christ (as in the revelations of St John and in Jewish apocalyptic literature) or a boat full of European goods (Wilson, 1973, pp. 50–2). The classic examples are the Amerindian movements of the nineteenth century or the Melanesian 'Cargo Cults' in the early part of this century. Both were movements of an ecstatic, hysterical nature that mobilized support around the myth of a historically predetermined new age.

This is not to say that the ecologist movement has ecstatic or hysterical elements within its ranks, nor that it awaits a saviour. It is, however, to suggest that there have been instances in its short history of a 'new age dawning' vision of social reality. Dominique Simonnet picked up on this tendency quite early: 'Despite their quasi-scientific appearance, the alarmist warnings often sink into prophecies and sometimes mysticism. The initial ecologist discourse was an example of this type of millenarian anxiety' (Simonnet, 1979, p. 98). In 1986, Antoine Waechter was confident in predicting that 'the ecologist perception of human history constitutes the social revolution of the end of this century' (Waechter, 1986); three years later, we were informed that the future society would be ecologist or nothing (Bassot *et al.*, 1989).

Amid the wealth of ecologist literature there is also a strand of thought lying just beneath the surface that might be called futurist in that it conceives of a better future by means of technology:

> Ecologism does not, therefore, refuse technical progress as has often been said. On the contrary, the most radical strand, represented by Murray Bookchin, tends to be rather over-optimistic in suggesting that technological possibilities are unlimited and that the most sophisticated techniques, highly efficient products stemming from a meeting of biology and computer science, could be used to lighten the workload of man.
>
> (Simonnet, 1979, p. 72)

The question is, will the future society be technologically 'liberating' and ecologically acceptable or will it be a refined form of social and political domination? The hope is that new technologies will be conducive to the kind of convivial society to which ecologists aspire. The communications sector is a case in point. Many people would say that within the confines of the 'information society', communications are becoming a prerequisite to effective democracy. At the same time, IT (information technology) is a multinational product, much like any other commodity, bought and sold through telephones and computers. In France, the development of *télématique* (videotext) has opened up possibilities of individual and collective communication that inspire some ecologists who wish to work towards a more direct democracy with methods using less delegation, such as the referendum by popular initiative (RIP – Référendum d'Initiative Populaire). With this in mind, Les Verts suggest studying the possibilities of using *télématique* (Cochet, 1986). Such possibilities leave others cold:

> The RIP is a fair idea because it is democratic. However, it is meaningless unless the vote is the result of a real and serious debate. Otherwise, it becomes a fabulous means of manipulation and Le Pen has fully understood this with regard to immigrants and the death penalty.[6] I am very surprised to see that certain Greens want to study the possibilities of using videotext in this area. Where would the debate be?
>
> (Fournier, 1986)

One recent example of this ecologist attraction to new technologies is to be found in the voting system at the AGMs since November 1992. At the AGM of Chambéry and the emergency AGM of June 1993, votes were computerized and virtually instantaneously flashed up on the screen. Given the ease with which votes could be taken, the principal consequence of this high-tech democracy was that activists often spent as much time voting as they did debating.

The question of the advantages of modern technology in promoting a more participatory society has very ambiguous answers. The French sociologist Edgar Morin is of the opinion that certain rises in the standard of living can be a reflection of a lowering in the quality of life: 'the multiplication of means of communication can be tied to the impoverishment of personal communication' (Morin and Kern, 1993, p. 97). From another angle, it could also be maintained that IT can simply be another means of social control. In reality, this futurist source of French ecologism illustrates the type of contradiction often found within its discourse. On the one hand, it is suggested that a technique may be liberating in itself and, on the other, only if social relationships allow it to be.

The utopian tradition in the ecologist movement is, therefore, one which raises its head periodically in different forms. Since the outset of ecologism, the anarchist form is the most important, and traces can still be seen in Les Verts. It was, however, more visible during the 1970s, when extra-institutional political activity was at its strongest. More recently, since the 1980s, ecologists have spent a lot more time and energy in carving out their own political niche.

Values

Ecologism does not put on offer a 'perfect society' which can be brought about by the wave of a magic wand or by revolution. The road will be long before reaching sustainable development, a convivial society and peaceful international relations. It is within the web of daily routine and of decisions, big and small, that we need to reform, step by step, our way of doing things and of looking at the world. We need ongoing reforms which are not guided by dreams but by values.

(Les Verts, 1994, p. 27)

Every sociopolitical movement has a wealth of ideological sources which can modify its image and actions at different periods in history. Socialism has been through periods where the centralized state was seen as the best provider of individual happiness, and other periods in which emphasis was instead given to the decentralized community. Equally, ecologism in France has seen the 'back-to-the-earth' period of the 1970s give way to the present-day struggle against social exclusion. Given the rate of social change and the distaste with which ecologists worldwide greet the term 'ideology', perhaps a better description at this stage would be that of *axiology* (Lambert, 1990); that is, a system of values which leaves the future open and which represents more a kind of moral code than what we are accustomed to calling ideology: 'ecologist awareness also contributes in its own way to enforcing the idea of indispensable and common, minimal rules, a sort of "ecumenical morality"' (Lambert, 1990, p. 95).

When promoting their beliefs, the three most oft-cited values are those of responsibility, autonomy and solidarity. Individual and collective responsibility[7] towards the environment and the generations to come has become an important ecologist precept. Ecologism surfaced in the 1970s on a wave of concern over depleting natural resources, pollution and the subsequent questioning of economic growth. This concern was accompanied at the time by various warnings of imminent doom if production and consumer habits were not changed. Following the increase of pollution problems and accidents such as that of Chernobyl in 1986, such warnings were anything but superfluous, but care has been taken over the years by ecologist writers to hone down this general concern into a guiding principle. The natural environment is no longer considered to be a gift to humankind but rather a loan from future generations. This implies that the environment and future generations have certain rights to be respected in human choices. The idea that nature or non-existent humans have rights has been vigorously attacked as anti-humanistic. The ecologists, however, consider that unless behaviour such as that based on this belief becomes commonplace, the planet may soon reach a point of no return.

The question of responsibility towards future generations has, of course, given rise to the expression 'sustainable development', first popularized by the 'Brundtland Report' of 1987. Sustainable development would be designed to articulate present needs with long-term ones. That is to say, present-day needs should not have priority over future ones, the nature of which is not as yet known. This principle quite obviously puts into question individual and collective lifestyles which are often based on polluting industries. By way of a specific policy answer, the French ecologists support the introduction of an ecotax. An ecotax is designed to internalize external costs, which are often paid for by the community or by another profession further down the commercial line. Certain ecotaxes have, in fact, already been created in France. When, for example, a factory pollutes a nearby river, the factory's owner is now responsible for that pollution. It is no longer the local angler who has voluntarily to clean up the river.

Autonomy, as we have seen, is a concept made famous by Ivan Illich. French ecologists of the 1990s have refined the concept and see it as the ability to control one's own destiny, 'to have control over one's own productive activity' (Les Verts, 1994, p. 29). This somewhat general concept is intended as a guide to action in different domains, and one of the most important is, no doubt, that of technocracy in industrial and post-industrial society. The reaction of ecologists to what is seen as the technocratic state is reflected in the ideal of smallness, summed up in the title of Ernst Schumacher's famous book, *Small is Beautiful* (1980). Small may be beautiful but, above all, it is controllable in the eyes of ecologists, and this underlying idea is at the heart of their theories on human action; that is, the smaller an activity, the more manageable it is likely to be.

Within a technical context, certain construction projects are criticized for this reason. A highway project, for example, no doubt spoils the view of the countryside as well as developing the importance of the car in society. But it is also a case of the citizen being literally and metaphorically overtaken by a project. The hostility to certain dam projects also represents a mixture of opposition that is of a strictly environmental nature coupled to a refusal to accept technically gigantic projects which swamp the individual.

Politically speaking, ecologists' wishes for greater public participation in the decision-making process can be hampered by large-scale projects. The fear is that the larger a project, and the more expensive it is, the less likely it is that the opinions of individual citizens will be taken into account. Here again, the ecologist critique is centred on the power of 'technocrats' in contemporary society.

Finally, within the wider social context, the idea of the local community is at the heart of ecologist thought and action. However, this idea has given rise to a fundamental ambivalence in interpretation. When Antoine Waechter gained the leadership of Les Verts in 1986, he did so brandishing the myth that 'the municipality [*commune*], and especially the small rural municipality, is the focal point of the society to which we aspire. To forget this would be a profound mistake' (Waechter, 1986). This image of the small rural community has been heavily contested within Les Verts (and from outside), but it is an interesting one, as it ties up with a fundamental sociological problem: how do individuals form a society? How can social solidarity be maintained? These questions are even more acute in today's increasingly individualized and atomized society. The major theorists who contributed to the birth of sociology all broached the issue. In 1887, the German sociologist Tönnies referred to *Gemeinschaft* (community) and *Gesellschaft* (association/society) to distinguish between traditional and modern society. Traditional society was one of proximity and 'mechanical solidarity' (according to Emile Durkheim). Modern, complex society is based on the notion of contract (Henry S. Maine), heterogeneity (Herbert Spencer), rational bureaucracy (Max Weber) and 'organic solidarity' (Durkheim). Toing and froing between these two types of social organization is also central to ecologist thinking, given the desire to reconstruct the social bond of past rural communities whilst living in the modern world. The reference to the 'small rural community' gives the impression that the ecologists are leaning backwards, but, as ambiguous as such a reference is, it is rather a wish to rehumanize what is seen as an increasingly lifeless social body.

By way of an antidote to this atomization, solidarity has also been stressed by contemporary ecologists as a necessity in fighting the effects of increasing social exclusion due to mass unemployment. Solidarity is not egalitarianism but rather the ability for everyone 'despite any handicaps or mistakes in life to be helped back into a situation whereby he can control his life and live decently' (Les Verts, 1994, p. 31); life in a caring community, in other words. To be in any way meaningful, such sentiments have to deal with the question of work in our unemployment-ridden Western societies. The subject of work is the one on which the ecologists have made their greatest effort to go beyond their image of nature lovers by producing a quantitative and qualitative analysis of the place of work in contemporary and future society.

Quantitatively speaking, new production techniques (automation, computing, etc.) have made full employment a meaningless, misleading term which is now only fit for electoral campaigning. Ecologists believe that the only long-term solution to the structural unemployment caused by an ever-decreasing volume of work is some form of work sharing. Les Verts are in favour of a 35-hour week (moving towards 30 hours within a few years), backed up by an Act of Parliament leaving companies two years to adapt. Any wage reductions would target the higher salaries and no salary would fall below a fixed rate. Such a measure would create, it is claimed, between 1 and 2 million jobs (Les Verts, 1994, pp. 60–2).

Qualitatively speaking, these same new technologies, while contributing to overall unemployment, are creating a society in which people will no longer spend most of their lives at the workplace. Alongside a policy of work sharing, ecologists believe that the free time which is thus created could be used in a creative way, instead of simply being seen as wasted time.[8] In our society the expression 'Time is money' sums up the commercialization of the time factor in people's lives. To a large extent, lack of time prevents people from participating fully in social life. They no longer have the 'power to live'.[9] In order to change the underlying ethics of the system, French ecologists believe it is necessary to redefine the place of work in society, and the ramifications are, indeed, vast:

> For two hundred years our societies have been dominated by the pro-
> ductivist ethic ... It is not going to be easy to get rid of this ethic and
> replace it with one in which voluntary cooperation, self-determination,
> creativity and quality relationships with other people and with nature are
> the dominant values.
>
> (Gorz, 1982, p. 31)

It can be seen that the ecologist values of autonomy and solidarity are two sides of the same coin and take us back to the discussion of Personalism. Autonomy becomes individualism if it is not constantly checked by solidarity. The relationship between autonomy and solidarity also leads us on to the issue of social class in connection with French ecologism.

Ecologism as a Class Ideology?

In 1951, Rudolph Herbele declared that social movements are 'as a rule closely bound to certain classes and opposed by others' (Herbele, 1951, p. 14). With this in mind, can it be said that the ecologist movement represents a particular social class struggling for power and recognition in advanced capitalist society? The (manual) working class was seen as the natural social base for the socialist movement. Is there any equivalent for the ecologists and, if so, which is the class in question?

The orthodox Marxist analysis suggests that green politics is 'an attempt by a specific social group to come to terms with its incorporation into the social relationships imposed by capitalism' (Weston, 1986, p. 27) and that ecologists suffer from their 'narrow middle class base' (p. 29). Be that as it may – and more recent research has qualified this position (Prendiville, 1994) – Les Verts see themselves as a vehicle taking on board all those groups working for sociopolitical and economic alternatives:

> Be it in the organization of social or citizen pressure groups, or in the

search for social and economic alternatives, *Les Verts*, while respecting
everyone's independence, put themselves forward as a place in which
apparently different forms of militant action may meet.

(Bousseau *et al.*, 1988)

At this point in the debate the importance of post-materialist or post-industrialist theories comes into play (see Touraine, 1969; Bell, 1973; Toffler, 1981).[10] These concepts are often linked to the growth of the ecologist movement (Lowe and Rüdig, 1986) and postulate a society based on services rather than production, in which the control of knowledge and information is the key to political and economic power. In this type of society, blue-collar classes are gradually replaced by the white-collar ones, while a technocratic elite replaces the owner classes traditionally associated with capitalism. This general theory of macro-social change holds that the ecologists represent an emerging, post-materialist class whose basic material needs have been satisfied and who are now beginning to concentrate on 'higher order needs' (Lowe and Rüdig, 1986, p. 515). Some believe that they may even be beginning to 'pull up the drawbridge' by concentrating on 'quality of life' concerns while the lower classes try to satisfy basic material needs (Chafer, 1984, p. 38).[11] The new divide between materialists and post-materialists is seen as replacing the old divide between capitalists and workers in a different form, as a spokesperson for Les Verts indicated a decade ago:

However, it is not a question of a 'new class struggle' along the lines of 'proletarians versus capitalists' but rather of a *mosaic of social groups and citizens* (consumers, transport users, regionalists, feminists) struggling against certain groups called technocrats who, more than the political class, have the final power of decision in numerous sectors (e.g. energy, transport, urban and regional development).

(Cochet, 1984, p. 45)

This fragmentation of social conflict is seen as being at the heart of a fundamental shift in Western values, which now place qualitative demands on a par with, if not above, quantitative ones (Inglehart, 1971, 1977).

Are the ecologists the political representatives of post-materialism? The hypothesis is enticing in its simplicity, but a definitive answer to such a question is, of course, impossible. It is quite obvious that the ecologist movement has developed within a society undergoing fundamental social and economic change, and that its very existence is in part a result of these changes (for example, pollution, population explosion). It is also true that the generation of the 1960s, which is at the heart of the ecologist elite, was brought up amid the myth (if not always the reality) of the affluent society (Galbraith, 1961), and that the opposition movement of the decade in France which culminated in May 1968 was as much a protest against an alienating economic and social system as one in favour of a 'greater share of the national cake'. However, there would appear to be two problems with this hypothesis.

First, the Marxist interpretation of class considers that a degree of class consciousness is indispensable to the existence of a class as a historical actor. This process of maturity is coupled to the identification of the worker with his work. In contemporary society, however, as André Gorz points out, there is an increasing distance between the workers and their work: 'It is no longer a question of the worker freeing himself through his work or of mastering his work ... It is now more a question of freeing himself from work by refusing the nature, content, necessity and form' (Gorz, 1980, p. 103). In this context of weakening individual identification with the world of work, the conscious formation of a post-materialist class appears problematic.

The second problem concerns the inherent ambiguity of the term itself, which may be viewed in a positive or negative light. On the negative side, there is the underlying supposition that if the post-materialists are 'pulling up the drawbridge' of materialism, they are acting purely in their own interests as individuals. This brings the discussion to Anthony Oberschall's 'resource management theory' (Oberschall, 1973). Inspired by Mancur Olson's (1971) 'rational theory approach', Oberschall considers individual interest to be the major motivation in social movement activity. However, this type of approach does not appear to correspond fully to the ecologist movement.

While the importance of self-interest as a motivation towards social movement activity cannot be discounted, reducing collective behaviour to self-interest alone means denying the importance of the beliefs and ideals which are syncretized in ecologism. Moreover, the question remains: who stands to gain from a successful ecologist movement? While it is true that many social movements claim to act in the general interest, the ecologist movement claims to differ from the mainstream of (productivist) socialism and (economic) liberalism by aspiring to modify both the content and the form of contemporary society (that is, how the wealth is created as well as distributed). Clearly, this approach would not benefit ecologist activists alone.

In a more positive light, post-materialists are seen as those people who have seen the flaws in industrialism and who are beginning to contest the rationale of it:

> The ideological shift characteristic of post-materialists is not found among all ecologists, some of whom are quite comfortable with the dominant values of the system. The overlap is rather between post-materialism and those recently developing elements of the ecologist movement that have begun to articulate a critique of the techno-scientific rationale of industrial society.
>
> (quoted in Lowe and Rüdig, 1986, p. 516)

'Those recently developing elements' are, in fact, the ecologists who articulate social ecologism with natural ecologism, that is, the defence of the natural environment coupled to analysis and critique of social relations and power sharing in modern economies. Given the ambiguity of the term 'post-materialist', the question as to whether the ecologists are a political expression of post-materialism remains open.

Conclusion

Ecologists see their beliefs as forming a system; that is, bringing together diverse but complementary strands of thought into a coherent whole. However, there are times when the strands of thought in question seem quite contradictory. Such a belief system has its advantages, in that people of apparently different social and political horizons can come together under the ecologist banner. It can also have its disadvantages when the contradictions in perspective between these different beliefs appear in the full light of day. It is possible that the choice of stressing the social side of the term 'environment' in the 1990s, having stressed the natural side during the previous decade, is an attempt at bringing together the two major strands of ecologism. The values which ecologists themselves put forward (responsibility, autonomy, solidarity) quite clearly show the two complementary sides of ecologism in defence of the natural and social environments. However, ecologist activists have made few inroads into certain classes, particularly the manual working classes. If one accepts that ecologism represents a new 'post-materialist' class in a 'post-industrial' society, this may not be a problem in the medium and long term. If one considers, however, that ecologism should reach into all social classes, it may represent an obstacle to the movement's progress.

As for the future, ecologism in France has entered a new phase since the departure in 1994 of the ex-leader Antoine Waechter, widely seen as the leader of the 'naturalist' tendency within Les Verts since 1986. This change in leadership has been altering the traditional image of the 'birds and the bees' ecologism with which Les Verts had been labelled during the 1980s, and from which they had also made political mileage. Ecologism would seem to have shifted in the mid-1990s from a somewhat confusing ideological mix to a clearer set of values which encompass both the natural and social sides of the ecologist coin. If and when the general public and the media realize the shift, a great leap forward will have been made.

Notes

This chapter is a revised version of a section of my *Environmental Politics in France* (1994). I wish to thank Westview Press for allowing me to reproduce material from the book.

1. Conservationism is the apolitical protection of the natural environment. Environmentalism is the politically conscious protection of the natural environment (e.g. Greenpeace, Friends of the Earth). Ecologism is a political belief system linking the natural and social environments and based on the values of autonomy, responsibility and solidarity.

2. See, for example, Association Plein Air Nature, presentation brochure of 'Salon Vivre et Travailler Autrement', 19–27 March 1988, Paris. This exhibition was the second of its kind, wishing to publicize the French 'alternative' under its many different guises (for example, health foods, naturism, alternative work practices) and not solely, therefore, a manifestation of organized ecologism. Nevertheless, the themes (both progressive and slightly dubious) present at this exhibition cannot be totally dissociated from it. The following extract sums up this idea: 'l'APRI [Association pour la Protection contre les Rayonnements Ionisants], forerunner to the 1970s anti-nuclear movement in France, has given birth to quite a number of sometimes old associations which were created for a specific reason: vaccinations, naturism, organic agriculture, hygiene by plants, etc., and which illustrate a strand preoccupied with a more "natural" lifestyle. If some members of this strand appear somewhat conservative, irrational or sectarian, there is, however, no doubt that the vast majority of these associations were the forerunners of the ecologist movement' (Collectif Ecologiste, 1977, p. 19).

3. Another example of the importance given to personal development in social change is shown in the following extract from a motion of the 1986 AGM of Les Verts: 'Personal development is a capital feature of social evolution ... Pacifism is built on an inner peace' (Lecuyer, 1986).

4. In the aftermath of the German state elections of 1986, the ecologist parliamentary 'fraction' was composed of 25 women and 19 men.

5. The reference to Vichy is to Marshal Pétain's reactionary, authoritarian regime which had its headquarters there in 1940–4. *Mon Oncle* is a film about the clash between old and new worlds. See also Alphandéry *et al.*, 1991.

6. On the ideology and policies of the extreme right-wing Front National, of which Le Pen is leader, see Chapter 4.

7. *Le Principe responsabilité* (1993) is the French title of a book by the German philosopher, Hans Jonas, which is rapidly becoming an ecologist reference.

8. In a brochure of Les Verts on work sharing, M. Rolant, ex-general secretary of the CFDT trade union and ex-director of the AFME (Agence Française pour la Maîtrise de l'Energie), summed up this idea: 'we have to combat the idea that working less hours in the factory or at the office means doing nothing. On the contrary, it means having more time for doing the things which matter most in life' (in Les Verts, 1985, p. 16).

9. *The Power to Live* (*Le Pouvoir de Vivre*; Aujourd'hui l'écologie, 1981) is the title of a seminal ecologist work. In the same vein, Les Verts have discussed the possibility of a guaranteed

160   *Brendan Prendiville*

minimum income (*allocation universelle*; Les Verts, 1994, p. 33) regardless of whether a person is in work or not. In the medium and long term, ecologists also remain convinced that a change of consumption habits is indispensable to any sustainable development. As one militant put it in 1987: 'consumption needs to decrease in order to get better' (Tête, 1987).

10. Speaking of Daniel Bell's *The Coming of the Post-Industrial Society* (1973), Toffler puts forward the following definition of post-industrialism: 'a society in which the economy is largely based on service, the professional and technical classes dominate, theoretical knowledge is central, intellectual technology – systems analysis, model building, and the like – is highly developed, and technology is, at least potentially, capable of self-sustaining growth' (1981, p. 443).

11. Anthony Chafer uses this expression as an allusion to Tozzi's (1982) argument that the ecologist movement could be seen as trying to prevent the working classes from obtaining the benefits which they themselves enjoyed from the polluting, consumer society.

References

Allan Michaud, D. (1979) *Le Discours écologique*. Bordeaux: Université de Bordeaux 1.

Alphandéry, P., Bitoun, P. and Dupont, Y. (1991) *L'Equivoque idéologique*. Paris: La Découverte.

Aujourd'hui l'écologie (1981) *Le Pouvoir de vivre*. Montargis: Ecologie Mensuel.

Barrier-Lynn, C. (1975) 'Ecologie, vers un despotisme super-éclairé?'. *Esprit*, September, pp. 184–96.

Bassot, E. *et al.* (1989) 'Ni droite, ni gauche: Verts' (Motion d'orientation), AGM of Les Verts (Marseille). *La Tribune des Verts* **3**.

Bate, J. (1991) *Wordsworth and the Environmental Tradition*. London: Routledge.

Bell, D. (1973) *The Coming of the Post-Industrial Society*. New York: Basic Books.

Bousseau, C. *et al.* (1988) 'Motion d'orientation', AGM of Les Verts (Paris). *Vert-Contact* **82** *bis.*

Capra, F. (1982) *The Turning Point*. London: Fontana.

Chafer, A. (1984) 'The Greens in France: An Emerging Social Movement?'. *Journal of Area Studies* **10**, 36–44.

Cochet, Y. (1984) 'Political Ecology in France 1974–1984'. *Journal of Area Studies* **10**, 45–6.

Cochet, Y. (1986) 'Construire' (Motion), AGM of Les Verts (Paris).

Collectif Ecologiste (1977) *Les Ecologistes présentés par eux-mêmes*. Verviers: Flash Actualité Marabout.

Ferry, L. (1992) *Le Nouvel Ordre écologique*. Paris: Grasset.

Fournier, A. (1986) 'Réflexions' (Text), AGM of Les Verts (Paris). *Supplément au Vert-Contact* **6**.

Galbraith, J. (1961) *L'Ere de l'abondance*. Paris: Calmann-Lévy.

Gorz, A. (1980) *Adieux au prolétariat*. Paris: Galilée.

Gorz, A. (1982) 'La Reconquête du temps'. *Aujourd'hui* **54**.

Grosser, A. (1992) 'Faut-il avoir peur de l'écologie?', in *Tout sur les écologistes*. Paris: Libération, p. 65.

Hascoët, G. (1986) 'Je dis oui' (Motion d'orientation), AGM of Les Verts (Paris). *Supplément au Vert-Contact* **6**.

Herbele, R. (1951) *Social Movements: An Introduction to Political Sociology*. New York: Appleton-Croft.

Illich, I. (1979 [1973]) *Tools for Conviviality*. Glasgow: Fontana/Collins.

Inglehart, R. (1971) 'The Silent Revolution in Europe: Intergenerational Change in Post-Industrial Societies'. *American Political Science Review* **65** (4), 991–1017.

Inglehart, R. (1977) *The Silent Revolution: Changing Values and Political Styles among Western Publics*. Princeton, NJ: Princeton University Press.

Jonas, H. (1993 [1979]) *Le Principe responsabilité*. Paris: Cerf.

Lambert, Y. (1990) 'Le Monothéisme des valeurs'. *Débat* **59**, 90–105.

Lecuyer, P. (1986) 'Alternatives écologiques' (Motion). AGM of Les Verts (Paris).

Lowe, P. and Rüdig, W. (1986) 'Political Ecology and the Social Sciences: The State of the Art'. *British Journal of Political Science* **16**, 513–50.

Morin, E. and Kern, A. (1993) *Terre-Patrie*. Paris: Seuil.

Mounier, E. (1985 [1949]) *Le Personnalisme*. Paris: Presses Universitaires de France.

Mouvement d'Ecologie Politique (1980) *Bulletin interne* 2.

Oberschall, A. (1973) *Social Conflict and Social Movements*. Englewood Cliffs, NJ: Prentice Hall.

Olson, M. (1971) *The Logic of Collective Action*. New York: Schocken.

Prendiville, B. (1994) *Environmental Politics in France*. Oxford: Westview.

Pronier, R. and Le Seigneur, V. (1992) *Génération verte*. Paris: Presses de la Renaissance.

Schumacher, E.F. (1980) *Small is Beautiful*. London: Abacus.

Simonnet, D. (1979) *L'Ecologisme*. Paris: Presses Universitaires de France.

Tête, E. (1987) 'Motion d'orientation', AGM of Les Verts, Paris.

Toffler, A. (1981) *Future Shock*. London: Pan.

Touraine, A. (1969) *La Société post-industrielle*. Paris: Denoël.

Tozzi, M. (1982) *Syndicalisme et nouveaux mouvements sociaux. Régionalisme, féminisme et écologie*. Lyon: Editions Ouvrières.

Vadrot, C.-M. (1978) *L'Ecologie, histoire d'une subversion*. Paris: Syros.

Verts, Les (1985) 'Travaillons tous, vivons mieux, gaspillons moins'. Brochure, Version 3, February.

Verts, Les (1987) 'Transformez votre vie par la pensée positive', brochure distributed at AGM of Les Verts, Paris.

Verts, Les (1994) *Le Livre des Verts. Dictionnaire de l'écologie politique*. Paris: Editions du Félin.

Waechter, A. (1986) 'Affirmer l'identité politique des Verts', AGM of Les Verts (Paris). *Supplément au Vert-Contact* 6.

Watts, N. and Wandesforde-Smith, G. (1986) 'Post-Material Values and Environmental Policy Change', in P. Lowe and W. Rüdig.

Weston, J. (ed.) (1986) *Red and Green. The New Politics of the Environment*. London: Pluto Press.

Wilson, J. (1973) *Introduction to Social Movements*. New York: Basic Books.

6

Feminism

MÁIRE CROSS

Women, might it not be high time we carried out a revolution among ourselves? Will women always be isolated from each other and will they never be at one with society except to malign their own sex and arouse pity in the other? For so long as nothing is done to raise women's minds and for so long as they do not help to make themselves more useful and consistent, the state cannot prosper.

Olympe de Gouges, 1791 (1986, p. 115)

Social, Economic and Political Origins

In 1982 Yvette Roudy, a minister in the socialist government, led an unsuccessful attempt to get her party to accept the principle of a minimum quota of 20 per cent of women on lists of candidates (Roudy, 1985, pp. 20–1). In 1992 a European Commission summit conference organized a debate on parity. The member states of the Community recognized the need to redress the gender imbalance in Parliaments and other elected bodies. In the European elections in 1994, five political parties in France (Lutte Ouvrière, the Parti Communiste Français, the Parti Socialiste, L'Union des Ecologistes pour l'Europe and L'Autre Politique, led by Jean-Pierre Chevènement) took this to heart and presented lists with an equal or greater number of women candidates. That did not save them from disappointing results.

France has a rich tradition of feminism: it is both reformist and revolutionary; theoretical and practical; universalist and particularist. It has developed in political discourse, in philosophical treatises, in literary works, and more recently in other cultural forms such as the cinema. Yet feminism is on the fringe of political activity. According to the numbers of women in power, France has one of the worst records for female political representation in Europe. The supreme court, the Conseil Constitutionnel, has refused to endorse any attempt to reform the constitution to ensure female and male parity in politics. For an analysis of feminism as a political ideology, however, we must go beyond mere counting. In order to measure the political success of feminism it has often simply been considered sufficient to count the handful of women in political posts or at the summit of the hierarchy of professional or cultural categories. The demand for parity between the sexes in all elected assemblies is proposed as a response to the continuing political exclusion of women, but it does not contain a solution to their social and economic exclusion. The debate over parity which has raged among feminists (Gaspard, 1994; Viennot, 1994; Le Dœuff, 1995; Trat, 1995; Varikas, 1995; Barzach *et al.*, 1996) is not the essence of feminist ideology, but it raises questions about the fundamental nature of women's exclusion.

This ideology has developed from the collective challenge by a relatively small number of women and men on behalf of a much larger group – all women – to the almost permanent exclusion of this group of citizens from power sharing. The challenge has undergone several changes of direction since it began during the French Revolution. It is rooted in nineteenth-century political and philosophical traditions, having been influenced in turn by 1789 individualism, liberalism, utopian socialism and Marxist socialism. It is rooted in nineteenth- and twentieth-century political actions of socialist and republican opposition movements, inter-war pacifism, post-1968 student activism, psychoanalysis, structuralism and deconstructionism. More often than not feminism allies itself to, or is a subculture of, another ideology, a class or a race. We talk about socialist feminism and liberal feminism. Bourgeois feminists of the early twentieth century were rejected by a small group of women within the socialist party. In the 1980s immigrant women in France of Islamic origin challenged the hegemony of white middle-class feminists. It has long been recognized that the term itself is totally inadequate to describe the many facets of feminism, either as direct protest or as intellectual theory, with aims as diverse as egalitarian reformism or radical revolution, a search for parity or political separatism. Indeed, because of the very diversity of feminist ideologies the plural term 'feminisms' is frequently used in contemporary debates.

Feminism as a recognized political ideology and as a collective movement has developed in France, within and outside the formal political process; prior to this, many individual calls for greater equality and demands for female emancipation did of course occur.[1] Since the early nineteenth century, feminism has been based on a belief that gender equality is a valid aspiration as a basic republican value, and that the transfer of that missing reality was possible through legal reform. Since this time, however, feminism has also recognized that republican institutions are part of patriarchy, and that legal reform is inadequate to end the oppression of one group by another. Many feminists claim that even to attempt to discuss feminism as a political ideology in electoral, party or governmental policy terms is questionable. Political activity must include all public manifestations of the recognition of the need for change, many of them unsuccessful so far, since gender inequality remains an integral part of French society. Campaigns have been carried on mainly through individual writing and pressure group activity. Many of the protests have gone unnoticed. This silence or invisibility is highly significant for women's continuing oppression.

Since its origins, feminism has been vociferously attacked in the press by satire and mockery or simply by direct antagonism, with the result that feminism has a constant problem of finding outlets of expression and avoiding being treated as an aberration of an insignificant minority. Furthermore, in France as elsewhere, because of this ostracism by the media, there is in general a difficult relationship between feminists and their sisters; many women distance themselves as much as possible from the strident images satirized in anti-feminist mythology. Traditionally in France this apathy or antagonism visible in the press is even stronger among politicians, who hold the key to changing the balance of power between the sexes through campaigns for legal reforms and through encouraging the equitable sharing of responsibilities in the formal political process.

One important consequence of the invisibility of the protest movement is a profound ignorance of the specificity and endurance of the struggle in France. Many of these points are common to Western feminism, but this chapter concentrates on the shaping forces of French feminism while recognizing that it originated as a philosophy common to many countries, and that the increasing speed of information at an international level in the twentieth century has rendered it open to many outside influences which have often seemed to reduce French specificity. For instance, it is claimed that in the 1970s the 'new – or second – wave' of feminism in France was sparked off by other feminist movements, in particular, the American movement:

France has been conscious that it had to catch up with other advanced industrial societies in economic development as well as in the socio-

cultural sphere. The more limited and belated development of feminism
and environmentalism has meant that France has tended to follow
foreign models.

(Hall *et al.*, 1994, p. 296).

While it is arguable that 'France' wished to respond to feminist demands simply to keep up with its neighbours, it is true that international
communications have accentuated the universal dimension of feminism. A further international common feature is the superficiality of
sporadic press attention which gave women the rare opportunity to tell
their (her)story,[2] the speed at which it declined, and the pervasiveness
of the supposition that sufficient gains had been made once the first
reforms were passed. It was assumed that there was no further need for
any feminist campaign. In France the 1975 Veil law ending the 1920 ban
on abortion was hailed as the great victory for feminism, yet four years
later in October 1979 Paris saw the biggest demonstration by women for
free abortion on demand. Curiously, this continuing struggle was rarely
mentioned in political circles. In the 1990s, there has been a shift away
from the attempt to impose equal rights through legislation to a drive to
change attitudes and create an awareness of gender issues through
language. The current obsessions with politically correct terminology –
also American inspired – have not removed the social, economic and
political roots of inequality, which are very real for millions of women in
a post-industrial capitalist country such as France or in the developing
economies of the world.

Forms of exploitation vary with evolving power structures, but genuine change is needed as much as ever. Feminism is a repressed ideology;
deprived of its own power base of a party or press outlet, it is constantly
marginalized or misinterpreted. The universal dimension is evoked to
suggest that women in France are treated much better than their
counterparts elsewhere in the world. Currently, extreme forms of *la
guerre des sexes* are depicted as specific to American feminism; to say
otherwise is seen as an attack on French specificity. Any acknowledgement that women have made progress in top professional jobs is
couched in guarded terms of assurance to men, assurance that women
have retained their essential female nature so that men respond with
appropriate tenderness and devotion, thereby rendering obsolete the
need for a feminist movement.[3] This assertion, while insisting that
French women have a unique capacity for finding a perfectly balanced
existence successfully combining their equally important possessions of
lover, career and home, has no explanation to suggest why French
political reality is so misogynist. Feminism bears all the hallmarks of the

ideology of an oppressed class; none the less there have been successful political campaigns to change the law in three areas – social, economic and personal – which have to some extent removed the most glaring aspects of oppression or inequality.

Socially the inferior position of women in French society was defined by the Code civil of 1803, set out by Napoleon I. This galvanized the early nineteenth-century feminists, outraged by the all-powerful role attributed to the husband and father over his wife and children, and by the double standard of morality, permitting men sexual privileges and reducing women to domestic slavery. Flora Tristan defined this oppression as a necessity of a despotic regime; she was one of many who campaigned for entitlement to divorce and equal marital and parental rights. The Code civil remained virtually intact until the end of the nineteenth century, when there began a series of reforms allowing divorce and financial independence to married women. As late as the 1970s, many of the inequalities remained (Dhavernas, 1978, p. 7).

One of the most glaring aspects of inequality is the economic. There is a long history of the political quest for economic equality before the law in France. Traditionally the Rousseauesque image of the angel in the home is far removed from reality, where women are in the worst-paid occupations and are prone to exploitation on many levels (Louis, 1994). Evidence of inequality in patterns of employment does contribute to a feminist ideology, as it is the inspiration for many to take up feminist issues in politics. Moreover, contemporary studies of female employment reveal that inequalities remain in constantly changing economic conditions, which in turn affect the evolving power structures in gender relationships. For instance, there has been a massive growth in women's employment, which could be interpreted as a positive step. According to a study by Marie-Thérèse Letablier (1995), the increase in the numbers of women in employment in France over the last ten years has been the mainspring of the growth of the labour force. At the same time this study argues that women are more affected by unemployment, despite the increase in the level of women's education. Furthermore, the increase in the number of women at work has increased job segregation. In spite of political support for equality of employment, expressed in the law of July 1983 and incorporated into the Labour Code, there has been little progress in the equality of job opportunities (Initiatives, 1995). Inequalities have been reinforced because of job shortages and, even more significantly, the time spent on domestic labour has not diminished in France.

A third area of inequality is the question of equality of the rights to sexual freedom of men and women, the ending of double standards of morality, the right to control reproduction with free access to contraception and abortion, and the right to freedom from domestic violence, rape and pornography. These issues are not new to politics, but they resurfaced in political campaigns in the 1970s in such a way as to dominate public perceptions of feminist politics. Now, to a certain extent, the campaign to make the personal political is paramount, almost to the exclusion of political and economic equality. Many feminists argue that this campaign is the more important because women's oppression is based on the exploitation and violation of women's bodies and sexuality. On the other hand, the prioritization of one aspect of oppression alarms socialist feminists, who present evidence to show that women's oppression is based on economic exploitation. French feminism has a long history of campaigns around personal issues. The campaign for information on family planning by the neo-Malthusian movement in the inter-war period was considered to be quite subversive. Today there seems to be an establishment barrier to forging historical links with previous struggles over such matters, as if the personal struggles of many for recognition outside normal codes of behaviour presented a threat to society as a whole (Ronsin, 1980; Bard, 1995).

The grass-roots campaigns for legal reform to achieve genuine gender equality take place far from the nerve centres of intellectual feminism. Although the term 'feminism' has become pervasive in a general way, feminists have only succeeded in forcing gender issues on to the political agenda in a restricted number of areas from time to time, and this through the actions of a minority. Feminists have only rarely organized into one single movement. They have often found allies within other political movements. Preoccupation with gender reform has not been the sole priority of either the right or the left. Feminism in France has not had a significant direct impact on political parties or other ideologies, which consider it to be a marginal issue. However, the political theories of feminism are highly sophisticated and deeply rooted in French philosophical and political traditions.

Defining Feminism

In the English language, feminism is 'a social movement claiming political and economic equality of women with men' (*Penguin English Dictionary*) or 'advocacy of the claims and rights of women' (*Shorter Oxford English Dictionary*). It is therefore either a belief or an organization or both. In French the word *féministe* is more recent (1872) than *féminisme* (1837). Defined as a 'doctrine which advocates extending the rights and the role of women in society' (*Le Petit Robert*), the word in its current usage existed long after a feminist movement had come into being. The English definition emphasizes equality, the French definition stresses difference. Karen Offen (1988) rightly points out the sloppiness of the definition of feminism since it became widely used at the end of the nineteenth century in France.

There is also a distinction to be made between the ideology of feminism and the demand for an increased role for women in politics. President Chirac's first prime minister, Alain Juppé, appointed a record number of women in junior posts in his first government in May 1995, none of them feminists. This number shrank significantly in his first ministerial shake-up in the autumn of 1995. The Communist Party boasts of having the most women elected to power since 1945, but rejects the feminist analysis of patriarchal oppression in favour of the Marxist concept of class oppression.

There is a difference between feminism and women's history. The relationship between them is that feminism interprets women's history in a specific way, that is, as the history of an oppressed class. Describing the role of women in the wartime resistance movement does not immediately transform them into feminists but records their presence and challenges traditional interpretations of history. There is a difference between feminism and the history of gender relationships. Describing the role of women as an economic group during the French revolution of 1789, or describing the role of women in religious orders, recognizes gender as a social category as important as class.

For the purposes of this chapter there are two specifically French interpretations of gender issues. Both have their inherent strengths and weaknesses. Both have contributed to the construction of French feminism as a political ideology. The first interpretation is based on the notion of equality, the second on that of difference.

Equality

The French conception, stressing the extension of women's rights and of women's role in society without actually using the term 'equality', contains the inherent contradiction of the French experience. The 1789 revolution, for example, endowed society with a formal set of egalitarian principles of citizenship from which women were excluded from the outset. Immediately individual women such as Olympe de

Gouges and Théroigne de Méricourt challenged this exclusion, but they were cruelly silenced.[4] In her 'Declaration of the Rights of Women', Olympe de Gouges spelt out the fundamental inconsistency of women's position in society. If women were liable for punishment by execution, they should be entitled to political rights: 'woman has the right to climb the scaffold; she must equally have the right to mount the tribune, provided that her actions do not disrupt public order under the Law' (Gouges, 1986, p. 104).

Legalistic formal discourse is very much part of the ideological inheritance in France, and French feminism developed along these lines. Throughout the nineteenth century women challenged exclusion on egalitarian grounds, but what feminist history has clearly shown is that monarchy, republic and empire were equally repressive; because men were in control, the minority protests were easily silenced and forgotten. Male suffrage was introduced by political leaders during the early stage of the Second Republic. When women protested and demanded the right to vote in the name of republican and social principles, they endured imprisonment and mockery for their pains. From then universal suffrage was synonymous with male suffrage and women were simply deemed politically inadequate. There began to develop arguments associating women with the dangers of clericalism, which pervaded French politics until the mid-twentieth century. Michelet and Proudhon, two influential political thinkers, articulated anti-feminist arguments. Michelet suggested that since women were more active in practising their religion they would be prone to vote for the policies advocated by the hierarchy of the Catholic church, by then right-wing and anti-republican. This effective but facile argument, which disguised the true misogyny of republican ideology and politicians, has recently been challenged by feminist historians (Reynolds, 1995; Bard, 1995). During the Third Republic, the suffrage question remained to the fore but unresolved in republican discourse. Three times in the inter-war period, while representatives in the Chambre des Députés voted for female suffrage, in the second chamber the Sénat refused to consider the suffrage question of women or voted against it, supposedly because of the clerical factor but basically because of deep-rooted conservative values about women in society (Macmillan, 1991). Ironically, through religion women found a window of opportunity for active public life denied to them by the state. They could participate in voluntary philanthropic organizations run by the Catholic church or in professional careers. Membership of female religious orders was high throughout the mid-nineteenth century, until the growth of state education and social services replaced the social role of the church (Macmillan, 1996; Mills, 1996).

Damage to the cause of gender equality had already been inflicted by the influential anarchist Proudhon, who successfully propagated a commonly held opinion in the labour movement, where men were fast becoming converted to the idea of the male as the sole breadwinner. According to Proudhon, women ought to have no say in politics and no right to work outside the home. Instead their role was to provide for men within the home and for the Republic by raising a family in republican virtue. The question of universal suffrage is now an embarrassment to republican and nineteenth-century historians of France, because it brings republican virtue into disrepute. If it is mentioned, the old chestnut of clericalism is frequently raised or is simply ignored. That republican France, so progressive in its revolutionary discourse, should be so reactionary and so misogynist has been one of the shaping influences of French feminism, simply in its power to silence and to render women's political impotence in the political process invisible.

Because of this it must be stressed that egalitarian feminism was never a monolithic movement, but has developed wherever circumstances have permitted. Many women join political parties in the hope of influencing them from the inside. Even at the height of the Radicals' antagonism to female suffrage many women joined the newly formed Radical party, which shows that not all women in politics are feminists. As a result of its chequered history, feminism now comprises many different definitions and actions crossing into politics in a variety of ways.

However pervasive the term 'feminism' has recently become, its influence on politics has been superficial. Whether it means recognizing women as an historical category or as an item on the political agenda of a party, there is a fundamental problem of marginalization within a patriarchal power structure. Feminism in the 1990s has the same potential for invisibility as it had a hundred years ago. It is difficult to retain a public profile when only a small minority of people – men and women – are engaged in the process of promoting equality of all women with all men. The end is such an ambitious programme that, like socialism, the magnitude of the cause weakens the prospect of success.

Difference

The second interpretation is based on the notion of the right to sexual difference. From the earliest manifestations of French feminism a core belief was that there is such a thing as male and female nature, as Rousseau had demonstrated, but that instead of demanding acquiescence from women, relegating them to the home and denying them equal access to the public sphere by declaring them incapable, their natural qualities should be equally valued by society. Instead, women are collectively segregated into the private sphere and unjustly exploited by men because of biological differences. As a result, claim feminists, society is badly organized because women have no part in running it. Male values alone make for an imperfect, violent society. This interpretation calls for a place for women in the public sphere to act in their natural capacity, which would benefit society since male-invented structures are faulty.

Late twentieth-century feminists developed the notion of difference in new ways. They concentrated on the importance of the denial of female self-expression as part of this exploitation. Simone de Beauvoir coined the phrase 'You are not born a woman, you become one'. Currently Luce Irigaray, among others, is an exponent of the sexual difference ideology. 'Essentialist' feminists claim that female difference is so valuable that the all-important aim of feminism should not be simply the attempt to instigate fairer conditions for women, but the search for self-expression culturally, socially, economically and politically. They believe that women would lose their own specific identity if they simply imitated male values. The feminists adhering to this interpretation believe that the patriarchal structures of society deny women power, but that as victims they cannot find ways of abolishing the patriarchal structure because it is so pervasive. Instead they have sought to develop ways of creating female space. During the 1970s, consciousness-raising groups throughout the world were the main focus of political activity, and university academics developed new disciplines around gender issues and women's history.[5]

The historical antecedents of this interpretation in France are little known; it was the basic premise among utopian socialists in the 1830s.[6] Saint-Simonians played a leading part in extolling the complementarity of the sexes and stressed the contribution women could make to civilizing society; instead of an exploitative and aggressive capitalist system, true feminine qualities would ensure that reason would replace physical violence. The belief in the unique nurturing qualities of women inspired the thousands of Frenchwomen who formed pacifist movements in the 1920s and 1930s, justifying their call for female suffrage by declaring that if women were in government along with men they would ensure that no war would ever again take place.

Belief in difference paralleled a revolutionary vision of marriage or sexual partnerships where the complementarity of the sexes would flourish. The utopian communitarian Charles Fourier wrote daring proposals for alternative lifestyles, with a redistribution of household tasks on a communal basis and new relationships beyond conventional monogamous marriage. The Saint-Simonian leader Prosper Enfantin proclaimed a messianic role for the couple of man and woman, but was imprisoned by the authorities for immoral behaviour when he developed theories of sexual liberation for women, usually to the benefit of himself. Pauline Roland, Jeanne Deroin and Suzanne Voilquin were only some of the many active revolutionary women who politicized their personal life choices in an attempt to end female exploitation. The utopian socialists did not have a monopoly in declaring women's redemptory role. The special qualities and redemptory role of women were constantly portrayed by the Catholic church in nineteenth-century France through the cult of the Virgin Mary (Warner, 1976; Michaud, 1985).[7] Thanks to the development of the railways, the shrine of Lourdes was a huge success. The extraordinary interest in the woman question unleashed by the Saint-Simonians did not seek primarily to instigate political equality; it was based on a general critique of society. The misery of the proletariat was of equal concern.[8]

This early socialist forum set in motion a sequence of events similar to the May 1968 movement. By challenging the status quo and encouraging the political assertion of a wider group, both movements inadvertently drew attention to blatant gender oppression within the left and right of French politics. Both of these movements challenged the power of the system in which women were and still are excluded from the formal political process of parties and parliament. Through their encouragement of the act of self-expression, many women became more assertive and began writing as individuals about their experiences of oppression. Saint-Simonian women developed the first women's collective movement eventually calling for emancipation (Adler, 1979). Although this movement did not last, these same women played a leading role in developing a feminist socialist agenda in a brief moment of political expansion and freedom of expression during the Second Republic of 1848, which conservative republicans and Louis Napoléon quashed in 1851 and 1852 (Moses, 1984; Riot-Sarcey, 1994). Similarly, during a period of political euphoria in May 1968, women students challenged the double standard of men, who contested the oppressive power of the French state but all the while refused to let them share power within their activist groups. The would-be liberators became the oppressors.

As a result of dissatisfaction with the rigidity of separate spheres, the hypocrisy of double moral standards, or a denial of their self-expression, feminists in the 1830s and 1970s challenged the values of patriarchal society by searching for a new, essential, universal woman, which some feminists later criticized as being too prescriptive. Furthermore, if there was a chance of freedom and greater control over selfhood for some intellectual women, this did not positively alter the situation of the silent majority. The question was raised, however, as to the feasibility of defining the collective identity of women and the impossibility of access to a political identity.

This interpretation based on gender difference continued to develop during the 1980s and 1990s with French feminists' application of psychoanalytic, structuralist and deconstructionist theories to feminism. There was a conscious decision to use male-centred philosophies and apply them to feminism. The intention was to criticize existing theories as being too exclusive, but also to transform them to find a feminist identity. For the purposes of expressing feminist thought this was highly successful; it enabled a huge output of feminist cultural creativity. Recent works in English on feminism in France have tended to stress the importance of this aspect. But while it is true that there was a tremendous flourishing of philosophical, sociological and literary works in the search for feminine identity (Marks and Courtivron, 1985; Duchen, 1987; Fraser and Bartky, 1992),[9] this in itself could not be termed a feminist movement, since it lacked any reference to pressure group activity. Polemical issues soon flared and divisions occurred around questions of the degree of rejection of patriarchy, of objections to the imperialism of substituting a female version of universalism for a male one, and of the identity and creation of a new culture to express female difference, all of which have been fiercely debated in the past twenty years among academics. After an initial period of solidarity around the abortion issue in the early 1970s, there have been many splits within already small groups, all claiming feminist authenticity.

The current intensity of intellectual debate and the forms of its discourse reflect the highly sophisticated philosophical tradition in France, but any organized political action stemming from this theoretical aspect of feminist ideology has been virtually negligible. Instead, an intense, inward-looking tendency of French feminists in a restricted, academic, hot-house environment is only nurtured further by feminist academics on an international network, in particular those from American universities. Feminists such as psychoanalyst Antoinette Fouque (now a member of the European Parliament) and writers including

Hélène Cixous, Monique Wittig, Julia Kristeva and Luce Irigaray have become household names in French feminism, but these few women who preferred to create alternative female space in cultural and philosophical terms and turned their backs on mainstream political institutions have had little inclination to cultivate the broader movement of solidarity, which existed for a short while in the 1970s.

Already there are myths around the events which led to the 1970s women's movement. The highly publicized actions of a few are now interpreted as a spearhead for a mass movement. Roles of leadership and decisions are wrongly ascribed to particular individuals, whereas the structure of most groups was anti-hierarchical and informal. Nevertheless, individual actions of protest, already interpreted by the general press as representative of an umbrella notion of feminism, have inevitably contributed to the development of the ideology of feminism (Delphy, 1994). Without the historical references crucial to the flourishing of an ideology, actions are lost in the past. This weakens the potential for a mass movement of feminism. One handicap of being overly esoteric is that there are too few ideological references in common parlance to counter the many misconceptions which restrain feminism as a political movement. Many precedents of collective and individual struggles exist. Yet women will remain ignorant of the roots of their own oppression until the dissemination of the findings of a feminist history programme can serve to counter anti-feminist ideology. No matter how sophisticated the construction of feminist theories in the past twenty years has been, without a more widespread pressure group for reform of social structures, women activists in a feminist movement are helpless. They are imprisoned as stringently as ever by a patriarchal society, the power of which is ensured by political, economic and social structures. In the 1990s feminism seems to have reached another impasse; cultural potency has not been a remedy for political impotency.

Political Difference

The overriding feature of French feminism or indeed Western feminism is heterogeneity: because this excluded group has no obvious forum for debate and militant action, it often seeks alliances with other movements such as the ecologists or the socialists. Women are united only by their exclusion; sisterhood is divided by loyalty to class, religion, race, family and many other sociological factors. Gender is only one element of a person's social existence and, although many feminists would disagree, other elements such as class, education, work, family or religion are equally vital in determining the ideological and political adherence of individuals. Women as individuals have little opportunity to act in solidarity, hence the absence of a coherently structured feminist organization; but that is not to say that they have little opportunity to intervene in politics or contribute to the political ideology of feminism through other allegiances. The complexity of gender relations and gender politics has only recently been identified in political and social science. Women with feminist aspirations have not always acted according to a consistent political strategy, or demanded the same agenda.

Feminism could be described as a latent ideology. It seems to have a fluidity that makes it more dependent than any other ideology on sudden shifts in politics. The shake-up of power relationships at times of crisis such as 1789, 1848 or 1968, or at a change of government as in 1974, 1981 or 1995, seems more likely to provide sudden and unprecedented opportunities for a very small number of feminists to appear on the political stage and define what they are seeking on behalf of all their sisterhood. From these historical experiences we are able to surmise and analyse the demands and conflicts among political activists during the Second Republic, or in the pacifist and left-wing movements of the 1920s and 1930s, or after May 1968. Feminist campaigns have been transient in the public eye but not so in the background. When women were enfranchised in the immediate aftermath of 1944 there was no active feminist movement, but women had been increasingly active in public life since World War I. However, until the tremendous growth of women's history in France over the past twenty years, an important part of the process of the exclusion of women was a collective amnesia. There is a disjointed history of militancy in French feminism, and the greatest problem has been to retain the memory of previous actions, since the voices of feminists had so little opportunity of being heard.

Conclusion

The isolation of intellectual feminists is an inherent weakness. The interpretation based on the search for gender equality might seem more politically straightforward, more easily expressed in rights, and a central theme in French politics, but it is not without its basic weaknesses. Equality for women, in a society based on inequality, raises many conflicts. However, the small number of diverse organizations which together produce a highly sophisticated political ideology, and the establishment of feminist historiography, have proved that feminism was never far from the agenda either in political parties or in republican politics. The important characteristic of this egalitarian ideology is that it was more often than not associated with another movement, for this interpretation covers individuals often engaged in public debate and movements in different capacities – Masonic circles, international pacifists, trade unions, communist or socialist parties, women's leagues, Catholics, engagement in the Resistance movement often at high personal cost. The essential is: what kind of equality? Equal rights to men's rights which are far from being equal? Or equal rights among all women? Or equal rights in a society which also abolishes social and racial inequality?

We have seen that, in French history, there is a strong culture of emphasizing sexual difference but that this expression does not automatically lead to a strong demand for political equality. The feminist demand for the right to be different permanently marginalizes women by insisting they cannot fit into a man's world. They provide patriarchy with an excuse for denying them their rights and pushing women back into their traditional roles, in the name of 'femininity'. In some instances there has been a direct conflict between difference and equality: the national controversies in 1989 and 1994 over the wearing of headscarves in the classroom by Muslim schoolgirls following Islamic codes of dress raised many questions, and divided feminists and socialists over female emancipation, cultural pluralism or respect for republican secularism.

The changes in French society in the latter half of the twentieth century have been many. Women are more articulate because of better educational opportunities, more visible economically, more assertive socially, but politically still in the background. The consequences for feminism have been significant. There has been a development of the ideology and of the movement for change, and changes in women's lives have occurred through their direct impact on political events. Nevertheless, these changes are far from adequate for the majority of feminists, and they cannot be considered permanent gains. Many of the nineteenth-century legally imposed gender inequalities within the Code civil have been eradicated,[10] but a society of true gender equality remains a dream and seems as remote as ever. Indeed, many believe there is a political backlash (Kauffmann, 1995), and the few recent gains made by women are equally liable to be eroded by any right-wing government that so chooses. The current debate on abortion is possibly the best-known example. The extent of antagonism to abortion was made apparent when doctors and clinics were physically attacked. The question for feminists is how to become a stronger movement in order to gain access to decision-making processes in society for the good of women and men.

Recently the influence of psychoanalysis, postmodernism, theoretical literary and linguistic discourse has become a specific part of French feminist ideology. Faced with the enormity of exclusion from power, it tended to become introverted and remain marginalized, to the benefit of patriarchy, in the absence of a sustained rights-based campaign for social, economic and political equality. In the 1980s and 1990s there has been a stalemate in the ability of the legislators to implement reform within the existing capitalist system. This boosts the argument that exploitation under the class system is the more significant form of oppression. In the 1970s in France, feminist intellectual development was quickly marginalized. This only exacerbated the vicious circle of exclusion from power and reduced the search for other outlets of power sharing or power challenging. It is only recently that French feminists have turned once more to questions of gender-specific equality campaigns and of reverting to a discourse of equal rights. Once more the question of parity is on the agenda, but there is even debate as to whether there should be qualitative or quantitative parity (Fouque, 1995, p. 32).

I have argued that the importance of history in preserving the value of political acts of protest and constructing an ideology is particularly important for feminism. I have suggested that current reinterpretations of difference by academics and their appropriation of French attempts to create a female identity have been to the detriment of long-term objectives. Intellectual feminists dominate discourse, stressing aspects of sexual difference, whereas political activists such as Arlette Laguillier, leader of the small, extreme left-wing movement Lutte Ouvrière, the first woman candidate in the presidential elections, reject the restriction of the term 'feminist', preferring to be known as revolutionary since they argue for social and economic equality for all. There is a need for feminists to assert their ideology in social and political engagement, to assert gender solidarity within women's struggles in a constantly evolving economy. There is also a role for feminist academics, because there is a need for a more accessible history of feminism so that other feminists are alerted to the dangers of creating an ahistorical conception of feminism, just as feminists have rightly refused the universalist claims of patriarchy and the simplistic notion of egalitarian feminism.

Notes

1. For the purpose of this chapter I am making a rather simple distinction between feminism as a modern ideology and political movement and the various demands for female emancipation expressed throughout history prior to 1789. For further reading on the period immediately

prior to 1789 see Spencer, 1984, and Haase-Dubosc and Viennot, 1991. For a general history see Albistur and Armogathe, 1977.
2. In English, 'herstory' is a useful linguistic tool without an equivalent in the French language. It was coined to convey an important feminist intellectual action, namely, the reinsertion of women into their rightful place as subjects, previously missing from history, which was henceforth declared the patriarchal version of the past. I use this term here to demonstrate one aspect of feminism with an international dimension, to which academic feminists have actively contributed and which has become an integral part of the feminist movement.
3. 'Neither the feminist advances in the recent past nor the present crisis have unleashed a war of the sexes. In all circumstances French women have been able to keep men's ear and to receive tenderness from them. As befits the modern age, women of influence have been replaced by influential women. They have gained the public right to have a career beyond the antechambers. The well qualified no longer pass the dishes but the files of documents in ministers' private offices and ... committees. They have abandoned planning table settings in favour of planning strategies' (Coignard and Guichard, 1994, p. 45).
4. Olympe de Gouges was guillotined and Théroigne de Méricourt was incarcerated in a lunatic asylum. For a comprehensive study of the role of women and women's issues in the French Revolution see Brive, 1989, 1990, 1991.
5. French feminist academics claim that women's studies has never been taken seriously by the establishment and that deprivation of funds and university posts makes it a poor relation of international feminist academia. It is therefore a continued part of oppression. See Armengaud and Jasser, 1994, and Roudy, 1995.
6. The historical dimension of feminism based on difference is not often evoked in current literature. See Fraser and Bartky, 1992, and Butler and Scott, 1992.
7. This position was reiterated by Pope John Paul II in his *Letter to Women*, July 1995.
8. For an analysis of the utopian socialists' theories of 'the woman question', as it was often described at the time, see Grogan, 1992.
9. The group Psyche et Po epitomizes the work of French feminists.
10. For a discussion of the limitations of these reforms see Dhavernas, 1978.

References

Adler, L. (1979) *A l'aube du féminisme: les premières femmes journalistes*. Paris: Payot.

Albistur, M. and Armogathe, D. (1977) *Histoire du féminisme français du moyen âge à nos jours*. Paris: Des Femmes.

Armengaud, F. and Jasser, G. (1994) 'Une offensive majeure contre les études féministes'. *Nouvelles Questions Féministes* 15 (4), 7–20.

Bard, C. (1995) *Les Filles de Marianne: histoire des féminismes 1914–1940*. Paris: Fayard.

Barzach, M. *et al.* (1996) 'Le Manifeste des dix pour la parité'. *L'Express*, 6 June, pp. 32–3.

Brive, M.-F. (ed.) (1989, 1990, 1991) *Les Femmes dans la Révolution française*, Actes du Colloque 12–14 avril 1989, 3 vols. Toulouse: Presses Universitaires du Mirail.

Butler, J. and Scott, J.W. (eds) (1992) *Feminists Theorize the Political*. London: Routledge.

Coignard, S. and Guichard, M.-T. (1994) 'Les Françaises'. *Le Point*, 24 February, pp. 45–59.

Delphy, C. (1994) 'Les Origines du mouvement de libération des femmes en France'. *Nouvelles Questions Féministes* **16–18**, 137–48.

Dhavernas, O. (1978) *Droits des femmes, pouvoir des hommes*. Paris: Seuil.

Duchen, C. (ed.) (1987) *French Connections. Voices from the Women's Movement in France*. London: Hutchinson.

Fouque, A. (1995) 'Jospin pour les femmes'. *Le Nouvel Observateur*, 13–19 April.

Fraser, N. and Bartky, S.L. (eds) (1992) *Revaluing French Feminism*. Bloomington, IN: Indiana University Press.

Gaspard, F. (1994) 'De la parité: genèse d'un concept, naissance d'un mouvement'. *Nouvelles Questions Féministes* 15 (4), 29–44.

Gouges, O. de (1986) *Olympe de Gouges, Oeuvres* (ed. B. Groult). Paris: Mercure de France.

Grogan, S. (1992) *French Socialism and Sexual Difference: Women and the New Society, 1803–1844.* London: Macmillan.

Haase-Dubosc, D. and Viennot, E. (eds) (1991) *Femmes et Pouvoirs sous l'ancien régime.* Paris: Rivages.

Hall, P., Hayward, J. and Machin, H. (1994) *Developments in French Politics.* Basingstoke and London: Macmillan.

Initiatives (1995) 'Femmes: l'objectif d'égalité n'a pas résisté à la crise'. *Le Monde* (supplement), 5 July, pp. i–iv.

Kauffmann, S. (1995) 'La Revanche des "hommes blancs en colère" contre les féministes américaines'. Paper presented at *Le Monde* Conférence Mondiale sur les Femmes, Beijing, 31 August.

Le Dœuff, M. (1995) 'Problèmes d'investiture (de la parité, etc.)'. *Nouvelles Questions féministes* **16**(2), 5–80.

Letablier, M.-T. (1995) 'Women's Labour Market Participation in France: The Paradox of the Nineties' (trans. C. Simpson). *Journal of Area Studies* **6**, 108–16.

Louis, M.V. (1994) *Le Droit de cuissage: France 1860–1930.* Paris: Editions Ouvrières.

Macmillan, J. (1991) 'Religion and Gender in Modern France: Some Reflections', in F. Tallet and N. Atkin (eds) *Religion, Politics and Society in France since 1789.* London: Hambledon Press, pp. 55–66.

Macmillan, J. (1996) 'Wollstonecraft's Daughters, Marianne's Daughters, and the Daughters of Joan of Arc: Marie Maugeret and Christian Feminism in the French Belle Epoque', in C. Campbell Orr (ed.) *Wollstonecraft's Daughters: Womanhood in England and France 1780–1920.* Manchester: Manchester University Press, pp. 186–99.

Marks, E. and Courtivron, I. (1985) *New French Feminisms.* Brighton: Harvester Press.

Michaud, S. (1985) *Muse et Madonne: visages de la femme de la Révolution française aux apparitions de Lourdes.* Paris: Seuil.

Mills, H. (1996) ' "Saintes Soeurs" and "Femmes Fortes": Alternative Accounts of the Route to Womanly Civic Virtue, and the History of French Feminism', in C. Campbell Orr (ed.) *Wollstonecraft's Daughters: Womanhood in England and France 1780–1920.* Manchester: Manchester University Press, pp. 135–50.

Moses, C. (1984) *French Feminism in the Nineteenth Century.* Albany, NY: State University of New York Press.

Offen, K. (1988) 'Defining Feminism: A Comparative Historical Approach'. *Signs* **14**, 119–57.

Reynolds, S. (1995) 'Le Sacre de la Citoyenne: Pierre Rosanvallon and the Significant Other'. *Modern and Contemporary France* NS3 (2), 208–12.

Riot-Sarcey, M. (1994) *La Démocratie à l'épreuve des femmes: figures critiques du pouvoir.* Paris: Albin Michel.

Ronsin, F. (1980) *La Grève des ventres: propagande néo-malthusienne et baisse de la natalité en France XIXe–XXe siècles.* Paris: Aubier.

Roudy, Y. (1985) *A cause d'elles.* Paris: Albin Michel.

Roudy, Y. (1995) *Mais de quoi ont-ils peur?* Paris: Albin Michel.

Rowbotham, S. (1992) *Women in Movement: Feminism and Social Action.* London: Routledge.

Samia-Spencer, I. (ed.) (1984) *French Women and the Age of Enlightenment.* Bloomington, IN: Indiana University Press.

Trat, J. (1995) 'La Loi sur la parité: une solution en trompe-l'oeil'. *Nouvelles Questions féministes* **16** (2), 128–39.

Varikas, E. (1995) 'Une représentation en tant que femme? Réflexions critiques sur la demande de la parité des sexes'. *Nouvelles Questions féministes* **16** (2), 81–127.

Viennot, E. (1994) 'Parité: les féministes entre défis politiques et révolution culturelle'. *Nouvelles Questions féministes* **15** (4), 65–89.

Warner, M. (1976) *Alone of All her Sex: The Myth and Cult of the Virgin Mary.* London: Weidenfeld and Nicolson.

Multiculturalism

ALEC HARGREAVES

Introduction

Multiculturalism is a taboo concept in French political discourse. Like Alphonse Daudet's Arlésienne, a character often referred to but never seen, it is frequently alluded to – almost always in a condemnatory tone – yet seldom professed or practised, openly at least. The taboos associated with multiculturalism are rooted in some of the country's most powerful ideological traditions, above all those pertaining to the republican concept of French nationhood. If ideologies are defined broadly as bodies of ideas shaping political action, none has been more potent than those associated with the republican myth of the French nation. For over two hundred years, that myth has played a fundamental role in French political life. Its apparent blindness or outright hostility to cultural diversity is deeply revealing of the historically situated nature of all ideologies, including those which, like French republicanism, claim 'universal' validity. Basic assumptions which have often gone almost literally without saying are unmasked when we begin to scrutinize the forces which have banished multiculturalism to an ideological 'no-go' zone. In this way, a seemingly marginal phenomenon can help to illuminate some of the core features of French political culture. The analysis proposed in the present chapter falls into three parts. I begin by illustrating the breadth of the current consensus against multiculturalism, then consider in greater detail its historical foundations, and finally examine a relatively short-lived period in the 1970s and 1980s when a greater openness to cultural diversity appeared possible.

An Alien Concept

The term 'culture' has been described by Raymond Williams (1976, p. 76) as 'one of the two or three most complicated words in the English language'. For present purposes, we may define it broadly as the human production of meaning and value. Beyond this generic sense of culture, it is also common to speak of cultures in the plural as particular codes, i.e. systems of meaning and value, shared by certain groups of people. Languages are among the most fundamental codes of this kind. Other important examples are religious systems, which lay down codes of personal morality and provide believers with a sense of cosmological understanding. In the modern world, few if any states exercise sovereignty over a territory whose inhabitants could be said to share a wholly self-contained and homogeneous culture, for the political frontiers between states seldom coincide neatly with the boundaries between cultural systems. In Western Europe, most states nevertheless claim to be the political embodiment of a nation, i.e. a culturally homogeneous people.

The (con)fusion of state and nation was quintessentially expressed in the pivotal act of the French Revolution, the 1789 Declaration of the Rights of Man and of the Citizen, which declared that sovereignty, i.e. political authority, resided in the nation, whose 'general will' was embodied in law.[1] The idea of unified nation states has since played a central role in European history (Hobsbawm, 1990). Styling themselves as nations, regionally based groups united by the sense of a common culture have, in a variety of circumstances, sought to achieve political sovereignty; in so doing, they have often challenged the integrity of existing state boundaries. Conversely, states have attempted to protect or extend their boundaries by promoting the sense of a shared national culture among the population(s) actually or potentially under their authority. As we shall see later, control over the means of cultural reproduction, above all the educational system, has been of crucial importance in this process. During the post-war period, this dynamic has been further complicated in France and other West European states by the settlement of immigrant minorities, particularly those originating in former colonial territories in Africa and Asia. It is principally with reference to these post-colonial minorities that the term 'multiculturalism' has entered widespread use in the English-speaking world to denote the acceptance or promotion of cultural diversity within the territorial boundaries of a given state.

While the term itself is largely avoided in France, a vigorous debate over the phenomena associated with multiculturalism has arisen there with reference to recent migratory inflows. Large-scale immigration from countries with radically different cultural traditions is widely believed to have challenged the very foundations of French national identity, as codified in the laws governing access to French nationality, which in turn is coterminous with citizenship within the French polity. This debate, in which fears over the breakdown of social cohesion have found expression in calls for more effective policies of 'integration', reached a symbolic culmination in the 1993 reform of French nationality laws enacted by the centre-right government headed by Prime Minister Edouard Balladur. In their joint election manifesto issued earlier that year, the neo-Gaullist Rassemblement pour la République (RPR) and its centrist partners in the Union pour la Démocratie Française (UDF) had explained the need for this legislation in the following terms: 'The reform of the nationality code ... will help to clarify the conditions for successful integration. In this connection, we favour an approach to education which aims at transmitting a common culture, shared principles and values, not "multi-culturalism"'. (*Le Monde*, 1993a). The quotation marks placed around the term 'multi-culturalism' by the authors of the manifesto are clearly designed to emphasize the alienness of this concept within French political culture. Politicians and intellectuals representing almost every shade of the political spectrum commonly dismiss multiculturalism as an unacceptable 'Anglo-Saxon' import.

The desire to protect French republicanism from the 'threat' of multiculturalism is often reflected in caricatural misrepresentations of British or American approaches to the management of ethnic relations. For instance, the leftward-leaning social anthropologist Emmanuel Todd writes:

> British society gives a racial definition of the differences associated with immigration, whereas French society gives a cultural definition. In the eyes of French public opinion, Islam embodies unacceptably anti-feminist customs. But it is important to note that cultural differences are by definition less absolute, less eternal than racial differences ...
>
> On our side of the Channel, the weakness of racial feelings and the absence of communitarian separatism enable the receiving society to exert pressure ... which leads more often than not to the assimilation of the children [of immigrants] ...
>
> The British political system is now stable because the immigrant question has been settled, at a symbolic level at any rate. White identity is

to be preserved by the separation of communities, by a multiculturalism which is the logical by-product of a racial concept of society.

(Todd, 1992, p. 19)

The idea that British laws and institutions designed to combat racism – most notably those associated with the Commission for Racial Equality – actually serve to strengthen racial separatism is a grotesque caricature, as is the equation implicitly drawn by Todd and many others in France between multiculturalism and communitarianism. The latter term is generally used by the French to denote cultural separatism, i.e. a form of social organization designed to maintain cultural purity by minimizing contacts between different ethnic groups. The alleged superiority of the French approach to immigrant minorities is extolled – and some of its limitations are tellingly exposed – when Todd asserts:

British tolerance is based on a mentality of 'differentialism', that is to say, the idea that different races exist and that it is best to keep them separate. The British start off from the principle that the Pakistani community must not dissolve into theirs: a Briton does not want his son to marry a Pakistani woman. By contrast, the French approach starts out from a universalist assumption: if people behave in a similar way to us, they are welcome! We are in favour of inter-mixing, in favour of populations coming together – and that is incompatible with the maintenance of immigrant cultures.

(Todd, 1994, pp. 27–8)

This assimilationist view of the French nation typifies important core values of the left dating back to the Revolution of 1789. It is based on a rationalist view of human nature inspired by the Enlightenment, according to which individuals are capable of making free choices in response to their circumstances, instead of being mere passive components in some wider scheme of things. The right, by contrast, has traditionally been associated with a more closed, deterministic view of the French nation, which at various times has been identified with a hereditary monarchy, a biological race, or some form of trans-historical collective spirit. The alleged universalism of the republican tradition is not without its own limits, however. Newcomers are welcome to equal status with every other member of the national population only on condition that they abandon their pre-migratory traditions and assimilate as individuals – rather than as ethnically distinct groups – into pre-existing French cultural norms. The openness of the republican tradition stops where cultural differences begin.

With biological racism now an ideological anachronism and any notion of a hereditary monarchy equally lacking in credibility, most

mainstream politicians on the right have long since rallied to republicanism, where they have taken up the cry of assimilationism with a
vengeance. Shortly before taking office as Interior Minister in the
Balladur government, Charles Pasqua, a leading member of the RPR,
declared that he would not allow

> certain communities to form, refusing our culture and trying to impose
> theirs – their own customs and habits – on us … If France doesn't suit
> them, they should clear off and go home … A multi-ethnic or a multi-
> racial society [is tolerable], but not a multi-cultural one. Those who want
> to live on French soil must become French and assimilate our culture;
> there is no reason why we should put up with the others.
>
> (*Le Monde*, 1993b)

A decade earlier, when the left came to power in the early 1980s, the
French state had engaged in a brief flirtation with something akin to
multiculturalism (Safran, 1985). Even then, most of those who favoured
such a policy studiously avoided the term 'multiculturalism', preferring
to speak instead of 'le droit à la différence' ('the right to be different').
By the mid-1980s, even that expression and the ideological project for
which it stood had been largely abandoned (Vichniac, 1991). The
Islamic headscarf affair of 1989 drove the final nail into the coffin of
multiculturalism. Although the socialist Education Minister, Lionel
Jospin, successfully resisted calls for an outright ban on the wearing of
headscarves by Muslim girls attending French state schools, many on
the left sided with the dominant voices on the right in calling for a firm
stand against Islamic influences deemed to be incompatible with the
French republican tradition (Berris, 1990). In the immediate aftermath
of the affair, socialist Prime Minister Michel Rocard set up the Haut
Conseil à l'Intégration (HCI) to advise him on how best to 'integrate'
immigrants and their descendants into French society. Though less
brutally expressed, the HCI's message was fundamentally similar to that
of Pasqua:

> Notions of a 'multicultural society' and the 'right to be different' are
> unacceptably ambiguous. It is true that the concept of the nation as a
> cultural community, as put forward in the French tradition by Renan,
> does appear unusually open to outsiders, since it regards an act of
> voluntary commitment to a set of values as all that is necessary. But it
> would be wrong to let anyone think that different cultures can be allowed
> to become fully developed in France.
>
> (HCI, 1992, p. 30)

The HCI's reference to Ernest Renan's highly influential 1882 lecture, 'What is a Nation?', is emblematic of the republican tradition, which is often appealed to by opponents of multiculturalism. Renan's celebrated definition of the nation as a 'daily plebiscite' (Renan, 1992 [1882], p. 55), by which he meant a sense of community constantly reaffirmed by acts of personal volition on the part of individual members, was used as an epigraph for its recommendations by a forerunner of the HCI, a special commission set up in 1987 by the prime minister of the day, RPR leader Jacques Chirac, to consider proposed reforms to French nationality laws. The Nationality Commission was chaired by Marceau Long, Vice-President of the Conseil d'Etat, France's highest administrative court. The fact that Long was subsequently appointed chairman of the HCI by Rocard, Chirac's socialist successor as prime minister, reflects an underlying continuity in important policy areas which has to a considerable extent transcended the alternation of left and right in government. This underlying consensus was articulated by the Nationality Commission, as by the HCI, in terms of an overarching commitment to the republican conception of the French nation, which the Commission described as an elective entity based on rational processes inspired by the values of the Enlightenment, in contrast with an organic, deterministic idea of the nation associated with German romanticism (Commission de la Nationalité, 1988, vol. 2, pp. 89–90).

The Nationality Commission explicitly based this part of its report on testimony which it had heard from the philosopher Alain Finkielkraut, whose essay *La Défaite de la pensée* (1987) in turn owed much to Renan. Summarizing his argument in an interview with Thomas Ferenczi, Finkielkraut emphasized the contrast

between two different concepts of the nation: the elective model proclaimed ... by the [French] Revolution, based on the idea of a pact made between rational human beings, and the ethnic model, which responded to the revolutionary challenge by characterising each people as a unique entity slowly fashioned by a particular language, race or land. In one case, justice opposes heredity, as the sovereign nation opposes the monarchy; in the other, justice and heredity are one and the same thing, for the monarchy enjoys legitimacy which is in the full sense of the word national, rather than divine, in origin. On the one hand, the nation is composed of individuals brought together by a conscious, freely made decision to work in unison; on the other hand, the individual simply is the nation, and I, as a German, a Frenchman, a Russian or a Persian, am shaped by and speak for the nation whether I like it or not.

(Finkielkraut, 1989)

This distinction between an open, elective form of nationhood based on Enlightenment rationalism, typified by France, and a closed, deterministic concept of the nation bathed in romantic irrationalism, typified by Germany, is a piece of myth making on a grand scale. Not the least of its paradoxes is the fact that it implicitly bases the legitimacy of the French model partly on its historical lineage: a sense of heritage (a negative trait when invested in monarchical regimes) generates a warm glow when linked to France's republican tradition. No less importantly, the claim that 1789 created a voluntaristic model of nationhood is, from a strictly historical point of view, at best little more than a half truth: viewed in the light of the contemporary debate over multiculturalism, it is dangerously misleading. This is not to deny that the revolutionary heritage has had a profound effect on French attitudes towards cultural diversity. To understand that heritage, and the ways in which it has been reworked in the light of changing circumstances, we need briefly to examine the revolutionary period itself in greater detail.

The Revolutionary Heritage

The revolutionaries' main aims, as defined in the 1789 Declaration, were to replace the supposedly divine right of kings by democratic controls over the affairs of state, and to place all members of the national community on an equal footing before the law, ending the privileges enjoyed by a relatively small minority largely on the basis of heredity. Taking the existence of the nation for granted, the revolutionaries redefined the rights and responsibilities of its members. Nowhere does the Declaration define the conditions of access to French nationality, a term which had indeed yet to be invented. The Declaration certainly embodies important voluntarist features. It explicitly bases sovereignty, i.e. the authority of the state, on 'the general will', this being the collectively formulated project of the nation instead of the personal prerogative of a monarch. In line with this, the Declaration lays down that 'all citizens have the right to be involved personally, or through their representatives' – but not, it should be noted, through the mediation of preordained Estates of the kind that characterized the *ancien régime* – in exercising sovereignty (Fenet and Soulier, 1989, p. 7). In abolishing the system of Estates, which had institutionalized personal and social inequalities on a group basis, the Revolution asserted instead the principle of universalism, i.e. the equal treatment of all individuals whatever their origins, and by the same token denied any intermediary organization the right to stand between the state and the individual.

In theory, all members of the nation were citizens. In practice, political rights were restricted during most of the revolutionary period to so-called active citizens: women, a full half of the nation, together with men of low socioeconomic status, were relegated to the rank of mere passive (i.e. unenfranchised) citizens. It was not until the second half of the twentieth century, with the enfranchisement of women and the liquidation of the overseas empire (most of whose inhabitants had been denied political rights), that French nationality finally coincided almost exactly with French citizenship (Guillaume, 1991).

During the Revolution, access to what we now call French nationality was still based essentially on principles inherited from the *ancien régime*, according to which a person born on French soil and/or of French parents was deemed to be French provided he or she also resided in France. Various constitutions drawn up during the Revolution, most notably that of 1793, enabled foreigners to become French citizens if they expressed the wish to do so, provided they were deemed to be politically loyal and/or socio-economically integrated (Stora, 1990). As a proportion of the total population, foreigners choosing to take up French citizenship – whose political or socioeconomic integration presupposed a significant degree of acculturation – were relatively few in number. The overwhelming majority of the population became French without engaging in any act of volition. They were part of the French nation simply because they were born in France (a legal provision known as *jus soli*) or because their parents were French (*jus sanguinis*). By the same token, the circumstances of their birth made it practically certain that they would internalize the cultural codes traditionally present in France, either through parental influences and/or as a consequence of their wider social environment.

Renan's definition of the nation as a daily plebiscite was inspired by very different circumstances from those prevailing in 1789. Whereas the revolutionaries had been preoccupied with the redistribution of rights and responsibilities among the members of a nation whose boundaries were taken for granted, Renan gave his lecture in the wake of France's defeat in the Franco-Prussian war of 1870, which had resulted in the north-eastern provinces of Alsace and Lorraine being annexed to Germany. Convinced that the inhabitants of these lost provinces would, if given the opportunity, vote to be reincorporated into France in spite of their close cultural affinities with Germany, Renan argued that in the definition of a nation, the volition of its members should enjoy primacy over any other consideration, such as culture or tradition.

As Weil (1994, p. 323) has observed, this part of Renan's lecture –

which was cited repeatedly during the hearings organized in 1987 by the Nationality Commission and enshrined in its report as the *summum bonum* of France's republican values (Hargreaves, 1988) – is, from an empirical point of view, little more than a red herring. The external circumstances which prompted the lecture and shaped its argument bore little resemblance to the concerns which had fired the revolutionary process almost a century earlier. Statistically, the act of volition so prized by Renan, and which is today held up as a republican norm with which to guard the gates of French nationality in the face of recent immigration, has never been more than a marginal feature in the making of the French nation. Weil (1994, p. 323) has calculated that French nationality was never requested by 95 per cent of those who currently hold it; they received it automatically as a consequence of their place of birth and/or because their parents were French. In this respect, little has changed since the revolutionary period or, for that matter, since the *ancien régime*. Moreover, a close reading of Renan's lecture shows that even he was far from immune to the idea of the French nation as a trans-historical entity exerting a powerful cultural hold over the volition of its members (Silverman, 1992, pp. 19–27).

It is true that German nationality laws prioritize the biological fact of filiation over place of birth, whereas the French nationality code accords an important role to *jus soli* alongside *jus sanguinis*, and that foreigners who wish to naturalize face more obstacles in Germany than in France (Brubaker, 1992). In both countries, however, all but a small minority of the population owes its nationality to an accident of birth rather than to an act of will. Popular images of the French nation as an entity constituted through inherently more rational processes than those at work in Germany are thus of doubtful validity.

France and Germany do differ profoundly where the historical relationship between state and nation is concerned. Most of the geographical area now governed as a single entity by the French state was united much earlier than the majority of German-speaking territories, where it was not until 1870 that unification was brought close to completion. The territorial unification of France was largely (though not entirely) completed well before the Revolution of 1789. In Germany, the formation of a unified state lagged behind the development of a shared culture. In France, by contrast, the inhabitants of many of the territories brought under the control of the monarchy as it widened its authority beyond the Paris region during the later part of the Middle Ages spoke languages or dialects other than 'standard' French, and felt only a limited affinity with the sovereign power.

The monarchy's policy of encouraging and in many cases imposing cultural homogenization was to a large extent sustained after the Revolution, albeit with some important modifications. While religious belief was made a matter of personal choice, the state continued to pursue linguistic unification by discouraging or outlawing the use of languages other than French. These centralizing instincts were strongest among the radical faction known as the Jacobins, whose sympathizers sat on the left in revolutionary assemblies, where they gained the upper hand over the Girondins, who argued unsuccessfully for a less centralized form of government known at the time as federalism. As the forces of counter-revolution were at their strongest outside Paris, deviation from the cultural norms of the capital was fiercely opposed by the Jacobins, who insisted that the Republic must be one and indivisible. Hostility towards the linguistic diversity which was particularly strong in peripheral regions of France was summed up by Bertrand Barrère de Vieuzac, a prominent Jacobin, when he remarked: 'The language of federalism and superstition is Breton; the language of emigration and hatred against the Republic is German; the language of counter-Revolution is Italian and the language of fanaticism is Basque' (quoted in Schlegel, 1986, p. 35).

Laws banning the use of languages other than French for public purposes left the broad mass of the population in many rural areas relatively untouched in their everyday lives until the introduction of compulsory nationwide education, which came in the early years of the Third Republic. Introduced in 1882 by Education Minister Jules Ferry, compulsory attendance at state-run secular primary schools by every child in the land was a far more significant step in the construction of French national identity than the theoretical lecture delivered the same year by Renan. Instead of being left to exercise spontaneous acts of volition, this and succeeding generations in every part of the country would be educated, through the sole medium of the French language, to identify with France and its institutional incarnation in the form of the Republic. In contrast with Renan's ethic of free-standing voluntarism, school textbooks created at this time were to become famous for legitimizing the Republic by (re)constructing a continuous line of French nationhood dating back through the medieval monarchy and beyond to 'our ancestors the Gauls' (Weber, 1976; Citron, 1987).

The introduction of a state-controlled mass educational system coincided with the rise of large-scale immigration into France from neighbouring European states. By the closing decades of the nineteenth century, France's low birth rate had induced widespread fears that the country lacked not only an adequate supply of labour power for its economic needs, but also sufficient conscripts for its armies in the face of an ever more dynamic and populous Germany. Contrary to what might have been expected in the light of Renan's lecture, in 1889 French nationality laws were reformed with the express purpose of reducing the scope for personal choice among the descendants of immigrants. By greatly widening the applicability of *jus soli*, the Third Republic ensured that unless they specifically formulated a request to the contrary, most second-generation foreigners residing in France would automatically become French nationals on reaching the age of majority, and the third generation was denied any right at all to renounce French citizenship (Masson, 1985; Decouflé, 1992). While France's military needs were addressed in this way, the compulsory schooling founded by Ferry was to ensure that young citizens of foreign origin were inducted into a common culture alongside their peers of native stock. There was no trace in any of this of the voluntarism so extolled by Renan.

Ferry played a key role not only in the domestic construction of French national identity, but also in shaping the French encounter with external cultural diversity, for it was under his premiership during the 1880s that France began rapidly to expand its overseas empire. By the eve of World War I, it stood at the head of a colonial empire second in size only to that of Great Britain. During much of the colonial period, France officially pursued a policy known as assimilation, the avowed aim of which was to transform the indigenous inhabitants of the overseas empire into cultural replicas of their colonial masters (Betts, 1961). In reality, native cultures were disrupted as and when the interests of the colonizers required this, but very few educational resources were spent on assimilating France's colonial subjects into the culture of the motherland. As French subjects, they were subject to the authority of the French state, but because all but a tiny minority were denied citizenship, they had no role in legislative or executive decision-making. Even in Algeria, which was regarded juridically as an integral part of French territory rather than as a colony, citizenship was open to the indigenous Muslims – who accounted for the vast majority of the population – only if they formally renounced their Islamic status. Very few chose to do so. In this way, the external gates of French citizenship were guarded by a test of cultural assimilation (Bruschi, 1987).

The Politics of Cultural Diversity in the Post-War Period

World War II marked the beginning of the end of the overseas empire, but it was not until the bitterly fought Algerian war of independence, which ended in 1962, that France was finally forced to accept that the colonial period was over. It was at the same time that the left, which until then had mainly acquiesced in or positively promoted the colonial enterprise, began to take a more sympathetic view of ex-colonial peoples, who, in a transposition of terminology borrowed from the French Revolution (in the course of which the *ancien régime* had been overthrown by the Third Estate), now became known collectively as the Third World. These same peoples – particularly those originating in North Africa, and above all Algerians – have been the most dynamic elements in post-war migratory flows to France, increasingly supplanting Europeans. In this way, ex-colonial peoples whom France failed to assimilate culturally or politically when the empire was in place have now established a significant presence within the home territory of the former colonizing power (Hargreaves, 1995).

It is often suggested that the 'threat' of multiculturalism is a consequence of the resistance of immigrants from former colonial territories to the cultural norms dominant in the receiving state. The indignities and brutalities which characterized the colonial system certainly induced attitudes of caution and distrust among many immigrants with personal experience of it. However, far more important in the emergence of multiculturalist thinking in France (albeit with only minimal usage of that particular term) were changes within the French political system itself.

After the French Revolution, the left had developed into new forms with the rise of industrialization. By the twentieth century, it had split into two main camps: the socialists and the communists. While divided over many issues, both regarded class conflict as the central motor of social and political development, and both favoured a strong centralized state. Political movements sympathetic to regional cultural diversity tended to be conservative or openly anti-republican in character. During World War II, the right was deeply compromised by the willingness of regionalist movements in areas such as Brittany and Alsace to collaborate with the Nazi occupation forces in France. Semidormant in the early post-war period, regionalist movements began to gain a new lease of life in the 1960s, when for the first time they became primarily associated with the left (Beer, 1977, pp. 143–6).

Two main factors contributed to this realignment: decolonization and disillusionment over traditional forms of class-based politics. The Algerian war showed that culturally distinct territories which were regarded juridically as part of the one and indivisible French Republic could become independent if organized groups among their inhabitants mobilized in a sufficiently determined way (Loughlin, 1993). It also indicated that a far more vigorous dynamic of change was at work among colonized peoples than in Europe, where the left had traditionally expected revolutionary leadership to be shown. The events of May–June 1968 revealed a marked lack of enthusiasm for radical political change among the working classes and their supposed political mentors in the Communist Party (PCF). Many on the non-communist left began to look at alternative lines of social cleavage – such as gender and ethnicity – as potential areas for progressive politics. During the 1970s, the reconstituted Socialist Party (PS) committed itself to the principle of decentralization, which it began to put into effect when the left came to power in 1981 (Safran, 1985). The PS was also committed to granting voting rights in local elections to immigrants, despite the fact that, except for brief moments during the revolutionary period, the acquisition of French nationality had always been regarded by both the left and the right as a prerequisite for the rights of citizenship in France.

It was during this period that PS leaders enthusiastically embraced 'the right to be different' as one of their slogans. Mitterrand (1981), for example, promised during his 1981 presidential campaign that if elected he would favour 'the development of the right to be different, the right to an identity sustained by the promotion of [immigrants'] homeland languages and cultures'. He used the same slogan in support of regional cultures, and as soon as the left took office Culture Minister Jack Lang appointed a working party headed by Henri Giordan to draw up recommendations on how best to protect and promote cultural diversity in the regions. The title of Giordan's report, *Démocratie culturelle et droit à la différence* (1982), incorporated alongside the fashionable 'right to be different' the concept of 'cultural democracy', which had been developed during the 1970s, initially under the auspices of UNESCO, and later by the Council of Europe. Cultural democracy was contrasted with the so-called democratization of culture, typified by the policies of Gaullist Culture Minister André Malraux, who during the early 1960s had set up a network of provincial arts centres with the aim of disseminating elite cultural forms downwards and outwards from their pinnacle in Paris. By contrast, cultural democracy denoted a bottom-up process emphasizing popular cultural forms, often anticolonial in character in the context of UNESCO, or driven by internally disempowered groups in cases highlighted by the Council of Europe (1982, pp. 21–2).

The leftist vogue for what in English-speaking countries would be called multiculturalism was to prove relatively short-lived in France. Its rallying call, the 'right to be different', was indeed steeped in political ambiguity from the outset. Well before the socialists came to power, it was embraced by members of the centre-right administration presided over by Valéry Giscard d'Estaing, who believed it would serve their strategy of encouraging or even forcing the mass repatriation of immigrants originating in Third World countries, particularly Algeria. Between 1977 and 1981, responsibility for this policy rested with the Minister of State for Immigrant Workers, Lionel Stoléru, who would later serve as a minister under Mitterrand. To prepare the way for repatriation, sending states were encouraged to finance the teaching of homeland languages and cultures (*langues et cultures d'origine* – LCO) to the children of immigrants in French schools. In setting up a working party in 1979 to advise him on cultural policy, Stoléru declared that the children of immigrants were 'legitimately demanding the right to be different and to choose their own future' (Commission mixte 'Culture et immigration,' 1980, p. 99). The superficially generous tone of these remarks contrasted cruelly with the government's attitude towards unwanted foreign youths who wished to choose a future in France: to the extent that the law allowed it, they were summarily expelled. Although LCO teaching did in the short term appear to open the door towards a certain type of cultural diversity, France under Giscard was never committed to a genuine policy of multiculturalism. On the contrary, far from being designed to make France more culturally diverse, the LCO programme was regarded as a stepping stone in a policy aimed at ridding the country of Third World minorities.

Simultaneously with these initiatives in the field of public policy, an emerging group of theorists led by Alain de Benoist and known collectively as the New Right was enthusiastically expounding its own version of cultural differentialism (Taguieff, 1994). Fear of American cultural domination led Benoist (1986) to compare the plight of France to that of Third World countries in the face of homogenizing globalization. The ideas of the New Right, which first came to public attention in the late 1970s, were successfully adapted for electoral purposes by the extreme right-wing Front National (FN) during the early 1980s, when immigration became a major political issue. FN leader Jean-Marie Le Pen (1985, p. 112) seized on the 'right to be different' to justify the rejection of immigrants from Third World countries, arguing that every people had the right to protect its cultural integrity from foreign influences.

One of the most important features of these arguments has been a tendency to reify cultural differences so that they effectively serve as a thinly disguised substitute for more old-fashioned ideas of biological racism (Taguieff, 1987). Immigrants and their descendants are held to be 'unassimilable' into the French nation because they are trapped within alien cultural systems. Yet as Charlot (1981) observed in a perceptive early critique of the 'right to be different', this slogan was to a large extent an invention of well-meaning sympathizers among the native French population, rather than a demand formulated by people of immigrant origin. Far from being trapped inside a rigid cultural shell inherited intact from pre-migratory experiences, immigrants and their descendants have proved adept at internalizing and manipulating a wide variety of cultural codes, including those dominant in the receiving country. Indeed, for most second- and third-generation people of minority ethnic origin, the attraction of those dominant norms is far more powerful than the pull exerted by the pre-migratory codes of their ancestors (Hargreaves, 1995; Tribalat, 1995).

If the socialists all but abandoned their commitment to multiculturalism (as expressed in the 'right to be different') after only a few years in power, this was no doubt in part because their own slogan, deftly exploited by the right, had helped to convince a majority among the French public that cultural differences associated with immigration were threatening the very foundations of national cohesion. These anxieties were orchestrated to great effect by the right in a series of major controversies during the late 1980s and early 1990s over French nationality laws, citizenship and the principle of *laïcité* (secularism) in the national education system.

French nationality has traditionally been a necessary though not always a sufficient condition for political citizenship. In the face of hostile public opinion, the PS's proposal to break this link by granting local voting rights to immigrants without their being required to take French nationality was shelved within months of the left taking office in 1981.[2] Mitterrand remained on record as favouring such a step, but by the mid-1980s the initiative had passed to the right, which proposed to move in a contrary direction. With the FN calling for French nationality to be based essentially on the biological principle of *jus sanguinis*, the longer established centre-right parties sought to retain electoral support by proposing more modest but nevertheless important restrictions in the operation of *jus soli*, which until then had bestowed French nationality automatically on most children born in France to immigrant parents. In the face of a vigorous opposition campaign, and with only a wafer-thin parliamentary majority, the Chirac government of 1986–8 pulled back from these proposals and played for time by setting up the Nationality Commission (Wayland, 1993). When the centre-right parties returned to power with a landslide majority in 1993 under the premiership of Balladur, their first major legislative act was the reform of French nationality laws. As a consequence of this, the children of immigrants must now specifically opt for French nationality instead of having it automatically bestowed upon them.

A major justification advanced in support of this reform was that it conformed with the republican tradition of voluntarism, which was purportedly fundamental to the construction of the French nation. The RPR's Pierre Mazeaud, *rapporteur* (spokesperson) for the new legislation, told Parliament:

> National membership should not be passively borne but should result from an act of choice: as the nation would not exist without the consent of its members, what is wrong with a law facilitating the expression of the wish to be a member of the nation?
>
> (*Le Monde*, 1993c)

As we have seen, this was at best a highly selective view of the historical facts. The main aim of the nationality reform was to reassure the majority population that minorities of immigrant origin associated with alien cultural traditions would in future be excluded from citizenship, for it was assumed that they would be reluctant to declare their allegiance to the French state, signalled implicitly by the act of opting into French nationality. Mazeaud pointed to the main suspects when he declared: 'The role of Islam stands out more and more – Islam, and particularly the fundamentalist threat, which refuses all adherence to our society' (*Le Monde*, 1993c). Yet there is in principle still nothing to prevent such minorities from taking French citizenship for pragmatic purposes while at the same time remaining attached to cultural norms distinct from those dominant in France.

Having renounced the project of mass repatriation in the early 1980s, and having placed little more than a symbolic barrier between the French nation and people of recent immigrant origin through the nationality reform of 1993, the traditional centre-right parties decided on a show of force on what they regarded as a key battleground in the fight for the cultural cohesion of the nation: that of the state education system. The terms in which this battle was fought encapsulate in many ways the plasticity with which the ideology of republicanism has been used in support of historically contingent purposes. In 1994, five years after the first Islamic headscarf affair, the UDF's François Bayrou, Minister of Education in the Balladur government, issued a circular aimed at prohibiting the wearing of such scarves in French state schools. The circular justified the exclusion of allegedly ostentatious religious symbols by an appeal to republican values:

> In France, our sense of purpose as a nation and as a republic has found expression in a certain idea of citizenship. By its very nature, this French idea of the nation and of the Republic respects convictions of all kinds, notably religious and political convictions, as well as cultural traditions. But it refuses to countenance any splintering of the nation into separate communities indifferent towards each other, concerned only with their own rules and laws, in a mere state of coexistence. The nation is not simply a collection of citizens holding individual rights. It is also a community with a shared destiny.
>
> That ideal is forged first and foremost at school. School is the place par excellence where education and integration take place, where all our children and young people meet and learn to live together in mutual respect. The presence within school of emblems or behaviour indicating an incapacity to respect the same obligations, to follow the same classes and programmes as everyone else would negate this mission. Discrimination of all kinds – sexual, cultural or religious – must halt where school begins.
>
> This secular [*laïque*], national ideal lies at the very core of the Republican school system. It is the foundation of the duty which is incumbent on that system to provide civic education.
>
> (*Le Monde*, 1994b)

Freedom of conscience and of speech are enshrined in Articles 10 and 11 of the Declaration of 1789, which in this sense could be read as multiculturalist in spirit. Yet the same document is frequently appealed to by opponents of multiculturalism, who argue that the revolutionaries' rejection of intermediary bodies between the individual and the state constitutes a core republican principle incompatible with the official recognition of organizations claiming to represent separate ethnic groups, which in turn is held to rule out a multiculturalist policy (Noiriel, 1992). This line of reasoning clearly informs the above extract from Bayrou's circular, which is a masterpiece of double-talk. It begins by invoking the founding values of French republicanism in support of the principle of freedom of conscience, and ends by insisting that these same values require a uniform educational system imposing strictly identical obligations on every child. In theory, this circle is squared by the magic principle of *laïcité*, which was formally introduced under the Third Republic with the aim of keeping religious influences – at that time, mainly Catholic – out of state schools, where it was claimed that neutrality was to be observed in matters of religious or political belief. The laws on *laïcité* were aimed primarily at imposing a limited kind of neutrality on teachers; they are now being turned against certain groups of pupils – above all Muslims – who are felt to be threatening an educational project of cultural conformity which is anything but neutral in its intended effects. Far from leaving the construction of value systems to individual pupils, Bayrou stands four-square in line with the spirit of the educational system instituted by Jules Ferry when he explicitly declares that state schools must inculcate a sense of national belonging and shared civic values. The more contingent concerns lurking behind Bayrou's seemingly lofty restatement of the principles of republicanism were made clear when he told the press that the whole *raison d'être* of his circular was to ban Islamic headscarves from state schools while continuing to allow the wearing of Catholic crucifixes and Jewish kippas (*Le Point*, 1994). The wish of young people of immigrant origin to participate in the life of the nation through its educational system was not enough; they must first renounce emblems of cultural particularity that jarred with historically conditioned notions of French universalism.

Conclusion

France, like every other 'nation state', has always been a place of cultural diversity. Yet while proclaiming the right of individuals to choose their own values and beliefs, only rarely has the state pursued policies which could be described as multiculturalist. Most politicians on both the left and the right appear unable or unwilling to distinguish between multiculturalism and communitarianism; it is feared that any official recognition or support for cultural diversity will inevitably threaten the political integrity of the one and indivisible republic. Today, resistance to cultural diversity is at its most acute in the face of post-colonial minorities originating in Islamic countries. A study co-authored by socialist activist Françoise Gaspard, a leading proponent of the 'right to be different' in the early 1980s, points out that the furore sparked off by the Islamic headscarf affair stemmed at root from 'another form of communitarianism – in this case, republican – hiding behind so-called universalism, which in fact is simply the credo of a majority which, because it feels unsure of itself, is intolerant and deaf towards minorities' (Gaspard and Khosrokhavar, 1995, pp. 65–6). While seemingly open to outsiders, the ideology of assimilation is indeed deeply ethnocentric. Its rejection of multiculturalism embodies the hard core of contingency lurking behind the principled exterior of French republicanism.

Notes

1. The text of the 1789 Declaration is reproduced in Fenet and Soulier, 1989, p. 7.
2. In 1992, the Maastricht treaty granted voting rights in local and European elections to citizens of European Union states regardless of where they resided within the EU. However, the right to vote in national elections was withheld, and non-EU citizens were granted no voting rights at all. The treaty was only narrowly approved by a referendum in France, and after taking up office the following year the Balladur government announced that France was unlikely to implement local voting rights for EU nationals before the year 2001 (*Le Monde*, 1994a).

References

Beer, W.R. (1977) 'The Social Class of Ethnic Activists in Contemporary France', in M.J. Esman (ed.) *Ethnic Conflict in the Western World*. Ithaca, NY: Cornell University Press.

Benoist, A. de (1986) *Europe, tiers monde, même combat*. Paris: Laffont.

Berris, D. (1990) 'Scarves, Schools and Segregation: The Foulard Affair'. *French Politics and Society* 8 (1), 1–13.

Betts, R.F. (1961) *Assimilation and Association in French Colonial Theory and Practice*. New York: Columbia University Press.

Brubaker, R. (1992) *Citizenship and Nationhood in France and Germany*. Cambridge, MA: Harvard University Press.

Bruschi, C. (1987) 'La Nationalité dans le droit colonial'. *Procès*, 18, 29–81.

Charlot, M. (1981) 'Peut-on parler d'un "droit à la différence" pour les jeunes Algériens?', in M. Charlot (ed.) *Des Jeunes Algériens en France: Leurs voix et les nôtres*. Paris: CIEMM, pp. 159–78.

Citron, S. (1987) *Le Mythe national: l'histoire de France en question*. Paris: Editions Ouvrières/Etudes et Documentation Internationales.

Commission mixte 'Culture et immigration' (1980) *Culture et immigration*. Paris: ICEI.

Commission de la Nationalité (1988) *Etre Français aujourd'hui et demain. Rapport présenté par M. Marceau Long au Premier Ministre*, 2 vols. Paris: Union Générale d'Editions.

Council of Europe (1981) *European Cultural Cooperation: Achievements and Prospects*. Strasbourg: Council of Europe.

Decouflé, A.-C. (1992) 'Historic Elements of the Politics of Nationality in France', in D.L. Horowitz and G. Noiriel (eds) *Immigrants in Two Democracies: French and American Experiences*. New York and London: New York University Press, pp. 357–67.

Fenet, A. and Soulier, G. (eds) (1989) *Les Minorités et leurs droits depuis 1789*. Paris: L'Harmattan.

Finkielkraut, A. (1987) *La Défaite de la pensée*. Paris: Gallimard.

Finkielkraut, A. (1989) 'La Nation disparaît au profit des tribus', interview with Thomas Ferenczi. *Le Monde*, 13 July.

Gaspard, F. and Khosrokhavar, F. (1995) *Le Foulard et la République*. Paris: La Découverte.

Giordan, H. (1982) *Démocratie culturelle et droit à la différence*. Paris: La Documentation Française.

Guillaume, S. (1991) 'Citoyenneté et colonisation', in D. Colas, C. Emeri and J. Zylberberg (eds) *Citoyenneté et nationalité: perspectives en France et au Québec*. Paris: Presses Universitaires de France.

Hargreaves, A.G. (1988) 'The French Nationality Code Hearings'. *Modern and Contemporary France* **34**, 1–11.

Hargreaves, A.G. (1995) *Immigration, 'Race' and Ethnicity in Contemporary France.* London: Routledge.

HCI (Haut Conseil à l'Intégration) (1992) *Conditions juridiques et culturelles de l'intégration.* Paris: La Documentation Française.

Hobsbawm, E.J. (1990) *Nations and Nationalism since 1780.* Cambridge: Cambridge University Press.

Le Pen, J.-M. (1985) *Pour la France.* Paris: Albatros.

Loughlin, J. (1993) 'The Algerian War and the One and Indivisible French Republic', in A.G. Hargreaves and M.J. Heffernan (eds) *French and Algerian Identities from Colonial Times to the Present: A Century of Interaction.* Lewiston, New York and Lampeter: Edwin Mellen, pp. 149–60.

Masson, J. (1985) 'Français par le sang, Français par la loi, Français par le choix'. *Revue européenne des migrations internationales* **1** (2), 9–19.

Mitterrand, F. (1981) Reply to election questionnaire in *Le Droit de vivre*, May, p. 17.

Le Monde (1993a) 'Le Projet de l'UPF', 11 February.

Le Monde (1993b) 'M. Pasqua contre une société "pluriculturelle" ', 21–22 March.

Le Monde (1993c) 'La Réforme du code de la nationalité à l'Assemblée nationale', 13 May.

Le Monde (1994a) 'Le Droit de vote des citoyens de l'Union aux municipales françaises est renvoyé à 2001', 12 July.

Le Monde (1994b) 'Le Texte du ministre de l'éducation nationale', 21 September.

Noiriel, G. (1992) 'Français et étrangers', in P. Nora (ed.) *Les Lieux de mémoire, iii, Les France. Vol. 1: Conflits et partages.* Paris: Gallimard, pp. 275–319.

Le Point (1994) 'Interview François Bayrou: "Plus de voile à l'école" ', 10 September.

Renan, E. (1992 [1882]) 'Qu'est-ce qu'une nation?', reprinted in *Qu'est-ce qu'une nation? et autres essais politiques* (ed. Joël Romain). Paris: Presses Pocket, pp. 37–56.

Safran, W. (1985) 'The Mitterrand Regime and its Policies of Ethnocultural Accommodation'. *Comparative Politics* **18** (1), 41–63.

Schlegel, J.-L. (1986) 'L'Immigration interroge notre identité nationale'. *Projet* **199**, 29–48.

Silverman, M. (1992) *Deconstructing the Nation: Immigration, Racism and Citizenship in Modern France.* London: Routledge.

Stora, B. (1990) '1789–1989: Nationalité et citoyenneté (histoire d'un couple, histoire d'une crise)', in *1789–1989: Actes du colloque organisé à la Maison de la Culture d'Amiens les 27, 28 et 29 octobre dans le cadre de la commémoration du bicentenaire de la révolution française.* Amiens: Association de Soutien à l'Expression des Communautés d'Amiens, pp. 20–41.

Taguieff, P.-A. (1987) *La Force du préjugé.* Paris: La Découverte.

Taguieff, P.-A. (1994) *Sur la Nouvelle Droite.* Paris: Descartes & Cie.

Todd, E. (1992) 'France-Angleterre: le tournoi raciste'. *Le Nouvel Observateur*, 26 March, pp. 18–19.

Todd, E. (1994) 'Invitons-les à devenir françaises'. *L'Express*, 24 November, pp. 27–9.

Tribalat, M. (1995) *Faire France: une grande enquête sur les immigrés et leurs enfants.* Paris: La Découverte.

Vichniac, J.E. (1991) 'French Socialists and the *droit à la différence:* A Changing Dynamic'. *French Politics and Society* **9** (1), 40–56.

Wayland, S. (1993) 'Mobilising to Defend Nationality Law in France'. *New Community* **20** (1), 93–110.

Weber, E. (1976) *Peasants into Frenchmen: The Modernization of Rural France 1870–1914.* Stanford: Stanford University Press.

Weil, P. (1994) 'Immigration, nation et nationalité: regards comparatifs et croisés'. *Revue française de science politique* **4** (2), 308–26.

Williams, R. (1976) *Keywords: A Vocabulary of Culture and Society.* Glasgow: Fontana.

Index